FACTS*

* and other lies

T0038382

Welcome to the Disinformation Age

Ed Coper

ALLEN&UNWIN
SYDNEY · MELBOURNE · AUCKLAND · LONDON

First published in 2022

Copyright © Ed Coper 2022

All rights reserved. No part of this book may be reproduced or transmitted in
any form or by any means, electronic or mechanical, including photocopying,
recording or by any information storage and retrieval system, without prior
permission in writing from the publisher. The Australian *Copyright Act 1968*
(the Act) allows a maximum of one chapter or 10 per cent of this book, whichever
is the greater, to be photocopied by any educational institution for its educational
purposes provided that the educational institution (or body that administers it) has
given a remuneration notice to the Copyright Agency (Australia) under the Act.

Allen & Unwin
83 Alexander Street
Crows Nest NSW 2065
Australia
Phone: (61 2) 8425 0100
Email: info@allenandunwin.com
Web: www.allenandunwin.com

 A catalogue record for this
book is available from the
National Library of Australia

ISBN 978 1 76106 570 5

Internal design by Peter Long
Index by Garry Cousins
Set in 12/18 pt Minion Pro by Midland Typesetters, Australia
Printed in Australia by Pegasus Media & Logistics

10 9 8 7 6 5 4 3

The paper in this book is FSC® certified.
FSC® promotes environmentally responsible,
socially beneficial and economically viable
management of the world's forests.

Ed Coper is a leading communications expert and was on the front lines when the internet collided with democracy, growing Australia's first online political movement GetUp to quickly amass more members than every political party combined. He powered Change.org's global expansion into over eighteen countries and pioneered techniques to bring politics into the digital age, and has been behind the scenes of many of the last decade's most prominent social movements. He has advised campaigns on every continent except Antarctica, and high-profile changemakers from Malala to Richard Branson. Ed founded the New York–based Center for Impact Communications, which has led efforts to safeguard US elections from disinformation and overcome vaccine hesitancy. Ed also founded a New York creative agency that serviced multiple Nobel Peace laureates and political and social leaders to scale their social impact. His groundbreaking campaigns have raised hundreds of millions of dollars for causes, won landmark social change and have featured in several museum exhibitions. Ed is based in Sydney and is director of the Populares communications agency.

Praise for *Facts and Other Lies*

'This is a timely account of a growing malignancy affecting all modern democracies, namely disinformation. Democracies have always contended with disinformation, but it has exploded with technological advancement and the consolidation of media power in the hands of Rupert Murdoch. Self-interested actors, both states and non-state actors, are well advanced in developing the science of disinformation. Coper makes a valuable contribution towards a fuller understanding of this problem, and laying the groundwork for the sober national conversations we need to have about protecting our democracy.

—**Kevin Rudd**, former Prime Minister of Australia

'Read this book if you want to save democracy. Disinformation is tearing apart the fabric of our society, and this is the handbook we need to fix it. At threat is the very trust that gives legitimacy to our democratic institutions and governments. I wish I'd had this book on my nightstand every time I faced malicious fake news. Ed Coper is a must-read for anyone who shudders every time they hear an anti-vaxxer, a conspiracy theorist or whenever Clive Palmer or Alan Jones opens their mouth.'

—**Wayne Swan**, former Deputy Prime Minister of Australia

'A fascinating and terrifying explanation for how we got into this disinformation mess, and a wise roadmap for how we might get out of it. Coper is both philosopher and pragmatist. This book illuminates so much about the place where humans and social media meet, for better and for worse.'

—**Bri Lee**, author of *Who Gets to Be Smart*

'Few have mapped our information dystopia more effectively—and entertainingly— than Coper. From the Ancient Greeks to the lockdown protests, via Hannah Arendt, Donald Trump, the Murdochs and many others, Coper has given us a detailed history of disinformation—and of how we used the magnificent connective tool of the internet to magnify our worst, most primitive impulses. Mapping the marching routes of bot armies, tracking the infection vectors of fake media, explaining the maths—and economics—of social media radicalisation, following the tortured logic of QAnon and anti-vaxxers and explaining the psychology of irrationality, Coper has plunged into a dark world indeed, but the analysis he returns with, and the solutions he proposes, are compelling.'

—**Bernard Keane**, Politics Editor, *Crikey*

'Exposed: Fiendish liars, "fake news" tricks, and their unwitting victims. This book is essential reading for anyone wanting to cut through the nonsense and get to the truth.'

—Eason Jordan, former Chief News Executive, CNN

'We live in a world that unfolds at a pace, and with the violent twists and turns in the plot, of a thriller. This book captures the intensity of our politics and connects it to the science of misinformation and its correction. Without losing our attention or slowing down, Coper manages to convey the main elements of the science in this page-turner. We learn about why people continue to rely on information they know to be false, why tribal bonds are not a thing of the past, and why we shouldn't try not to think of an elephant, but should inoculate ourselves against disinformation. This is a great read that gets across a lot of science in a hip narrative.'

—**Professor Stephan Lewandowsky**, Chair in Cognitive Psychology, University of Bristol

To Billie, Juno and the found Summer of 1987

Contents

Introduction

> 'Just remember, what you're seeing and what you're reading is not what's happening.'
> —President Donald J. Trump

Would your slightly younger self, even from as recently as 2015, believe the news of today?

An entire city block of a major American city blown up by a suicide bomber on Christmas Day over his concerns phone towers spread disease. Someone elected to the US Congress on a platform that Democrats secretly harvest an anti-aging chemical from the blood of abused children. Angry rioters in furs and horns overrun the US Capitol in a bloody carnage of insurrection, intent on hanging their very own vice-presidential candidate. The prime minister of Australia employing the wife of his friend who fronts a group the FBI have declared terrorists. A global pandemic which, even as they lie dying from it, people refuse to believe exists.

Many who sat in shocked disbelief as pictures of these events beamed around the world had the same question: 'How on earth did we get here?'

For those rioters adorned in Trump flags, red MAGA hats and various states of fancy dress, it was the culmination of a journey of online radicalisation that began with the weaponisation of disinformation by their political leaders, hyperpartisan commentators and foreign saboteurs.

By charting their journey of radicalisation, we will learn much about the broader social context into which they thrust themselves and their fanciful realities, ones which had no bearing in facts. We'll also learn how we can help to halt the process so that your next Christmas dinner isn't ruined by finding out Aunty Jane has been arrested for plotting to free imaginary children from the Victorian Premier's basement.

This book will help explain how disinformation has fractured society, why it is so potent and so hard to stop, and what people can do to help prevent its spread in Australia—where you may be surprised to discover federal politicians and shock jocks are already operating from the same disturbing playbook. The type of disinformation campaigns you read about happening overseas are dictating our political conversations right here in Australia, far under the radar from our less than observant gaze.

*Dis*information—which *deliberately* aims to deceive, as opposed to '*mis*information' which may be merely unintentional—is a very distracting symptom of a much deeper malaise: the breakdown of our traditional information ecosystem, and in its place the rise of a new information *dis*order that encourages falsehoods and disadvantages facts.

Some elements of disinformation are not new. We have always lied, especially in organised politics. We have always lived side by side with our own parallel truths that compete with one another. But rarely have we been so deeply embedded in echo chambers that are completely cut off from any unifying reference points of common information. We have lost our north star.

As a result, when society is challenged by a new circumstance—say, hypothetically, a novel coronavirus makes the leap to human hosts and then spreads around the globe, killing millions—we look to the things that have got us through previous crises: trust in our institutions of government and science to give us the plan we can compliantly follow to safety.

But instead we find that trust has rotted away with the damp of neglect. People see conspiracy in simple public health instructions to wear a mask or avoid physical contact, and proudly do the opposite as an expression of political opinion. People take their instructions from quack profiteers whose theories occupy the same social media real estate as the World Health Organization and the *British Medical Journal*. People embrace explanations that defy reason, and then lob casuistic pot shots at their peers before retreating into tribal fortresses.

Public confidence is smashed, and millions kiss their loved ones a last goodbye on FaceTime.

The rise of computers and the internet heralded an era of unfettered access to information and each other. We anointed it 'The Information Age'. With it came abundant optimism that the democratising effect of an informed citizenry would break down cultural and political barriers, free people from the yoke of suppression and spread knowledge previously hoarded in the dusty shelves of ivy-covered institutions.

Instead, these technologies enabled the opposite: people retreated into likeminded bubbles of groupthink, autocrats entrenched their rule through social media and knowledge was supplanted by 'alternative facts' that marched back and forth across the internet while the truth was still putting its pants on.

Welcome to 'The *Dis*information Age'.

It is an epoch marked not just by a few depressing milestones—here an election interference by Russia, there a country leaving the European Union, everywhere an increase in vaccine hesitancy—but marked by the entire reorganisation of our society, and with it the dynamics of how we relate to information and each other.

Closed-off groups develop their truth and reality in parallel to yours and never the twain shall meet. News systems spread opinion and inflammation where they used to offer news and information. Conversations take place in spaces geared to elevate our worst selves and suppress any mitigating forces of reason and restraint.

Facts can't compete with memes, and now Grumpy Cat has his own ready-to-drink coffee line, but doctors can't convince people to avoid Gwyneth Paltrow's potentially fatal coffee enema. Our information ecosystem has become so polluted that we will even, quite literally, inject coffee up our rectum, despite medical and scientific evidence clearly telling us not to. Our brains, like the enema, will push on undeterred.

Disinformation is a virus that spreads contagious information from person to person, leaving a trail of human wreckage in its wake. In 2018, more than twenty people in India were killed due to disinformation about child kidnappings spread on WhatsApp. The Myanmar junta used disinformation on Facebook to prosecute a genocide against the Rohingya in Burma, leading to the deaths of untold thousands and the forced displacement of many more. We can't yet quantify how many deaths can be attributed to the erosion of trust in public health measures and a vaccine against covid because of organised disinformation campaigns on social media. Half of all the Twitter accounts urging an end to covid lockdowns in America were found to be robots.

The stakes are very high. These incidents may seem scattered, disparate and remote, but they are the sum parts of a greater devastating whole: the foundations of our societies are being shaken to their core, and many deep cracks have already been exposed. If we don't act now, these cracks will become chasms that will devour our societies entirely. And nobody wants 'Swallowed by an information sinkhole' on their epitaph.

Given the recent proliferation of disinformation, and its increasingly obvious and alarming effects on society, social scientists have been studying the phenomena and various ways to combat it. Their work, however, is largely limited to academic publications and journals.

At the same time, cognitive scientists, social psychologists, psycho-linguists and even computer scientists have long studied the way we form and keep opinions. Other researchers are expert in radicalisation, conspiracy and cults. All of this expertise has come to bear on the spread of fake news.

But we are yet to pull all these threads together into an accessible understanding of how these cognitive, social and behavioural practices culminate in harmful disinformation, and how we can take practical steps to combat it and protect the things it threatens: civil order, fact-based policy debates and democracy itself. This book is an attempt to do so.

To effectively combat disinformation, we must first fully understand the backdrop which gave rise to it. To embark on that understanding, we have to take quite a circuitous route that begins in Ancient Greece and ends in the halls of our very own parliament thousands of years later. We'll meet a lot of old White men in robes—appropriate attire for the former, but not the latter.

We will study the converging forces of cognitive evolution, philosophical debate and media consumption, and how they came crashing into the information age and social media.

This is merely the latest chapter in a long history of searching for and speaking truth. We have long argued about reason and rationality, but the mistake we made over the last few centuries was thinking that our debate led ever onward and upward towards an enlightened society who worshipped on the altar of truth. Up until a few years ago, we thought we had finally arrived there.

Science was fact, and we agreed on those facts and then argued about what to do with them. But we had only been lulled into an 'end of history' moment where we thought we had found enlightenment. It turns out we were just getting more convincing at saying we were very stable geniuses. In reality we had merely made our less rational parts dormant.

Then they woke up. Now experts tell us that by 2030, anti-vaxxer conspiracies will be the norm and pro-vaccination opinions the exception.

Recent developments in cognitive science have made it clear that humans are much less rational than we had always thought, and that our brains are not geared to find the truth, but to find each other—even when doing so means we have to call a spade a diamond.

There are a host of psychological phenomena which show this, and many of them are shocking to discover. The collision between cognitive psychology and disinformation has upset the apple carts of political science and philosophy: we have been forced to learn that our opinions are not guided by the facts; the facts are guided by our opinions.

To make matters worse, into this context came the disintegration of our traditional media landscape and the rise of cheap 'infotainment' in its place, which in turn ran headlong into the sucking vortex of social media and the algorithms that drive it. Our information became disordered. The whole thing felt like stepping out of a Monet and into a Picasso—then finding out both were cheap forgeries.

The net effect of this was a 'perfect storm' into which a boat named *Disinformation* happily plotted its course, its sails full of new technologies that rewarded emotive opinion, suspicion and division, and punished rational facts, nuance and balance.

Worse still, those who seek to exploit these suspicions and divisions are now able to weaponise these new technologies with ruthless efficiency and brutal efficacy—often undetected.

In our scramble to adapt to this new age we are attempting to defeat disinformation in all the *wrong* ways—which are at best ineffective, but often do more harm than good. It is because we are yet to catch up to the reality that we have indeed entered a new age which merits new approaches, instead of clinging to the losing belief that facts are an antidote to falsehoods.

But all is not lost, my friend, as the following chapters will endeavour to set out. The same fields of research that taught us why disinformation has been so effortlessly effective are now beginning to discover some potential remedies.

And those remedies place you directly on the front line.

At a time when Australia is facing generational crises—climate change, a global pandemic, the rise of the extreme right—understanding and combating disinformation and regaining a shared reality is essential to our ability to meet these crises with the necessary responses.

Through gamification, social media etiquette, intentional conversations, political leadership, media literacy and more, we can reclaim a common reality, get back to solving society's problems and take conspiracy theorists and nefarious demagogues off the front pages to confine them to the dustbin of the internet's fringes.

A note on 'fake news'

This book will use the term 'fake news' interchangeably with 'disinformation' because everybody understands what fake news is, but disinformation is a long and complicated word. There is a lot of contention around calling it 'fake news', because many people who consume and believe fake news have in turn embraced it as a term to throw at real news. 'CNN is fake news!' bellows their demigod ex-president. Disinformation is of course broader than mere fake news, but you, dear reader, are smart enough to realise two things: first, that fake news is a catch-all term for disinformation, and second, that used here it refers to *fake* fake news, not real news. Writing should meet its audience, and you call it fake news. If you start calling it 'bullshit info' then I'll switch to start using that. As Italo Calvino said, 'It is not the voice that commands the story; it is the ear.'

On with the show.

Part One
The Information Ecosystem

1 / A Brief History of Lies

Part One
The Information Ecosystem

SOCRATES: Stop, and let us recall to mind what
you are saying; are you not saying that the false
are powerful and prudent and knowing and wise in
those things about which they are false?
HIPPIAS: To be sure.
—*Lesser Hippias*, Plato

We tend to judge lying pretty negatively. There is no doubt it is a dirty word; it is one of the earliest moral lessons we teach our children. But our effortless knack at lying is one of the more remarkable features of our species, and of the abilities of our brains to manipulate situations to our advantage.

There are many other animal species that deceive: capuchin monkeys will sound the predator alarm and then run off with the bananas while everyone else is in a mad panic; squirrels will pretend to bury a nut while others are watching to throw would-be nut thieves off; some cuttlefish will pretend to be female to sneak into a nest while the male is standing guard. But the scale and sophistication of human lies is unparalleled.

Why We Lie

Honesty is also an important value to us humans. It gave us an evolutionary advantage by allowing early humans to work together, knowing that, 'Yes, Frank, you go and scare that woolly mammoth and I promise I'll be waiting round the next corner with a spear.' We get a lot of value from honesty. It allows us to form social connections and to trust human communication.

So when we lie, it means there is a value at play that is even more important to us than honesty. It could be compassion ('No, that haircut looks great on you!'), self-deception ('I really can sing'), self-preservation ('I did not have sexual relations with that woman') or material gain ('Coal is clean'). But lies only work because we are programmed to be mostly truthful. Otherwise nobody would ever fall for a lie.

Lying is an essential human skill, like walking and talking.

Evolutionary psychologists think that lying emerged shortly after the development of language itself. It is as old as cooperation: as soon as we worked out how to work together, we worked out how to game the system. One study of primates found the more cooperative the species, the higher the rates of deception.

As our brains develop and mature, we get better at lying and are more willing to do so. I've lost the ability to tell if my eldest daughter is telling the truth, and she is only five. All of what I have learned about body language, facial expressions and vocal cues cannot reliably inform me whether she has actually cleaned her teeth or not.

Her ability to lie—and more so her inclination—is impressive. Science tells me to be reassured by her on-track cognitive development rather than concerned for what I have in store for her teenage years.

Researchers placed hidden cameras in a room to test young kids' truthfulness, and found that the percentage of kids who took a peek at a toy and then lied about it increased with age. Thirty per cent of the two-year-olds lied, 50 per cent of the three-year-olds. By age eight, a full 80 per cent of kids lied about it.

In the same experiment, the sophistication of the kids' lying grew apace with their likelihood to lie. At three and four, the kids were terrible liars. They gave the game away immediately, blabbing out information they only could have known had they peeked at the toy. But by seven and eight they were able to mask their deception. They either withheld incriminating evidence or created rational explanations to make their answer seem like a guess. One five-year-old who was allowed to feel the toy rather than see it (but had peeked) told the researchers she knew it was a dinosaur because it 'felt purple'.

Unfortunately that improvement in our ability to lie is not matched with a great ability to detect lies. We are great liars and terrible lie detectors. Even lie detectors, which are calibrated to detect subtle changes in physicality when we lie, are terrible lie detectors. Much of what we know about the world we have been told by others, and so we are hardwired to believe and trust. Deception is as much a part of human nature as our ability to be deceived.

Between the ages of thirteen and seventeen we hit 'peak lying'. Sixty per cent of teenagers tell up to five lies a day. As adults we lie on average twice a day, mostly to hide our own inadequacies or to protect others' feelings. It is an essential tool allowing us to uphold social norms. As Jim Carrey's character experienced in *Liar, Liar*, being forced to tell only the truth for even just one day is a curse. He relentlessly offends and insults, confesses to a fart in a crowded lift, tells a cop every traffic violation he's committed that day and an intimate lover that he's had better. In real life, these social bonds he breaks are more important to us than our desire to be truthful.

This aspect of human interaction explains the spread of online misinformation and disinformation. The social motivations that lead people to share and believe fake news are important to understand. Too often we get distracted by sorting 'fact' from 'fiction' rather than examining the powerful social and evolutionary forces at work that would lead a person to not get a simple vaccination against a virus that has shut down their entire way of life.

Truth is important to humans, but only to a certain extent. We are social creatures before we are truthful creatures, and that means an understanding of lying will only get us so far in understanding disinformation.

To do that, we need to instead examine the forces that compel us to lie more so than focus on the lying itself.

In fact, Hannah Arendt took a look at all the major religions, and wondered why throughout history nobody really cared that much about lying (other than Freddie Mercury's Zoroastrians—perhaps that was the inspiration behind Queen's hit 'Liar'). She saw our distaste for organised lying as a relatively recent phenomenon, arriving with some of the philosophical developments we will discuss in the next section on truth: 'Only with the rise of Puritan morality, coinciding with the rise of organized science, whose progress had to be assured on the firm ground of the absolute veracity and reliability of every scientist, were lies considered serious offenses.'

Arendt was much more interested in a different conflict than the one between truth and lying: that between truth and *opinion*. As James Madison said, 'all governments rest on opinion'. Therefore Arendt saw any political power as diametrically opposed to rational truth. This gave us a different creature altogether: the political lie.

The Political Lie

Here's a statement that will shock no one: politicians lie.

They have since there have been politicians, and as long as there have been political issues to debate there has been disinformation campaigns to muddy them. So any examination of today's forces of disinformation has to acknowledge that something has changed; something is new.

What hasn't changed is the lie. Conspiracy theories, outright falsehoods about a political opponent, scare campaigns, fake news: all of these things are as old as politics. As soon as societies had resources to protect and people to organise, we created political entities to govern them, and on day one the first order of business was to start lying.

Political lying really took things up a notch in the twentieth century with two global hot wars then a protracted cold one. The Nazis—whose entire rise to power was built on a lie about why Germany lost the first of those hot wars—made a dark artform of political propaganda, playing on people's fears, boiling complex issues down into racist generalisations and then blasting them repeatedly over every medium at their disposal. That lie, in turn about another 'big lie' Hitler accused the Jews of making, became the narrative foundation the Holocaust was built on. Political lies have consequence.

Just in the last twenty years our maps have been redrawn by lying. Britain has exited Europe based on a series of well-told lies (like the 'Leave' campaign manager saying he caught a train through London without hearing English spoken), and the Middle East and Africa are still reeling from the ripples caused by American lies that Saddam Hussein had weapons of mass destruction.

Australia's own recent political history is rife with it—*Crikey* published a dossier of 27 'significant lies and falsehoods' Scott Morrison had told in his first two years as prime minister. Bernard Keane documented how our highest leader 'lies openly and frequently, about matters large and small—Australia's carbon emissions, or an inquiry in relation to a sexual assault within the ministerial wing in Parliament House, or simply whether he spoke to someone who refused to shake his hand'. Their point was not to make a partisan attack, but to highlight the erosion of truth at the apex of our politics: 'We would publish exactly the same dossier about a Labor prime minister if he or she had lied as often, as brazenly, and with so little accountability . . . We don't want to live in a country where systemic lying by our elected leader has become so normalised that no one seems to notice.'

When Donald Trump assumed the leadership of the free world off the back of a sophisticated network of lies and professional liars (don't worry—we'll cover that one in great detail later), many people were shocked. But even their narrow political history of presidential elections are rife with lies, and should have come as no surprise.

It's not hard to find examples, so I'll just provide two—one old and one new—to demonstrate the ubiquity of political lies to influence elections, specifically US presidential elections.

The 1800 US presidential election was one of the most bitterly fought, considered by some scholars to still have the mantle of the nastiest election in American history. Perhaps not unrelatedly, it was the first to be run by political parties.

George Washington had won the first two presidential elections (in 1788 and 1792) unanimously—thereby achieving legitimately the feat that many tinpot dictators have sought to emulate since: 100 per cent of the vote. Back then, the president was the guy (they were all guys) with the most votes, and the vice president was the runner-up. Imagine President Biden with his Vice President Trump: the West Wing would be more like *The Odd Couple*.

Thomas Jefferson lost to John Adams in 1796, and so became his vice president. He unsurprisingly used the position to constantly undermine his president, and in 1800 they ran against each other again. This time the results would be different.

The election was essentially a convoluted tie between Jefferson and his own running mate, and the deadlock was only broken by Alexander Hamilton before he was an eponymous Broadway hit. Hamilton lobbied his party to throw their votes behind Jefferson, as, although he disagreed with Jefferson's principles, the other guy had no principles at all. The whole thing was so messy they had to amend the Constitution before the next election to stop the whole shemozzle from happening again.

Back then, the candidates thought the best way to fight an election was to not campaign at all. Horse-and-cart tours or town hall debates were tacky and beneath a distinguished statesman. Instead, the campaign was carried out through propaganda in partisan newspapers who tried to out-smear their opponents. Much classier.

Jefferson's winning strategy was to simply remind voters that he wrote the Declaration of Independence (then still on the 'recent bestsellers' list). The sympathetic papers were unsubtle in their praise:

> At an early age, he had the glory of conceiving and of composing the most sublime production of genius, which either the ancient

or modern world has exhibited ... When Mr Jefferson wrote the declaration of independence, even his mind could scarcely have penetrated the bosom of futurity, so as to have anticipated the astonishing effects of his own composition.

—*The Independent Chronicle and the Universal Advertiser,*
29 May 1800

Not even a climate denier in a Murdoch paper gets a better run than that.

So as the 24th anniversary of the Declaration approached, both sides knew it was going to be a July 4th dedicated to the celebration of one candidate. Adams' supporters had a cunning plan: rain on that parade by declaring in their newspapers that Jefferson had died.

In those days, news travelled slowly. So did fact checks. Voting ran from April until October, so electors were in the midst of casting their ballots while thinking Jefferson was in fact ineligible for office, due to the unfortunate fact of him being dead.

By the time the 4th of July rolled around the rumour had spread far and wide, but not yet its correction. The Jefferson papers were clear on the purpose of this rumour: 'a fabrication intended to damp the festivity of the 4th of July, and prevent the author of the Declaration of Independence from being the universal toast of the approaching auspicious festival'.

It was one lie in an election characterised by lies both sides told about each other, from Jefferson being an atheist to Adams being a fan of the Brits (at the time, two of the biggest insults you could muster).

In one of history's most curious asides, both Jefferson and Adams died on exactly the same day as each other twenty-six years later, on the very day of the 50th anniversary of the Declaration of Independence they had written. Adams, unaware Jefferson had died hours earlier, used his last words to lament the fact that Jefferson was still alive. Jefferson's last words: 'is it the Fourth?'

Fast forward exactly 200 years and not much had changed. Elections, while now featuring TV ads, debates and cable news punditry, still contained the slanderous mud flung back and forth between candidates.

Most people remember the 2000 US presidential election for the conservative Supreme Court determining the Florida recount, but few recall that it was almost another man who got in the way of George W. Bush's ambitions to follow in his father's footsteps: John McCain.

McCain was the early frontrunner for the Republican nomination. He won New Hampshire handsomely, one of the first states to have a primary, and was on track to cement his position with a win in South Carolina, and likely with it the eventual nomination.

Enter the Turd Blossom.

That was Bush's affectionate nickname for his man behind the curtain, Karl Rove. In South Carolina, voters received an onslaught of anonymous leaflets accusing McCain of everything from being a homosexual to having committed treason while a POW in Vietnam.

Then came the real clincher. South Carolinians (not the most progressive or inclusive bunch) started getting phone calls from 'pollsters' asking the question, 'Would you be more likely or less likely to vote for John McCain for president if you knew he had fathered an illegitimate Black child?'

One of McCain's children was adopted from a Bangladeshi orphanage. It was enough for the South Carolina voters to put two and two together and come up with five: not only did it torpedo McCain's efforts in South Carolina, it sank his momentum from which he never recovered. Bush won the primary, stole the presidential and then once in power remade our century with grander lies.

McCain gave up on his attempts to reform the Republican party into one that the *New York Times* described 'would be divorced from religiousness and without dogmatic socially conservative notions', and instead stood back as it devolved into the party that came to rally behind Trump's worst excesses.

Lies, while consequential, have been a constant in shaping our politics and therefore our societies. But something fundamental has changed.

Most historical lies have been fleeting: an opportunistic ploy to capitalise in the short term before the lie can be exposed, like Thomas

Jefferson's 'death'. False narratives, like John McCain's 'illegitimate child', have also been fringe. The dominant story reverts to the truthful mean.

Today the lies are much the same, but the results are different. They are fed into a hyperconnected vacuum where they can spread unadulterated by a central truth and untarnished by contrary opinion. Information exists in bubbles that circumvent the usual flow of information from trusted, curated news sources to voters, creating alternate realities that stoke fear, spread rumour and relentlessly smear.

The key artery of our democratic pact—that voters have the information necessary to make judgments favouring their interests and values—has been severed. James Madison, who succeeded Thomas Jefferson as president in 1808, warned that 'A popular Government, without popular information, or the means of acquiring it, is but a Prologue to a Farce or a Tragedy; or, perhaps both.' The central question to examine is whether disinformation has prevented people from attaining that information to the point where we can declare the farce and tragedy is upon us.

2 / A Brief History of Truth

'The more often a stupidity is repeated, the more it
gets the appearance of wisdom.'
—Voltaire

We take many things for granted these days: surviving once-deadly, now-routine maladies by merely popping a pill we can buy at the same place we get our chewing gum; flicking a switch on our wall and—hey presto!—conquering the darkness with photon-emitting electrons in a tube of ionised mercury vapour; pushing a few buttons on a compact mash of minerals and glass in our hand and having an underpaid student visa-holder on a scooter turn up at our door twenty minutes later with a warm Portuguese chicken burger in hand.

The simple idea that there is a knowable 'truth' we can all agree on, supported by an agreed set of facts we can find in science books, is another.

That notion is a relatively recent invention. We take it for granted.

The truth has, throughout history, been a closely guarded and hotly contested concept usually kept locked far away from public view. As has our ability to interact with it as informed, supposedly rational beings.

When we worry about disinformation, what we are really saying is 'there are things we know to be true and know to be false, and the spreading of those false things is dangerous'. That formulation is much older than our concept of truth.

But are we just kidding ourselves when we think that our 'truth' (e.g. that vaccines work, that Joe Biden won the election, that 5G towers don't spread coronavirus) is any more valid than anyone else's truth (that vaccines cause autism, that Donald Trump won the election, that 5G towers emit infection)?

As we will discover, what we think is our educated and rational brain is in reality a machine geared to defend our moral and political beliefs, not discover empirical reality. This fact has given rise to millennia of spirited debate about not just what those truths are, but how we as humans can understand what truth is.

It was a topic of much discussion at the original toga parties. That gaggle of verbose Greek men we usually trace our Western ideas back to (and made famous to a larger audience through Keanu Reeves' philosophical masterpiece *Bill & Ted's Excellent Adventure*) had a fairly simple explanation: the truth was what you got when describing things you could actually see and touch.

For the next few millennia, concepts of truth were bound up in theology. In the Middle Ages the truth became something that only a few people could know: more old men, this time in Christian garb. They hoarded truth by keeping it recorded in a small number of carefully hand-copied books, inaccessible to people thanks to them being illiterate and it being in a language they didn't speak even if they could read it.

The Catholic Church knew that an individual's ability to form reasoned and informed thought would lead them to contest that very 'truth' from which the church derived its power.

That's exactly what happened once the masses (or, more accurately, a slightly larger number of wealthy, educated Christian men) got their hands on the ability to do so when Gutenberg 'invented' his printing press (only a few centuries after it was invented in China and Korea).

Truth for the Many

The printing press not only allowed ideas to spread much further and faster—it allowed for a more widespread agreement on what the 'truth' was. Prior to the printing press, the small handful of written texts (the Bible chief among them) were really a centuries-long game of 'telephone' (the American name for that whisper game Australians have a less politically correct name for). Every time the text was transcribed it changed slightly, so that after thousands of years what may in some versions say 'No one whose testicles are crushed shall be admitted to the assembly of the Lord' (Deuteronomy 23:1) might in other versions become 'purple monkey dishwasher'.

The printing press allowed for the harmonisation of all versions into one single accepted 'truth'. There was a rub, however: what the church gained in codification they lost in autonomy. As more people could print, and more people could read what they'd printed, the church fragmented into almost as many splinters as there could be pamphlets printed.

Heretics who questioned the church's singular version of the truth could go 'viral' before their ideas could be brutally quashed at the end of a papal lance or on top of a bonfire. Martin Luther, the original *Old York Times* bestselling author, had copies of his manuscript show up in London just seventeen days after he first nailed it to the door of a German church. He sold 5000 copies in just two weeks (the equivalent of a record going multi-platinum despite only 10 per cent of people owning a record player). What did the text itself do? It challenged the idea that the Pope was the arbiter of truth and the false certainty the church offered. It cleaved the Western world into Protestants and Catholics.

The Reformation, as the process is now known, has been credited as giving us everything from increased literacy and education, through to states, welfare and the 'Protestant work ethic'. In reality it changed Europe's relationship to the truth.

We moved from the Greek concept of truth being something we get from our senses (which, they acknowledged, could be fallible) to one where truth was something we could arrive at through rational thinking. We generally still live with that concept, despite everything we witness in our Facebook feed or on Sky News.

Printed material enabled an accuracy in scientific data that meant scientists could faithfully interrogate and learn from each other's work, rather than learn from a third-hand approximation of something Nancy's cousin had heard on her way to market. A proliferation of technological invention followed in the next century—it was as if a world-wide web of information had spread, giving unprecedented access to ideas and each other.

Information technology created a different power dynamic. Enlightenment logically followed, marked by a questioning of the religious orthodoxy of the day—a wresting of a central truth out of the hidden hands of a papal few and into the hands of an interconnected enlightened class of thinkers, scientists, artists and writers (still all European men).

The Enlightenment was an effort to supplant blind faith with critical inquiry, superstition with logic, and belief with rational justification. It was, as the great Australian philosopher and intellectual John Farnham coined it in his seminal work, the 'Age of Reason'.

Reason had a democratising effect. It gave rise not to the replacement of one absolute truth by another, but the possibility that differing religious and political ideas could be tolerated at the same time—even by the powerful. Catherine the Great of Russia was one such ruler who embraced the concept of spreading knowledge and ideas.

Of course, these enlightened monarchs added, as long as it doesn't come at the expense of their absolute power. Hence was born the idea of the 'benevolent dictator'. You let me rule; I'll rule in the interests of the people—or, as the motto of the enlightened despots became, 'everything *for* the people, nothing *by* the people'.

Readers who spent their covid lockdowns exhausting the available library of streaming content may know this concept from Hulu's hit *The Great*, where Catherine, agitating to get out from under the yoke of her oppressive husband's rejection of Enlightenment ideas ('women are for seeding, not reading!'), declares, 'You can cut a man's head off, or you can change what's in a man's head. Do the latter, you have a warrior for your cause. Do the former, you have a head with a lot of blood pouring out.'

Others were more optimistic that the Enlightenment would bring power to the masses in a way that challenged established authoritarianism rather than entrenching it. In a view that presaged the Change.org petition by 232 years, French writer Louis-Sebástien Mercier declared in 1778: 'Public opinion has now become a preponderant power in Europe, one that cannot be resisted . . . one may hope that enlightened ideas will bring about the greatest good on Earth and that tyrants of all kinds will tremble before the universal cry that echoes everywhere.'

Two years earlier, the Enlightenment had been imported to the nascent American colonies in the form of the Declaration of Independence. The French Revolution would shortly follow, although that quickly devolved into a bloody collective lesson in the limits of human reason. The Enlightenment saw itself as the reasoned pursuit of truth, to overcome the afflictions that the enforced ignorance and religious dogma of the church and the absolute monarchies had foisted on Europe.

As literacy expanded and technology improved, more and more people were exposed to ideas and concepts that had previously been the domain of a privileged few. Truth became something that was accessible, knowable and open for debate.

It also, according to the conventional thought of everyone since Plato, set us apart from the animals. That lasted until one of the less slapstick Marx Brothers, Karl, said it wasn't reason that set us apart from the animals, it was menial labour. He thought we should stop philosophising about 'truth' and start doing something to change it—which his adherents interpreted as meaning violent revolution. We then proceeded to test his ideas out for the next hundred years. It got a bit messy.

The Enlightenment has recently been making a comeback. In response to our recent descent into a 'post-truth' era of alternate facts, many people are calling for 'a return to The Enlightenment'.

Many Truths

What scholars are failing to see, when they present a neat dichotomy between an era of 'truth' and one of 'untruth,' is that of course there has never been a single accepted truth of anything. Whether we are dressing it up as religious debate over doctrine, or shouting it drunkenly at a pub debate over sporting records, at the end of the day very little of our world is actually objective.

This thinking found most currency in the 1960s when a bunch of academics declared we should basically move on from the concept of truth itself. They said that when we had patted ourselves collectively on the back for discovering and declaring universal scientific truths, all we had been doing was merely replacing one superstitious dogma for another: every 'truth' was merely a product of the historical, cultural and social lens we view and tell them through.

Instead of one truth, there are multiple truths. There is no objective reality, only constructs in our minds that sit somewhere between abstract ideas and concrete reality. I found this particularly useful in my undergraduate degree, where I saw it as an excuse to not learn the syllabus but instead argue that the syllabus was in fact unknowable. All it proved in the end was that my lecturers were firmly rooted in the Enlightenment tradition, more Descartes than Derrida.

Of course, in reality it doesn't help us to abandon truth completely, much in the same way it didn't help my grades to give a post-structuralist critique of my tasks rather than complete them.

It does help, however, to acknowledge that context, language, bias and politics colour our understandings of the world. As the world of criminal evidence has long accepted, the same set of events witnessed by ten people can lead to ten different conclusions.

The latest cognitive science is making it clearer and clearer that our brains are simply not wired to find nor particularly concerned with rational thought and empirical truth. Those are just things we invent to further our real evolutionary motivations: belonging and fitting in.

Yet still we are all inclined to see 'facts' as the ultimate panacea to fake news. As we will discover together in the chapters to come, that instinct is wrong.

In this current Disinformation Age, we are undergoing a similar splintering into multiple subjective truths. But the script is flipped. Whereas in the Middle Ages the central truth was a closely guarded theology that then splintered into competing rational arguments over science, in the Disinformation Age the central truth was an agreed set of rational scientific facts that then splintered into fringe ideas like QAnon that more closely resemble theology.

It is the departure from the *Encyclopaedia Britannica*—one knowable and curated central repository of agreed truth—into Wikipedia, the infinite, open-sourced interpretations of reality interminably edited by anyone with access to a computer and an axe to grind. Yet Wikipedia is equally regarded by those who read it as truth. We have lost the ability to distinguish between the two.

And so continues our complicated relationship to the truth. Add to this our natural predilection to lying as part of our normal cognitive behaviour, and you have a perfectly fertile ground on which to sow disinformation campaigns.

When we see external events in our world (take, for example, an unprecedented set of bushfires burning up and down our country) traditionally we have looked for guidance in the same places as each other: the nightly news, the words of our leaders, a newspaper following normal journalistic standards of fact-checking and accuracy.

Now we are more likely to receive our information from sources that fracture a common understanding of what the truth is: extreme voices on the internet with a barrow to push; shock jocks seeking political relevance through contrarianism; misleading memes that conflate current events with ideological crusades. This takes a bushfire and makes it an easel onto which you can paint anything, from climate denialism to anti-Semitic theories about space lasers (yes, this is a real example).

Now our central truth is obscured by a false equivalence between all sources. Peter Overton is indistinguishable from Pete Evans.

It makes us no more enlightened than the thirteenth-century French peasant, whose truth was a mishmash of arcane religious doctrine and a hangover of pagan superstition. We just have fancier memes and fewer boils.

At least the French peasants knew they were ill-informed. We *feel* enlightened, even when we are not. The common refrain from an anti-vaxxer, a conspiracy theorist, an anti-lockdown crusader: 'Wake up; read the research; we know *the facts.*' They lay their wackiest claims on the foundation of empirical truth. They appeal to the framework of rationality outlined above, that there is a knowable truth and they lay claim to it, based on the scientific evidence they demonstrate.

So maybe we can declare a victory of sorts: that truth these days is so paramount that even the most misinformed in our society make their justifications through the broken lens of facts and science.

We have been from Ancient Greece to Reformation Germany, through the rational humanism of revolutionary America and the absolutism of an Enlightened Russia, detoured through the confused streets of a postmodern Paris, before we made our way back again to the primacy of a universal truth.

If we want to stay there, enjoying the fruits of progress that knowledge and science deliver (especially as we face challenges like climate change), then we'll need to reflect on our collective concept of truth and find a way to combat the deliberate disinformation that threatens to undo many of the gains made in the last few centuries of rational thought.

As Harvard psychology professor Steven Pinker argues when pointing out the progress we have made as a society, those gains were made because of the adherence to certain values:

> They valued reason: the conviction that logic and evidence are better than authority, charisma, gut feelings or mysticism. They valued science: the idea that we can understand the world by proposing explanations and testing them against reality. And they valued humanism: the idea that the well-being of men, women and children is more important than the glory of the tribe, race or nation.

But these are not *truths*, they are *values*. And as we will discover when we explore the way a brain works, our values colour our view of what is true and untrue. Rational thought is indeed useful, and key to our progress as a society, but it is in fact *irrational*.

The next step is to understand just how irrational we are. After centuries of slapping ourselves on the back at how clever and rational we had become, we are now discovering that it is all an elaborate delusion: we have merely invented rational ways of covering up our emotional wiring that will happily ignore evidence if it doesn't align with our values and beliefs. This, in a nutshell, is what allows disinformation to thrive in the face of facts.

Our key to defeating disinformation lies in first understanding this irrationality.

3 / A Brief End of History of Truth

Bill S. Preston, Esq: 'The only true wisdom consists
in knowing that you know nothing.'
Ted 'Theodore' Logan: 'That's us, dude!'
—*Bill & Ted's Excellent Adventure*

Just as one brave shopper in Beijing was playing *Frogger* with a tank on his way through Tiananmen Square in 1989, a young American policy analyst on the other side of the world published an article in a little-known journal with a circulation of about 6000 readers, all of them inside the bubble of the Washington DC beltway. Unbeknownst to the shopper in Beijing as he was momentarily halting the advance of a column of tanks towards students agitating for democracy in China, the American analyst had confidently declared that whole struggle was over. Democracy had won a total victory.

The little-known author gave his article a provocative title, 'The End of History?', and then proceeded to address the question mark at the end of the title with an emphatic answer: with the imminent disintegration of the Soviet Union, American liberalism would be the last man standing, having seen off fascism in World War II and now communism with Gorbachev's embrace of the free market and blue jeans.

History was over! We won!

What we may be witnessing is not just the end of the Cold War,
or the passing of a particular period of postwar history, but the end
of history as such: that is, the end point of mankind's ideological
evolution and the universalization of Western liberal democracy as
the final form of human government.

The author, Francis Fukuyama, became something of an overnight intellectual celebrity. His article quickly became a book, and his phrase 'the end of history' became more of a slogan, shorthand for the victory lap the West could run around their old foes vanquished to the dustbin of the USSR as the Iron Curtain was drawn open.

In pre-internet terms, it 'went viral'. The *New York Times* described how: 'In Washington, a newsdealer on Connecticut Avenue reported, the summer issue of the *National Interest* was "outselling everything, even the pornography".' The article marvelled at how:

> Within weeks, 'The End of History?' had become the hottest topic around, this year's answer to Paul Kennedy's phenomenal best seller, *The Rise and Fall of the Great Powers*. George F. Will was among the first to weigh in, with a *Newsweek* column in August; two weeks later, Fukuyama's photograph appeared in *TIME*. The French quarterly *Commentaire* announced that it was devoting a special issue to 'The End of History?'. The BBC sent a television crew. Translations of the piece were scheduled to appear in Dutch, Japanese, Italian and Icelandic. Ten Downing Street requested a copy.

His thesis became the philosophical foundation for Bush I, and the moral justification for the 'benevolent hegemony' (read: invading countries you don't like) of Bush II that would follow.

In his arguments, Fukuyama borrowed heavily from the German philosopher Hegel—the guy who also declared he represented the 'end of philosophy' because his thinking was the historical culmination of all previous philosophical thought. Hegel, to his credit, was the first major Western philosopher to acknowledge people were a product of their social and historical environment instead of merely having 'natural attributes', but he also believed that history had a beginning, a middle and an end.

But whereas Hegel inspired the view that a final victory for progress would come in the form of a communist state, Fukuyama saw things differently.

Without any hint of irony that it was Hegel who gave us Marx, who then gave us communism who in turn gave us Ivan Drago in *Rocky IV*, Fukuyama decoupled Hegel from all that socialist nonsense to focus purely on Hegel's view on history: 'a moment in which a final, rational form of society and state became victorious'. To Fukuyama we had clearly reached that final victory. No other forms of government need apply. Game over.

Of course, we can say with the predictable benefit of hindsight that it was *not* game over. As a young Christopher Hitchens decried when Fukuyama's article first came out, it was mere 'self-congratulation raised to the status of philosophy'.

Bold predictions that China was democratising in favour of Western liberalism fell as flat as those other shoppers who bravely tried to stand up to the Chinese tanks, and Donald Trump gave his best shot at putting a big dent in the idea that American hegemony is a given. Free trade faces a renewed protectionism, now wielded as a blunt force instrument of diplomacy—from Trump's tariffs on EU steel to China's tariffs on Australian wine.

Democracy did nothing for the UK's free market ideals when it forced an exit from the EU, Cold War tensions thought long put to bed have bubbled up to the surface again, and unchecked authoritarian rule that enriches its leaders from Central Asia to Central Africa is doing nothing for the bold claim that democracy is the only road to riches. The assumption that you can't have capitalist wealth creation without freedom and liberalism is laughable, and just ask anyone who lost their house in the 2008 crash whether laissez-faire economics is the key to prosperity. As Thomas Piketty laid out in *Capital in the Twenty-First Century*, free markets have not only enlarged the gap between rich and poor people, but also reduced average incomes in both rich and poor countries. The very nature of how we organise our societies and economies is once again up for debate. Even the small government–loving Liberal Party of John Howard embraced big government when the shit hit the economic fan during covid. History might just have a little more in store for us.

And what does this all have to do with disinformation?

Bold declarations of the end of anything rarely stand up to the test of time, no matter how certain they feel at the time—to Fukuyama and his contemporaries, the collapse of the Soviet Union after decades of Cold War and a century of ideological warfare really did have a feeling of finality about it.

We had a similar collective feeling, before this recent disinfodemic, that the triumph of reason had been permanently realised. The Earth was round, vaccines worked and science was fact.

Now, we are caught in our own 'end of history' moment when it comes to truth and reason. Fukuyama's final triumph is anything but. The seamless spread of disinformation to become so dominant has taken most of us by surprise—we had become conditioned in telling ourselves we had experienced the triumph of truth, science and information over myth, superstition and ignorance. An 'end of history' to the entire process of Western civilisation's journey to find and define truth.

We won! We found the truth! Our millennia-long attempts at distinguishing the line between truth and falsehood have been accomplished! Our accepted liberal ideal that eliminated all other competitors was that if you give facts out you receive universal truth in return.

It has been a common theme throughout intellectual history to see our cognitive and social evolution as linear: we are continually progressing towards an end point (full enlightenment, a meaning of life, a crimeless society, a 'war to end all wars').

But recent developments in science have made it clear that we are much less rational than we think, and our brains are not geared to find truth, but instead to find each other (and yes, I acknowledge I turn to scientific thought to dispel the notion we are rational). We are social first and rational second, and the former will almost always win out over the latter. There are deep behavioural instincts that drive our cognition, and sometimes trump it.

This means disinformation is about more than just a few disrupted electoral cycles. It represents an abrupt deviation of the arc towards truth we had assumed was a linear trend. It has thrust us into a new epoch, one where emotion rules over reason.

The collision of cognitive psychology and disinformation, as we will explore in depth, has upset the apple carts of political science and philosophy: we are not rational creatures marching ever onwards and upwards to enlightened progress through market liberalism—we were just nodding in furious agreement with Jenny when she suggested it to us in the seminar, for fear of her not joining us for a drink after the meeting was over. Religion, culture, group dynamics, upbringing and the social setting are far greater determinative factors in whether or not we will agree with Francis Fukuyama's ideas than the merits of his arguments or the evidence he presents. We will just reverse-engineer an intellectually convincing rationale for our opinions *after* we have formed them.

Almost every great philosopher from Socrates to Descartes assumed this happened in reverse: that human beings are presented with information, and form their opinions based on what they receive.

Instead, it is the other way around.

When you read an article about how our ice caps are melting at an even more alarming rate than previously thought, you *think* you are filing that away as another data point in your forming opinions about climate change. In reality, you have already formed your opinions and instead are filing it based on whether it supports them or not.

Navigating Truth

There are good reasons for our reluctance to embrace this reality: our opinions are not worth much unless we maintain the illusion they are based on truth.

It would serve no one if our political leaders got up in a press conference and declared, 'What you are about to hear is purely based on my pre-existing political biases and in no way should be construed as the truth.' They have to tell their truths to govern, to make policy and to define our national narratives.

In reality we are better off sailing right past the thorny reality of our cognitive biases and the question about whether truth is even knowable, because of the very reasons those biases exist in the first place: we need to belong, and to do that we need to convey shared truthfulness through which we connect with each other.

James Clinch, who has researched disinformation from a psychology viewpoint, calls the big question of whether truth even exists 'an intellectual and cultural whirlpool with serious sucking power' from which it is difficult to get away in any discussion about shared truths.

In order to reason with each other we need to agree on a certain set of rules. One of those rules we have agreed on is that facts exist and are knowable, and that causes exist and are reliably linked to effects. Without those premises the whole house of cards of social cooperation and shared understanding collapses.

Imagine if two teams showed up on a sporting field, one with cricket bats and the other with footballs. It's not going to be a very good game unless the teams can first agree on what sport they are going to play—a shared set of rules makes a game possible. We are much better off continuing under the fiction that the truth is knowable if we want to play science.

It's like the difference between Newtonian physics and quantum physics: quantum physics tells us that everything is pretty much random and immeasurable, whereas the old Newtonian physics it replaced told us that everything worked like a predictable machine. The quantum physicists may be right, but for most people Newton is much more useful. Warning someone that an apple is about to fall on their head will always win you more friends than explaining to them that the apple is really just an unpredictable combination of random waves and particles.

Likewise, it is much more useful to society to warn people of the harms caused by fake news (like 'covid isn't real') than to explain to them the flaws in philosophical thinking that caused their understanding of the concept of 'fake' in the first place.

We won't get far by throwing the truth out with the bathwater. Postmodernist philosophers like Jacques Derrida tried, but it made people so uncomfortable it was dismissed as 'fashionable nonsense'. Whatever Derrida derided, dear reader, de reader desires de reason.

As Friedrich Nietzsche said, in a broad swipe at the type of culture wars he didn't even know were coming, a version of history that is more like art would be more useful than a history that is actually truthful: 'The history that merely destroys without any impulse to construct will in the end make its instruments tired of life; for such men destroy illusions.' He gave the example of religion, which if studied scientifically and historically, would be 'destroyed at the end of it all'. John Howard would have agreed. He wanted an end to this annoying obsession historians had with telling the truth about how Australia was colonised, because he believed 'as a nation we're over all that sort of stuff'.

What Nietzsche and Howard were really saying is that their versions of truth were more *useful* than the actual truth. It sounds absurd, but it actually embraces the reality of how truth is not really knowable—we have the ability to establish facts, and we then rationalise them into our own worldviews. The most convenient way to do so is to just skip over the whole part that questions the concept of 'truth' in the first place.

It is extremely difficult to fully grasp our disinfodemic without understanding the contested nature of truth and reason. But at the same time, once we gain that understanding it is then near unworkable. It is impossible to do anything about disinformation without retaining some kind of fidelity to truth itself. Facts are real, our interpretation of them is contested. My interpretation is my truth; your interpretation is your truth.

Without any commitment to facts, as contested as they are, we lose the whole compass steering this grand human experiment. So instead we need a better acknowledgement of their subjectivity.

Hannah Arendt, writing in the 1960s, had a similar reflection on this point in her essay 'Truth and Politics' when she too was examining the shortcomings of centuries of philosophical thought about truth and reason.

She distinguished between *factual truths*—things that happened, like 'in 1492 Columbus sailed the ocean blue', and *rational truths*—things that we 'work out' to be true, through processes like maths and science, like '2 + 2 = 4'.

To argue against a rational truth you merely need to make an error, but to argue against a factual truth you need to be deliberately deceitful, which the ancient philosophers never predicted people would do on a grand scale. This was best summed up by a lesser-known philosopher, Trump spokeswoman Kellyanne Conway, when she argued in favour of 'alternative facts'.

For Arendt, factual truths were in conflict with political power. It wasn't until Trump came along that this reality was brought out into the light of day, and the whole pretence of political truth was dropped entirely. Until then, political power had still draped its lies in the cloak of truth.

But acknowledging the subjectivity of all truth shouldn't mean we then give a green light to brazen lying, and a free pass to those who do it—lest we are all, in Nietzsche's words, 'destroyed at the end of it'.

We can instead agree there is good reasoning and bad reasoning. It's not merely my cultural biases and political beliefs that lead me to conclude climate change is real; there is a body of scientific evidence to give my truth a universality, even if the motivations are contested.

If I present you evidence of something walking like a duck, talking like a duck, and meeting the agreed scientific consensus for possessing the constituent characteristics of a duck, then my reasoning that it is a duck is superior to your reasoning that it is a blimp.

Our brains have evolved to be able to define a duck from that information, and it is a critical part of our human cognition. What we then need to understand is that the cognition that allows us to reason that it is a duck is also in competition with other things our brain does: like wanting to eat the duck.

We layer our reason on top of our instincts, and then the brain works overtime to make the two impulses compatible. If in the course of doing so we have to fudge our cognition of the facts, or ignore them completely, then the brain will happily do it.

Neurologically, this is broadly a battle between the prefrontal cortex, where our executive function lives (I'm going to reason this is a duck based on the information I see), and the deeper parts of the brain, particularly the amygdala, which drives our emotional lives (I am going to crack the skull of that guy holding that delicious duck so I can eat it).

Take this comment on a Facebook post from a Fox News viewer in America: 'I'd rather receive false information and keep my conservative views then [sic] receive true information and follow a socialistic agenda.'

 I'd rather receive false information and keep my conservative views then receive true information and follow a socialistic agenda.

2m   Like   Reply

While we can rightly mock their reasoning, the poster is merely articulating the reality of our cognitive process: the brain would much rather keep beliefs than change them due to facts.

Thinking otherwise has been the undoing of our response to the crisis of disinformation. Consider how social media platforms treat this person if they are served misinformation: show them facts to the contrary, in the expectation they will change their beliefs. This policy has no basis in neuroscience.

As creatures, we are made up of parts of us that favour reason and parts that disdain it. Often they are in conflict with each other. And so, in society we have experienced times where the parts that favour reason have been ascendant (like the Enlightenment), and times when the parts that disdain it were ascendant (like the Inquisition).

Reason is a human capability that is useful for getting important stuff done, like science and cryptic crosswords. However, it's only one force within human psychology, and there are other forces within us that are distinctly anti-reason. The interplay of those two forces, within individuals and societies, is one of the great themes of our history.

The Khmer Rouge emptied the cities of Cambodia and killed everyone who wore glasses in their attempt to revive the glory days of 'anti-reason', and history is rife with similar purges. America's presidents bemoaned reason long before Trump made it an artform; Woodrow Wilson said over a century ago: 'What I fear is a government of experts.' An anti-reason platform is often a prerequisite for their election, perhaps owing to America's Puritanical roots, which proclaimed, 'The more learned and witty you bee, the more fit to act for Satan will you bee.' Reason most often fought its wars with religion, the two standard bearers for our conflicting brain functions.

Rather than a linear progression towards truth and reason with an enlightened end point, as thinkers have traditionally approached the question, what we have really experienced is a constantly shifting battle over our hearts, minds and brains where reason is just one of the combatants. There is nothing in the make-up of our brains to say it is the dominant one.

Sometimes the technological, social, economic and political conditions favour the form of human cognition known as reason, and sometimes they don't.

The fundamental thing to understand is that in the Disinformation Age, we are now sliding down from one of the peaks of our love affair with reason, and entering another trough. What we're experiencing right now is a set of conditions far more hostile to reason than anything since Gutenberg started printing bestselling pamphlets. Technology is probably the main reason why, as this book will endeavour to explain.

One of the other big myths we have lived under is that the advance of progress and reason was evenly shared. Even during those periods we thought reason was universally prevailing, the 'truth' was always elitist. Look throughout history to see how it was a small privileged few who owned it, interpreted it, debated it and shared it.

Truth and reason never conquered falsehoods and ignorance. A privileged handful could say that of themselves, but not of society writ large. They merely proclaimed it as universally shared—that's our own biases if we believe it. Just look at how my treatise ignores all other thought than Western liberal philosophical history: Fukuyama was similarly blind to China when he had his eyes fixed on Europe's embrace of free markets and freedoms.

The participants in the debate over reason have always been propped up on the foundations that the privileges of literacy, education and leisure provide. The masses never had that luxury, and instead learned to live with our inbuilt ignorance.

Throughout history, knowledge, truth and reason were kept locked away from them in intellectual ivory towers, just as Plato had foreseen it in his famous cave analogy—where most people lived happily in ignorance in a cave looking at shadows, while only a small number of philosophers knew the truth of the sunlit outside world of reality.

We declared the printing press a breakthrough for the mass dissemination of ideas and information, and we hung our society's shingle on the idea of mass enlightenment.

But it was always a myth. The truth, even as it was in the ascendancy, was never evenly distributed. When we see a decline in reason, perhaps we are only witnessing an incline in the number of people able to be heard. We have always been just as unenlightened as we are now, but armed with disinformation handed down from the elites, the masses now have a willing megaphone to amplify it. Social media has laid this bare by inverting the balance between reason and ignorance.

Finding the truth is really difficult; we've been trying since the Greeks. Even basic 'facts' are not handed to us from on high—they have to be established. Historically there were few participants in this game, then technology opened the floodgates for everybody to participate. During the Enlightenment we got quite serious about discovering one single truth, but by the mid-twentieth century we'd largely given up on finding it.

The intellectual claims of many competing truths is not only the backdrop to the current disinfodemic—it is actually our best understanding of the true nature of reality. As Clinch put it to me, 'For whatever reason, our current era is one in which reason is taking a pounding. Seeking to return to a mythical world of "one truth" is a fool's errand. Instead, we need to learn to operate in the jungle of competing realities.'

While we might not have seen the end of history, we have now seen the end of a golden age of truth and reason. That's a disconcerting shift, and why your everyday conversations are dominated with the disbelief of how crackpot conspiracy theories seem so much more mainstream these days.

To understand the technological forces that pushed us from the peak of reason into the trough of disinformation, we need to first understand the history of information.

4 / A Brief History of Information

'We become what we behold. We shape our tools
and then our tools shape us.'
—attributed to Marshall McLuhan

If I had to write all of human history onto a matchbox, it would look something like this: we started off hunting and gathering, then moved on to farming, then built factories, and lastly moved on to computers.

Helpfully, historians have already come up with clever names for these eras.

In 'Pre-History' (a cunning concept to cover everything we have forgotten because nobody bothered to write it down), as hunter-gatherer nomads we mastered fire, put on clothes, made art and played music.

In the 'Agrarian Age' we decided to put down roots. It seemed like a great way to take a load off, but in reality it just made things complicated: people had to be organised, crops protected, rules made and followed. We built the wheel, took wild animals and made them domestic, invented laws and government and wine, and learned how to write. Eventually we built empires and explored the globe. That age ran right from antiquity through classical history and into modern history. But that's all ancient history now.

When someone had the clever notion of replacing farm hand-tools with mechanical equipment, and powering them by coal and steam, things really got interesting. We call the ensuing reorganisation of the economy and society into mass urban centres of factory workers the Industrial Revolution, and the age of rapid population and economic growth it spawned the 'Industrial Age'. Many parts of the world are still living in it.

The Industrial Age gave us such gifts as unfettered capitalism, pollution and income inequality, although most economists prefer to focus on the overall increase in living standards and life expectancy. GDP per capita (that measure of the economy where Jeff Bezos standing in a room with ten homeless people means they are all counted as multi-billionaires) had remained fairly stable throughout most of human history, but with the Industrial Revolution it grew exponentially.

People left the farms and villages to seek work in the factories, and the owners of those factories became a new middle class who weren't the old landed gentry and nobility. It kicked off a period of sustained growth that continues to this day, save for a couple of hiccups along the way like the great toilet paper hoardings of 1929, 2008 and 2020.

We got taller (except for that weird thing—known affectionately as The Antebellum Puzzle—where American men started shrinking, as GDP growth doesn't automatically mean everyone gets enough food), healthier (except for the widespread epidemics of infectious diseases like cholera and typhoid from being crammed into unsanitary worker slums), lived longer (unless you were a child, they were surviving infancy better but then dying in greater numbers as miniature miners and labourers), and ate better (if you could afford it, as—bear with me—linear growth in food production couldn't keep pace with exponential growth in population, otherwise known as your classic Malthusian trap).

But growth is good, and it gave us conditions so bad we had to unionise, and the unions gave us eight-hour work days, and eight-hour work days gave us leisure time for the first time, and some smart people used that spare time to invent computers.

That's when shit really got crazy.

An Information Explosion

Depending on your age, computers might not seem that exceptional, so pervasive are they in our lives now. You might even have been born into a world that was already governed by them. (Remember Y2K, when we realised just how dependent we'd become on computers, only to be relieved that instead of Armageddon we only suffered a few astronomical overdue video fines?) You might even be reading this on one, or on a tiny version of one that fits in your hand and can also tell the time, make phone calls and record and broadcast you dancing the 'Renegade' to millions of TikTok users around the world.

Computers are truly a remarkable invention that have remade our world. Just as the human brain is made up of billions of tiny interconnected neurons that fire together to enable us to dance those 'Renegade' dance moves, physicists were able to create little transistors that can do the same thing by amplifying signals in circuits. Memory chips in our computers are made up of billions of them.

One of the early inventors of those transistors, William Shockley, explained to his student how they work :

> If you take a bale of hay and tie it to the tail of a mule and then strike
> a match and set the bale of hay on fire, and if you then compare
> the energy expended shortly thereafter by the mule with the
> energy expended by yourself in the striking of the match, you will
> understand the concept of amplification.

These microscopic mule bonfires kicked off the world as we know it.

Pretty soon these transistors allowed us to assemble a machine that could process and manipulate more data than a human could, all the while taking up an entire room and costing only $3 million in today's terms.

When I was a kid, the technology had become so advanced I could load our Commodore 64 with a cassette, and after only a few short hours of playing outside, a game of *Pac-Man* would be ready to play. With its whopping 0.064 MB of computing power (one photo on your smartphone today is about 3 MB, or 47 times larger for comparison), it was a triumph of miniaturisation and home computing power. The laptop I am typing this manuscript on, which cost about the same as a Commodore 64 adjusted for inflation, has 16GB of memory. That's roughly 250,000 times more powerful.

This revolution was one in how we store and communicate information.

Think about the amount of information you can store on a USB stick, compared to the bulk of that information if you had to print it all out onto physical paper. If all the world's information storage capacity was apportioned equally to everyone on Earth, in 1986 each person wouldn't have even gotten a full CD-ROM's worth of storage (remember them?). By 2007 they had 61 CD-ROMs worth each, and in 2022 we each have the equivalent of more than 19,000 per person.

It's grown 58 per cent per year on average. We're even running out of words to measure it with. We only have one more prefix before '-byte' left after we exhaust our current ones. And who is going to remember how much a 'Yottabyte' is?

So what did we become able to do with all this information, all this storage?

An Optimistic Promise

When dishing out your $3 million for your IBM supercomputer, there was one big problem: you could only access it there at your standalone terminal. You couldn't take your work home with you, and your computer didn't speak to any other computers. This was a big problem if you were concerned about a large Soviet bomb landing on the one computer you had, thereby wiping out your entire data system (this was not a hypo-thetical—the original computer, the German Z3, had been destroyed by an Allied bomb falling on Berlin in 1943).

So in 1959 the US military designed a network of machines that could talk to each other, and so therefore survive a Soviet nuclear attack and preserve the ability of the military to communicate in the messy aftermath (cute of them to think there would be an 'aftermath' of the Cold War turning nuclear hot, but hey, it gave us the internet).

Imagine making a Lego model in Sydney, and wanting to share it with your cousin in Perth. You could break it up into its constituent pieces, stuff them in an envelope with assembly instructions, and mail it to Western Australia where they could reassemble it at the other end. That, essentially, is how the network of computers the military built worked. They took information, reduced it into tiny 'packets' that could be reassembled back into the information at the other end, and sent them travelling around the network.

It wasn't until 30 years later in 1989 that a guy named Tim Berners-Lee proposed a way to do this on every computer assembled all over the world.

To do this you needed a common language (a *'protocol'*—maybe a *hypertext* one to *transfer* information? We'll call it 'http' for short), and a bit of common software in order to read, or 'browse', the information when it comes through (let's call that a 'browser'). He even came up with a catchy name for the information reader: the 'World Wide Web' (let's just say 'www' for short).

By 2018, despite glaring inequality and technological apartheid, the majority of the world's population was using the internet—many of them never having even had a landline telephone.

Crucially, Berners-Lee open-sourced the code and protocols rather than privatising it under the protection of a commercial patent. All of a sudden, for the first time in human history, information was free and accessible.

When I did my undergraduate degree, assignments were a process of going to the library, finding books on the shelves, photocopying the relevant pages and taking those sheets of paper home to assist with writing an essay. If I wanted to get technical, I might look at a microfiche.

It was an exercise in privilege, afforded to only the slim minority of people lucky enough to have access to that trove of intellectual thought and information.

Now I don't need a library card, I just need Google. I source information for this very book you are reading on websites, archives, online journals and newspapers that are as accessible to me as they are to anyone with access to a computer and an internet connection (and yes, that still excludes a great many people, and yes much of it is now paywalled), whether they are in Outer Barcoo or Uttar Pradesh. Having never met them or been to these places, I can even socially engage with those people over the material we can both access from a thousand miles away.

The world, now connected by the internet, would never be the same again. Satellites, fibre optic cables, microprocessors, video-conferencing, social networks, 5G: our world is one interconnected and interdependent web of information technology.

I never realised just how true this was until I was plunged into the dark ages for a week when I was living in lower Manhattan during Hurricane Sandy (which, as a sidenote, was also the subject of a great deal of disinformation, including images of sharks swimming in the subway). No power, no phone signal, no internet, no news other than what your neighbour heard from their neighbour through word of mouth. My family only knew I was alive thanks to a working payphone and its underground copper wire connection, ironically scheduled at the time to be ripped out due to its obsolescence. When I was delivered back to a technological time of yore, it was disconcerting to discover just how dependent life had become on what were only very recent technological advances.

This is to say nothing of business and government dependence on the internet. It's why the only real battlefront of interstate conflict these days is through armies of cyber attackers trying to disrupt a nation in the most devastating way possible: by taking down their information networks.

In May 2017, the entire British Airways fleet was grounded on one of the busiest travel weeks of the year because an IT contractor accidentally turned off the big switch labelled 'uninterruptible power supply', thereby proving that label wrong. There was nothing wrong with the planes, but without a working website, app, call centres and IT system, the baggage couldn't move, passenger credentials couldn't be issued, nor could they be moved onto other flights. Airport staff resorted to using whiteboards. The outage lasted three days and was estimated to have cost the airline $150 million and the British economy even more.

Our rapid dependence on these technologies grew because we embraced them as liberating and democratising. One of the first scholars to look at the internet, political scientist Ithiel de Sola Pool, called it a 'technology of freedom' in 1983.

The internet made us a lot of promises, many of them utopian. We had always been a networked society—that is our human nature—but for the first time we were a globally connected network society.

It heralded an era of unfettered access to information and each other: hence we anointed it 'The Information Age'.

It was a time of abundant optimism.

In 1996 the self-styled 'cyberlibertarian' John Perry Barlow, who also moonlighted as The Grateful Dead's lyricist, created the 'Declaration of the Independence of Cyberspace'. In it he spoke for the new age of democratised information that would liberate us from the old world. It magnanimously opens—with all the poetic stonerist imagery of a Grateful Dead song—with the new world addressing the old: *'Governments of the Industrial World, you weary giants of flesh and steel, I come from Cyberspace, the new home of Mind.'*

The declaration captured much of the idealistic optimism that the internet promised:

> We are creating a world that all may enter without privilege or prejudice accorded by race, economic power, military force, or station of birth.
>
> We are creating a world where anyone, anywhere may express his or her beliefs, no matter how singular, without fear of being coerced into silence or conformity.
>
> Your legal concepts of property, expression, identity, movement, and context do not apply to us. They are all based on matter, and there is no matter here.

It was a form of techno-utopianism that said that though industrial machines had enslaved us, information networks would set us free. In hindsight, it was overly optimistic.

The internet promised us freewheeling intellectual liberation, but in reality delivered us cat videos.

It promised to break down cultural and political barriers through the democratising effect of an informed citizenry, to free people from the yoke of suppression by connecting them to a liberated global network of ideas, and a new enlightenment through the universal spread of knowledge previously hoarded under academic lock and key.

But somehow, these technologies also enabled the opposite.

The Information Age promised a breaking down of barriers, but the Disinformation Age has thrown up walls around narrow groups hostile to outside thought. The Information Age promised liberty through truth but the Disinformation Age has encouraged oppression through lies. The internet was not the democratising force we had first hoped.

In later chapters, we will examine just why that optimism was misplaced. The internet, as it turned out, was not immune to the forces of corporatism, censorship and state power that it promised to overthrow. In fact, it reinforced them.

It was unwittingly the perfect tool to undermine the things it promised to lift up: democracy, knowledge and freedom. It concentrated power in a few omnipotent companies with control and knowledge about every tiny facet of our lives that governments could only dream of, gave governments a tool to monitor their citizens without oversight, and destroyed the one true defence we had against those consequences: a functioning free press.

We now inhabit an information ecosystem of closed networks, corporate paywalls and government firewalls. Worse, its algorithms encourage and reward fear, ignorance and innuendo, and punish facts, nuance and common ground.

The internet created a perfect storm which weaponised disinformation could sail through unperturbed, while truth, reason and rationality lay wrecked on the jagged rocks of technology's own creation.

The Disinformation Age is threatening to undo many of the last few centuries' greatest achievements. It places on all of us a supreme responsibility to recognise and counter the forces of disinformation when we see them—which is probably every time we open our phones to look at social media.

This book is a tool to do just that.

5 / A Brief History of News

'The man who never looks into a newspaper is better informed than he who reads them; inasmuch as he who knows nothing is nearer to truth than he whose mind is filled with falsehoods & errors.'
—Thomas Jefferson

The rise of disinformation was precipitated by the decline of something else: the news industry, as your grandparents knew it.

We can't fully grasp the current disinfodemic without first charting the course of how the news media, once a fertile and abundant crop nourishing us all in abundant supply, disintegrated to instead become mere sod-forming waste nutrients for the crop that was to grow in its place: clickbait infotainment masquerading as news.

We can tell the story of the news over the last century through the tale of two Murdochs: Keith Sr and Keith Jr.

The Rise of News

In 1915, a letter from Keith Murdoch Sr reached the Australian prime minister Andrew Fisher's wartime desk:

> I now write of the unfortunate Dardanelles expedition . . . It is undoubtedly one of the most terrible chapters in our history. Your fears have been justified . . . This unfortunate expedition has never been given a chance. It required large bodies of seasoned troops. It required a great leader. It required self-sacrifice on the part of the staff as well as that sacrifice so wonderfully and liberally made on the part of the soldiers. It has had none of these things.

News travelled incredibly slowly back then, and even the highest political office relied on a drip-feed of censored British army briefings to keep updated on the progress of a war fought a world away. The Australian wartime leaders had not even been informed of the plan to land at the Dardanelles until after it had already happened.

The Australian public, like the prime minister, had little idea that the corps of fresh Australian youth, fighting in the uniform of a country less than fifteen years old, that they had waved off overseas, had become futile fodder for the Turkish machine guns perched high along the ridges of Gallipoli.

Keith Murdoch had a journalist's turn of phrase. He had ostensibly been sent to report back on the delays in mail reaching the troops, and his description of the post office, 'an inert mass of congealed incompetency', would appeal to a reader in any era as timelessly accurate.

But he also had an agenda. He viewed the British officer class he had met in the Mediterranean as grossly incompetent, and tragically wasteful of the Australian lives they commanded.

The news media had always been proudly activist, like the glowing praise of Thomas Jefferson from sympathetic newspapers mentioned previously. Murdoch now had a mission.

He agreed to defy the military censors and smuggle out a letter from British war correspondent Ellis Ashmead-Bartlett about the stark realities of the Gallipoli campaign. But the British caught wind of his plan and sent word ahead to the port of Marseilles, where the military police seized the letter in Murdoch's possession.

Not to be deterred by either the threat of punishment nor the absence of the only copy of a detailed account of an entire military campaign, Murdoch sat down straight away at his portable typewriter and tapped out an 8000-word letter of his own, based on what he could recall was written in Ashmead-Bartlett's letter as well as his own observations and conversations from his time there.

His letter detailed a costly and ineffective military campaign led by incompetence, and trenches full of disease and despondence.

It was a simultaneous feat of journalism, bravery and recollection. It also contained a generous dose of chutzpah.

More than this, it changed the course of history.

The letter set a political cat among the pigeons in London when Murdoch landed there, and ultimately resulted in the decision to evacuate the forces from the failed campaign on the Gallipoli peninsula. General Hamilton was recalled to London, ending his illustrious military career, howling complaints that Murdoch had violated his gentlemanly agreements to be bound by the usual military censorship and manners.

In Australia, it laid the foundation for the Anzac myth we still cling to today despite the choppy waters of its contested meaning in a modern national identity. The picture that emerged from Gallipoli was powerful enough to create a legend that converted a military defeat into a moral victory.

The context in which Murdoch was able to do this was remarkable.

Murdoch was able to show that under the same conditions as all other war correspondents, it was possible for a determined journalist to avoid censorship and provide first-hand accounts of what was actually happening. Ernest Hemingway, who himself saw action on the front lines in a Red Cross ambulance unit, wrote in 1918 that:

> The last war, during the years of 1915, 1916, 1917, was the most colossal, murderous, mismanaged butchery that has ever taken place on earth. Any writer who said otherwise lied. So the writers either wrote propaganda, shut up, or fought.

Phillip Knightley in his history of war correspondents called it 'a great conspiracy.' In the First World War he said, 'More deliberate lies were told than in any other period of history, and the whole apparatus of the state went into action to suppress the truth.'

The war correspondents were complicit in this sordid conspiracy, first because of the obstacles put in their way of finding out what was really happening on the front line (a heavily curated experience directed by the military brass) but second because of the nature of the horrors they saw once there. By London newspaper *The Times*' (now owned by the Murdoch family, incidentally) own account, 'such knowledge as was theirs inspired silence'. *The Times* wrote in their own official company history that the principal aim of the war policy of the newspaper 'was to increase the flow of recruits. It was an aim that would get little help from accounts of what happened to recruits once they became soldiers.'

Knightley goes so far as to suggest—referring to the Murdoch story—that 'if the war correspondents in France had only been as enterprising, the war might not have continued on its ghastly course'. Murdoch's account wasn't the perfect record of truth (in reality it was a highly coloured litany of editorialised gossip—like all good yarns), but it was pure journalism: an unsanitised account of events told in the face of the prevailing powers' wishes.

The allegiance of good journalists in Keith Murdoch's day was to the news. Profit was still the ultimate motive, but good news sold well. News and profit lived in handy symbiosis. Good journalism built audiences that, though still seeking to reaffirm their existing biases, would buy and read their newspaper with an unfailing fidelity matched only by Sunday church. In my household growing up, the morning newspaper was a more dependable appearance at the breakfast table than breakfast.

Murdoch, having doggedly beaten the military censors in the name of journalism, had shone a light on a story now so familiar we've learned it at primary school for generations. Flush with unprecedented political influence, he returned to Australia where he began a long Murdoch family tradition of buying newspapers and using them to promote or punish Australian prime ministerial aspirants.

When Keith Murdoch Sr died in 1952, his son Keith Jr took over the running of the family newspaper business.

To get out from under his father's shadow, Keith Jr let it be known he would prefer to go by his middle name: Rupert.

Keith Murdoch was everything that his son Rupert would become: cosy to political power and influence, shamelessly self-promoting, and an activist journalist bent on encouraging one outcome or another in support of his cronies. But Murdoch Sr represented a different era of news media, one built on a centralised machine of fact-finding and truth-telling that feared veering far from the mainstream, whose eyeballs they sold off in lucrative advertising deals.

Rupert Murdoch inherited an ailing business, as most of Keith's estate had gone to paying off his creditors. Murdoch Jr took one Adelaide newspaper still remaining and turned it into a global media empire, one that would come to own more than 800 titles in 50 countries, including the *Wall Street Journal* in the US and *The Times* in the UK.

But it was one business decision in particular that changed the shape of the media landscape forever: hiring an ex-Nixon and Reagan media adviser, Roger Ailes, to launch in 1996 a 24-hour cable news channel to be named Fox News.

Ailes had learned one simple lesson in his time working with Reagan, a political novice plucked straight from Hollywood films: people don't want to be informed, they want to be entertained. He summed it up less elegantly: 'If you have two guys on a stage and one guy says, "I have a solution to the Middle East problem," and the other guy falls in the orchestra pit, who do you think is going to be on the evening news?'

This 'Orchestra Pit Principle' was enough to make a media empire.

Roger Ailes had already given Richard Nixon to America. He took a 'sweaty, shifty-eyed, self-pitying, petulant, paranoid perpetual candidate whom Americans instinctively mistrusted' and made him president. That he was able to do so was thanks to Ailes' canny knack for what audiences wanted.

In later life he told *Esquire* magazine, 'If Richard Nixon was alive today, he'd be on the couch with Oprah, talking about how he was poor, his brother died, his mother didn't love him, and his father beat the shit out of him. And everybody would say, Oh, poor guy, he's doing the best he can.'

The same profile went on to describe the exchange when Ailes first met Nixon, as the presidential hopeful was preparing to go on a TV talk show Ailes was producing at the time:

'It's a shame a man has to use gimmicks like this to get elected,'
Mr Nixon is supposed to have remarked to Mr Ailes. 'Television is not
a gimmick, and if you think it is, you'll lose again,' Mr Ailes is supposed
to have remarked to Mr Nixon. And there the modern conservative
movement—not the ideological entity but the telegenic one—was born.

In 2011, a journalist was trawling through Nixon's presidential library
when he stumbled upon a startling memo from 1970 entitled 'A Plan for
Putting the GOP on TV News', with Roger Ailes' handwriting all over it.
The memo opens:

> For 200 years the newspaper front page dominated public thinking.
> In the last 20 years that picture has changed. Today television news
> is watched more often than people read newspapers, than people
> listen to the radio, than people read or gather any other form of
> communication. The reason: People are lazy. With television you just
> sit—watch—listen. The thinking is done for you.

It went on to outline in detail, down to the line item budget for the
number of cameras and other equipment needed, exactly how the
Republicans could get their message straight to local news services
around the country by bypassing the national networks.

There, as plain as day, under a heading of this secret plan entitled
'THE PLAN' it declares 'Purpose—To provide pro-Administration,
videotape, hard news actualities to the major cities of the United States.'
And why? 'It avoids the censorship, the priorities and the prejudices of
network news selectors and disseminators.'

It would take another quarter of a century before Ailes' plan was
fully realised in the form of a network leviathan that outsized even Ailes'
lofty ambitions of the memo.

It may seem obvious to us sitting here with the benefit of hindsight
that political aims could be served by controlling the TV news, but
Roger Ailes was well ahead of his time. His instincts to bypass the

mainstream national news to serve news content locally is the blueprint for how disinformation now works online, as we will discuss in detail.

His intuition for delivery of it predicted the way all news is now packaged, with the crusty old newsman in suit and tie supplanted by the telegenic young faces of the modern newsreader. It was all style and no substance, with the best story being the one that triggered the most emotional response, whether or not it had any grounding in truth—like Barack Obama being born in Africa or his healthcare plan consisting of 'death panels'.

Donald Trump didn't ride this model to victory; this model created Donald Trump—all style and no substance, appealing to gut feeling and intuition. This symbiosis between Trump and Fox News was best seen by the decline in ratings once Trump left office: the number of viewers was a staggering 40 per cent lower in April 2021 once Trump had crawled back under his Mar-a-Lago rock than it was in April 2020.

Fox News, as one of Ailes' deputies would later admit to a *Rolling Stone* reporter, was 'a 24/7 political campaign. Nobody has been able to issue talking points to the American public morning after morning, day after day, night after night.'

But to see Fox News through a purely political lens is to miss the main point: it became incredibly profitable as a *business*. It reshaped all news not because it was conservative, but because it invented a profitable product: emotive partisan outrage.

Within Rupert Murdoch's extensive business empire, the channel would routinely be responsible for over 20 per cent of the global revenue— matching the entire film division, which included 20th Century Fox and its frequent mega-cash cows like *Avatar* and *Titanic*.

Roger Ailes had political motives, achieving influence through realising his lifelong dream of remaking politics for the television age. Rupert Murdoch was always driven by profit.

Where Keith had succeeded as a journalist he had failed as a businessman. His son would not make the same mistake. But to do that, Murdoch Jr could not just expand his traditional news empire. There was a simple reason why: objective news reporting was failing as a business model.

Newspapers had been able to survive the arrival of television in the 1950s, but the arrival of the internet 40 years later would prove too much.

The Fall of News

When the pioneering editor in chief of *Time* magazine, Nancy Gibbs, first joined the newsroom as part-time fact checker in 1985, she entered a journalistic world of opulence. She told me of a golden age of publishing, where on publication-day Fridays bar carts full of top-shelf liquor would work their way up and down the rows of desks while waiters ferried steak dinner service on cloth napkins to eager writers who were happy to have landed jobs at media companies unfussed by any limits of the corporate expense account—rumoured to be virtually unlimited.

One story told of a publisher's wife who sent him on business road trips with his living room curtains in order to get the hotel to dry-clean them on the outlet's dime. Another former news editor recounted a moment of panic when they realised they hadn't budgeted enough on a company beach picnic for the 100 employees they were bringing with them: they hadn't accounted for the champagne on the bus, wine on the beach or the lobster dinner before the nightclub—only to have the extras obligingly signed off without hesitation.

Then came the internet.

By the time Gibbs took over the reins at *Time* three decades later, the entire media business landscape was vastly different, with profits in freefall and shrinking newsrooms expected to churn out a greater volume of stories more quickly, with fewer staff. The result for every magazine, newspaper, and even the new digital darlings of the news industry? Less Congress and more Kardashians.

A revolution within the way we consumed advertising laid bare the shaky foundations the news business had long been built on, despite its soaring success.

Just as Fox News was entering the American market on TV, the internet began diverting eyeballs away from newspapers. Print advertising revenue fell off a very steep cliff.

Within twenty years of digital advertising first rearing its pixels, print ad revenue in the US had fallen below where it had been in 1950 (when they first began tracking industry data), despite the population of America having doubled and the economy having grown seven times bigger. Between 2009 and 2014 alone, revenues fell by more than 50 per cent. In Australia over the same period, all newspaper revenue fell by 40 per cent. Classifieds, worth $3.7 billion in Australia in 2001, were only generating $225 million fifteen years later—a fall of a staggering 94 per cent.

The traditional news model had been simple: gather an audience through telling the news and then advertisers will pay you for ad space to sell to them.

And not just companies, too. If in 1950 Kathy wanted to sell her used lawnmower in Warrnambool, Victoria, she would pay to put a notice in the one place people would see it: the classifieds section of the *Warrnambool Standard*. These days she would list it for free on Facebook Marketplace. Of all Australian newspaper revenue losses in the last twenty years, 92 per cent have been from the loss of classified ads.

The vertigo-inducing free fall of newspaper ad revenue was perfectly mirrored by the dizzying incline in advertising revenue online. For the first time, in 2020 a triopoly of companies (Amazon, Google and Facebook) captured a majority of *all* US advertising. Not just digital advertising. Not just news media company advertising. *All* advertising. Out of every dollar spent on billboards, Super Bowl television ads, bus shelters, skywriters, every jingle on TV and every full-page ad in a newspaper—a majority of it went to just three digital behemoths.

Making a newspaper is very expensive. You need printing presses, trucks, reporters, warehouses and more. But once you have those things, putting things in the newspaper is relatively cheap. Printing a bunch of articles about politics? May as well throw an opinion section, obituaries

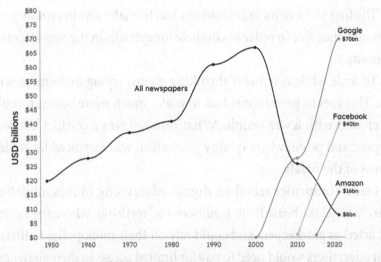

'For every action, there is an equal and opposite reaction': US advertising revenue, adjusted for inflation, 1950–2020.

and some personal announcements in while you're at it. It gave news companies a monopoly over a whole range of industries, much broader than just news.

With the internet came the removal of the advantage the news companies had, through the unbundling of the content found in the papers. Without the prohibitive barrier of needing a printing press and distribution network, websites popped up where you could list job postings, dating profiles, classifieds, commentary and local advertising. People started finding their apartments on Craigslist and their opinions on Craig's blog.

What had seemed like an impregnable fortress had actually been a house of cards. The news media business model imploded.

Once weaned from the lavish teat of advertising revenue, an inconvenient fact was exposed for those who had made a living off reporting the news: it doesn't sell.

The bottom line for news quickly became more important than the headline. A mad scramble to reinvent a centuries-old business model had some profound and chilling effects on our information ecosystem. Our disinfodemic was only made possible by these changes.

The first pivot news organisations had to make was to rapidly grow their audience size in order to compete for eyeballs in the new attention economy.

To scale while revenue is shrinking means trying to do more with less. This meant newsrooms had to make much more content, much faster, and with fewer people. What resulted was a conflict between purpose and profit, where quality journalism was sacrificed for topless photos of the royals.

News companies relied on digital advertising in this model: an entirely different beast from traditional advertising, where the outlets had acted as gatekeepers and could rely on their monopolies to dictate what advertisers would need to pay for limited access to their audiences. In the online world, the outlets would have to go out and compete for those audiences at a time the options for getting information were growing infinitely, most of it for free.

The more people that clicked on an article the more eyeballs the publication got, and the more revenue they could generate. To survive, media companies needed to publish things that would get the most clicks, rise to the top of search engine results, and be shared by more people.

Things that generate a lot of clicks: sensationalised headlines, celebrity gossip, race-baiting, polarised outrage and boobs. Things that do not generate a lot of clicks: democratic accountability, investigative journalism, policy analysis, nuance and balance.

The playing field was upended to heavily favour the *Naked News* (a real thing, where television newsreaders stripped) more than the nightly news.

If a novel coronavirus had escaped its Wuhan wet market in 1979 instead of 2019, would a different media landscape lead to a different outcome? Mainstream expert-based consensus news might well have led to more people taking the vaccine than the current media landscape where people are as likely to get their information from an established news site as a website saying the vaccine causes infertility.

Fed a healthy diet of quality information for decades, society was now served the equivalent of fast food in great measure, with predictable health results. Our news became dominated by junk information, which is cheaper and easier to produce at great volume—and let's be honest, tastes much better (even though we know we should be eating our meticulously researched investigative vegetables).

By 2013, number five on the top ten list of publisher rankings for most engaged-with news sites on Facebook (just behind CNN and the BBC and one ahead of the *New York Times*) was the liberal clickbait content farm Upworthy, with its headlines designed to get you to click at all costs, teasing their articles with nonsensical titles like, '*This Kid Just Died. What He Left Behind Is Wondtacular.*' (article views: 17 million) and '*His First 4 Sentences Are Interesting. The 5th Blew My Mind. And Made Me A Little Sick.*' (article views: 5 million).

A prize to any reader out there who can tell me what either of those articles are about. But that itching feeling you have, wanting to find out? That means the headlines are working.

Upworthy knew that winning the headline was the key to winning attention in a crowded feed. They called their formula that would test the potential virality of their articles the 'magic unicorn box'. It dictated all editorial decisions. As one-time editor in chief Adam Mordecai put it:

> We have a custom click testing system that I call the magic unicorn box which we built internally. I can't say how it works. All I can say is that I put my headlines in the box, and the magical scores come out, and then I make decisions based on that.

Upworthy, and other clickbait farms like *BuzzFeed* (whose more recent pivot towards traditional journalism led to mass layoffs), beat the mainstream outlets to a straightforward realisation of how to harness simple psychology by piquing our curiosity.

The Atlantic called the efforts at the time a 'cynical ploy to lasso cheap attention rather than fully engage an audience hunting anything more than a dopamine rush'. But for the mainstream outlets it was populate or perish. What did they do? Let me tease it for you: These Outlets Were Failing To Compete With Clickbait. What They Did Next Will Blow You Away.

Here's a sample of headlines from some Australian newspapers, on the day I am writing this sentence:

'It's set to be the defining image of 2021—will you take part?' (*Sydney Morning Herald*)

'This question makes Aussies uncomfortable' (*Daily Telegraph*)

'Shock reason potato farmer got busted with drugs' (*Bowral News*)

The 'shock reason', in case you are wondering, is that they found a box in the potato farmer's car labelled 'drug box'—*shockingly* it contained drugs.

The competition for eyeballs through tricks like clickbait headlines can't be decoupled from the nature of where those clicks come from: social media. We'll look at this in more detail in the next section, but it's important to state now that the rise of social media neatly correlates to the decline of media revenue. News designed to maximise sharing on social media platforms looks very different from news designed to tell the most accurate story. The efforts of news media companies to capitalise on new audience behaviours has been a race to the bottom.

To compete, they have to get into the gutter. Currently the biggest news website on Facebook *by far* is the right-wing bigotry factory the Daily Wire, which hardly even contains any original content. In May 2021 they had more than 70 million engagements to the *New York Times'* fifteen million. The playing field between news and hysteria is hardly level.

The next pivot the media industry made was one from an advertising-based revenue model (car ads in the car section) to a subscription-based revenue model (car fans paying for access to car news).

For outlets who didn't want to be reduced to sensational clickbait, this was the only card they had left to play. If only they could get their readers to pay directly for the content they produced, they would no longer be beholden to the advertisers or the cheap tricks for a volume of eyeballs.

The subscription model was heralded as the saviour of good news, but in reality it just put it behind a paywall. Those inside the paywall were fed a steady stream of opinion they already agreed with (for fear of losing them as paying subscribers), and those outside it received a steady diet of disinformation and sensation that grew in the vacuum the paywall had left in quality journalism's wake.

Disinformation has been the biggest beneficiary of the disintegration of our media landscape, thanks to the failure of the old-school business model and a lack of imagination to replace it with something that safeguards the quality of news. Facts have been the big casualty of this shift.

The Shrinkage of News

Compounding the effects of the decline in ad revenue was the market opportunity it created at the same time. The first media companies to suffer the implosion of advertising revenue as audiences moved online were the smallest ones, most likely your local news outlet.

As they went out of business in great numbers, countless towns and cities lost their only local news source. The only journalists covering town council corruption or local government elections. The only papers highlighting community environmental concerns. The only notice boards congratulating the overachieving high school kids, or letting the town know Betty from the hardware store had died.

Enter the big fish to eat up all the little fish, and the parallel crisis of media monopolisation. And re-enter our story Rupert Murdoch, whose media empire was on hand to pick the bones of the hundreds of local carcasses the internet had left scattered in 'news deserts' across the English-speaking world.

Nowhere is this more pronounced than in his native Australia. Through decades of deliberate government policy, news media in Australia has become super-concentrated into a couple of corporate hands while local and regional news outlets have all but disappeared.

Globally, newspapers have been shuttering at a disturbing rate since the internet devoured their advertisers. In the US, where in 1983 approximately 90 per cent of the media was controlled by 50 companies, that same 90 per cent is now owned by only five companies. In the last twenty years, nearly 2000 newspapers have closed across the States—a combination of market forces, declining ad revenue, digitisation and, like Australia, deliberate government policy.

But Australia makes media monopolising an artform.

One global study ranked Australia's concentration of newspaper ownership third in the world, behind only the state-run media giants of China and Egypt. Just one company, Murdoch's News Corp, controls about 70 per cent of the newspaper market. This is a serious problem when that same company uses its market dominance to push disinformation on a range of topics, climate change chief among them. In several Australian cities, Murdoch papers have no competition at all.

In 2020 alone, Australia lost more than 2000 newsroom and related media roles, compounding the thousands of journalism jobs already gone.

After gobbling up local and regional titles all over Australia, News Corp turned around and spat them out. On one day alone, Murdoch's company announced it would stop printing 112 local papers.

With one swing of the axe, under the cover of declining ad revenues, Australians from Caloundra to the Adelaide Hills found themselves without any local paper in print. Not long afterwards, News Corp merged the remaining local news sites with their capital city mastheads. People in Lismore wanting to find out how the works on their flood levee were progressing would now have to instead buy a subscription to the *Daily Telegraph*, based over 700 kilometres away, where they may find their Lismore news behind a paywalled section of the *Telegraph*'s website.

But they wouldn't do that. Instead, they turn to Facebook to consume their news from any source freely available. A sobering thought in Australia's anti-vaxxer capital, where businesses bar vaccinated people from entering their shops for fear of them 'shedding covid'.

Dozens of local newspapers now relegated to one tab on the *Daily Telegraph* website.

The loss of news sources for a community is larger than simply a void of information about what is going on there—it also severs a key artery of our democratic pact: that people have the information necessary to make judgments favouring their interests and values, the 'Prologue to a Farce or a Tragedy' of which Madison warned us.

Without quality news that is relevant to our community, we no longer have a shared baseline of facts on the issues that directly affect that community.

In the US the research on the effects of this have been startling. With the loss of local news, studies have shown citizens are less likely to vote, are less politically informed and are less likely to run for office.

Still not convinced? They have also found a link between the closure of local news outlets and local taxes going up.

With the decline of local news (and of watchdog journalism in particular) studies have been able to show that government officials conduct themselves with less integrity, efficiency and effectiveness. Even more worryingly, both government corruption and costs increase: salaries, taxation and county deficit spending go up, and federal funding goes down. Bad corporate behaviour, such as environmental degradation, goes unchecked.

We are acutely feeling the consequences in communities across Australia too: in the five years leading up to this most recent newspaper mass extinction event, a whopping eleven local councils were sacked for corruption—many of them thanks to the work of local reporters. It was a local paper, the *Illawarra Mercury*, that brought down the entire Wollongong council over bribes from developers, and it was another, the *Newcastle Herald*, that broke the Catholic clergy abuse story that led to the royal commission into child abuse.

Perhaps most disconcerting of all, we may not even know what consequences we are suffering, as the machinery designed to bring it to our attention has completely broken down. Local TV and radio have likewise been folded into their capital city parents. In 2019 the authorities counted 21 'news deserts' across Australia, and this was before the mass closures of 2020.

There is one enormous consequence of the information vacuum created in our communities: it gets filled with something entirely worse. When researchers from RMIT University surveyed those groups most vulnerable to covid, they found that during emergency-related events like a pandemic, 73 per cent of them would get their news from Facebook. Other studies have shown those who get their information from social media are less likely to be vaccinated. What is the 'farce or tragedy' that the breakdown of our news information ecosystem has heralded? It is the disinfodemic that has grown in the place where our shared baseline of facts used to be.

Meanwhile on TV, as the newspapers folded like . . . well, a newspaper, the message was received loud and clear that traditional journalism was bad for business. At the same time, Roger Ailes' polarised outrage machine was making money hand over fist. Fox News' ratings dwarfed those of the other 24-hour cable news channels like CNN.

It meant that in order to compete, the other TV news networks had to adopt the same model. This came at enormous cost to fact-based and balanced investigative news reporting—your information vegetables that no one is excited to eat. If my kids were left in charge of their menu choices, they would eat nothing other than the dietary equivalent of Fox News: cheap and nasty junk food bites that seem like a good idea when you crave it but leave you feeling sick and feral. Our media diets are now controlled by those baser instincts.

Keith Murdoch lived in a world where newsmen could garner respect and gather great audiences through their search for the truth—as coloured as their reporting of that 'truth' may have been, it was still a profitable search. His son lives in a world, partly of his own making, where the truth is bad for business—giving life to the now well-accepted adage that profit lies not in information but in affirmation. Affirmation is the motto of our social media ecosystem.

With the disappearance of the traditional places we would get our news, where has the news gone? To a place fully ill-equipped to host it. Our news is the square peg, and the round hole it now sits in is an entire infrastructure built not for news reporting but for viral advertising. The consequences have been deadly.

6 / A Perfect Storm

'We have met the enemy and he is us.'
—*Pogo*

We cannot paint an accurate picture of disinformation and its effect on our society without first describing in detail the canvas on which it is painted—hence this first part of the book breaking down how we got here in our journey on the information superhighway.

Parallel forces in news, technology, human thought, psychology and society all collided at once to give us our current predicament. Many of them we have broken down in detail already. But the big, hairy elephant in the room is where these conversations take place: online, largely on social media.

To understand what filled the vacuum left by our information ecosystem's disintegration we need to examine three key converging forces: the platforms where our conversations now take place, the algorithms that determine what we see on them, and the nature of our political conversations that take advantage of them.

Further in the background you also have an erosion of the trust in institutions just as people are given the tools to circumvent them. You can begin to see the perfect storm brewing . . .

In essence, this is a study in understanding how the technological processes that now govern our lives are ill-suited to the realities of human experience. And yet we have ceded complete control to them, and the handful of corporate oligarchs that control them. There's a guy writing code right now in a Palo Alto basement which will dictate what streets you choose to take when driving to work tomorrow morning.

We have traded away a lot in the name of convenience and expediency.

The Algorithm

When the grand human experiment entered the Information Age it set about digitally organising and categorising all human knowledge—no mean feat. Whereas in a brick-and-mortar library setting you chase facts by finding reference books in their totality, on the internet you chase facts through the snippets that search engines decide will be most useful.

Before the digital age, we searched for facts by asking to be pointed to documents and texts that would contain the answers. Now, we search for facts directly. We have been conditioned to expect the instant gratification of knowing the answer to whatever we are seeking, instantly. It has ruined pub trivia.

Google has tried to map all the world's information into a 'Knowledge Graph' that scans billions of available sources to give you the answer directly, rather than a list of links that may aid you in finding the answer yourself.

When you ask your virtual assistant—maybe Siri or Cortana or the unnamed Google Assistant lady who seems to prefer anonymity—a question, it's not going to be helpful for you if they read out a bibliography; you want the answer. So information has to be mapped directly to a definitive fact.

To demonstrate this point when writing this chapter, I entered one of the most searched-for phrases into my Google search bar—a question that definitely cannot be answered by 'facts,' one that has vexed philosophers since we first thought of looking down to gaze at that spot our umbilical cord used to be: 'What is the meaning of life?'

To my confected surprise, rather than suggesting I explore the great philosophical texts to inform my own understanding on this ultimate subjective and foundational question, Google just gave me the answer straight-up:

> The meaning of life is 'freedom from suffering' through apatheia (Gr: απαθεια), that is, being objective and having 'clear judgement', not indifference.

Huh. That was easy. There it is, plain and simple, presented as fact as if I had asked it 'how tall is Mount Kilimanjaro?' (5895 metres, FYI.)

---

what is the meaning of life   ✕   🎤   🔍

Q All   🖼 Images   ⊘ Shopping   🗐 News   ▶ Videos   ⋮ More   Tools

About 1,120,000,000 results (0.71 seconds)

The meaning of life is **"freedom from suffering"** through apatheia (Gr: απαθεια), that is, being objective and having "clear judgement", not indifference.

https://en.wikipedia.org › wiki › Meaning_of_life
Meaning of life - Wikipedia

❓ About featured snippets • 🏴 Feedback

When I go to the source that Google pulled that 'fact' from (the Wikipedia page for 'Meaning of Life'—itself a completely unverified source), that isn't what the answer says at all. The above quote is found buried halfway down a very lengthy page in context—that this is what a fellow named Zeno of Citium thought, from one school of philosophy called Stoicism. It is presented as one suggestion among dozens, within a subsection of 'Ancient Greek philosophy', in turn in its own subsection of 'Western philosophical perspectives'. The entire 17,000 word Wikipedia article—while being a surprisingly good summary of such a complex topic—does not offer any definitive answer to the question.

But in a society characterised by algorithmical thinking, where we worship the divinity of simplicity through outsourcing our mental processes to tiny machines, we are offered the simple answer as objective fact.

This is the power of a mathematical set of instructions that is used to solve a problem: *an algorithm.*

It's a word that has leapt from the lexicon of mathematicians and into the mainstream, thanks to its use in computer science. In the competition for customers, technology companies are engaged in a constant battle to grow the number of people using their platforms, and to keep them there as long as they can once they've won them over. Their ultimate mission is to become indispensable to as many parts of your daily life as possible, from when your alarm goes off in the morning to when you silence your phone at night. (But why stop there?! They will even monitor your sleep.)

To do this, social media platforms must become as intuitively useful and engaging as possible, and to do that they engage complex algorithms to understand you and serve you.

Just as the business model of media companies led to the disintegration of our information order, this business model of social media companies has created the information disorder that replaced it.

Information has become incredibly cheap to produce, now that you don't need a printing press or a video production unit, nor even to convince anyone to publish it for you. In fact, it is so cheap there is now too much of it—far too much for us to know what to do with, or to easily sort it into any kind of coherent system. Instead we outsource that function: we let the *algorithm* decide what we should see.

At the end of 2017, to another collective groan from every social media manager who had built their entire strategy around getting traffic from Facebook, Mark Zuckerberg announced yet another change in the way he would decide what information you would see in your feed:

> We will prioritise posts that spark conversations and meaningful interactions between people. To do this, we will predict which posts you might want to interact with your friends about, and show these posts higher in feed. These are posts that inspire back-and-forth discussion in the comments and posts that you might want to share and react to.

No doubt he didn't have a 'Let's storm the US Capitol!' post in mind, but that's exactly what we got—the most engaging content was highly emotive and performative, likely to be shared and elicit the most responses. If you put a 'storm the Capitol' post into this algorithm, the entire platform is designed to find those susceptible to that message, elevate it in their feed and make sure it ricochets around all like-minded users, until before you know it they've travelled to DC, donned their horns and flags and are putting their feet up on Nancy Pelosi's desk.

Maybe Silicon Valley simply has a too rosy-eyed view of human nature.

As one of the leading disinformation researchers, Claire Wardle, put it, the aspiration of these platforms never matched the reality, in the same way their rhetoric was overly optimistic about human nature: 'Designers of the social platforms fervently believed that connection would drive tolerance and counteract hate. They failed to see how technology would not change who we are fundamentally—it could only map onto existing human characteristics.'

In the same way serious news companies devolved into celebrity-driven gossip columns or partisan blowhard factories to have mass appeal, social media platforms were at the whims of the same desultory forces. Some things are more clickable and shareable than others, and we may not like the results when we hold up that mirror.

Wardle conducted the thought experiment of what would happen if a globally significant event like 9/11 were to happen in our new information environment:

> It is easy to imagine that, today, almost everyone in that scene
> would be holding a smartphone. Some would be filming their
> observations and posting them to Twitter and Facebook. Powered
> by social media, rumors and misinformation would be rampant.
> Hate-filled posts aimed at the Muslim community would proliferate,
> the speculation and outrage boosted by algorithms responding to
> unprecedented levels of shares, comments and likes. Foreign agents
> of disinformation would amplify the division, driving wedges
> between communities and sowing chaos.

In 2001, it took months before 9/11 conspiracy theories began gaining any currency, and in the US they didn't begin getting any serious attention until 2004. By that time they were swimming upstream against an established prevailing narrative about the meaning of the events. Today those theories would be swimming in parallel lanes in a race to meaning, where the conspiracy theories are wearing flippers and a sharkskin suit and the truth is Eric the Eel.

This runs headlong into what we will discuss later about cognitive biases and our strong desire to seek out and find those who agree with our existing beliefs. Social media algorithms are custom-built to help these cognitive biases win out over the parts of our brain that favour reason and rationality. In the same way that our brain deals with having to process too much information by simply filtering out everything that doesn't accord with our reality, so too do social media algorithms filter out everything except what it thinks you want to hear.

The algorithms will always reward sensationalism, tribalism and innuendo over science, truth and interrogation.

Layer onto this the features of automation, which removes the need for humans to be doing the labour of posting disinformation, as well as microtargeting, which allows that disinformation to find the exact person it will move while avoiding the attention of those who would flag it, and you have the cherry on the icing on the top of a perfectly formed disinformation cake.

It's as if in the great WWE wrestling match between competing parts of our human nature, social media was the 400 pound ogre waiting on the top rope to be tapped into the ring by their tag team wrestler, Anti-Reason. Rationality never stood a chance in this new ring.

These platforms are machines programmed to amplify the most engaging and shareable content, and so become ready-made vehicles for the amplification of disinformation.

The Connective Tissue

A piece of disinformation means nothing in a vacuum. But your consumption of information used to be private; now it is public. Once you elevate that piece of disinformation by sharing it on social media, you are imbuing it with the social capital you carry with your peers. It takes on a new gravitas as something you personally endorse and embrace, rather than just a random tidbit on the internet. Your peers are more likely to view it not on its standalone merits but through the lens of your relationship with them.

Our brains are hardwired to mistake popularity for quality, and social media has fed this cognitive bias to the extreme. This is the concept that explains something 'going viral'.

Once amplified, the machine then helps those who embrace that disinformation find each other and connect to them, often in closed groups far from the public eye. These groups then become hostile to outside opinion that may contradict the disinformation that has bound them together, and form strong tribes around their shared fake realities. And just like that what began as a health and lifestyle group is out on the streets flinging rocks at police in an anti-lockdown protest, over what they think is a secret vaccine plot to infect children with monkey flu microchips.

This is also a game about data collection—the most valuable currency of the networked age we live in. The more data a company has about you (what do you wear, where do you shop, do you have kids, are you renting...) the better they can target you with their product. But even more so, the more data these technology platforms possess on us, the more powerful their algorithms become.

Computer scientists at Stanford teamed up with psychologists from Cambridge and were able to figure out that once a computer program knew 300 things you had 'liked' on Facebook, it was able to more accurately predict your personality than your spouse could.

When you perform the same Google search I outlined above, you will not receive the same results I did. Your internet is personal to you. Nobody else has the same experience when surfing the web, because the platforms you are using know a scary amount about you and use it to serve whatever they think will be most relevant to you and whatever you are least likely to disagree with. Possessing this vast amount of data about you, search engines and social media platforms provide you personalised recommendations. Their algorithms will try their best to serve you the information you are most likely to agree with, with no filter for fact or truth, and try to shield you from information that might change your mind about it.

This is the filter bubble we will discuss later; what Cass Sunstein called 'cyber-balkanisation'—each tribe split into its own cocoons of partisan information.

Without the shared baseline of facts the news used to provide the masses, there is no central story to contradict any falsehoods. Safe inside our self-affirming bubbles, falsehoods can spread without ever meeting any contrary opinion—further reinforcing the falsehood and strengthening the bonds of those who share it.

French historian Pierre Nora called the places where collective memory is created 'sites of memory'. We are Australian, for example, not because of any geographic proximity to each other, but because we have our identity crystallised in these shared 'sites'—a statue in a park telling us who to commemorate; the faces we choose to put on a ten dollar note; our flag; an Anzac Day ceremony. That's why those things are contentious: it's in those 'sites' that our battle for collective identity takes place. Within filter bubbles, however, the things we have in common are fractured. Your online memory and experience is different from every other Australian's online memory and experience. Our 'sites of memory' are no longer collective.

Think about how these bubbles have bled into the physical world. In the 1950s a CEO might well have lived on the same street as his workers (albeit in a much nicer house). Now the managerial class is segregated from the working class (and consequently are much more easily able to make corporate decisions to harm communities they are now detached from). In the same way, people within neighbourhoods are now much more likely to reflect the same opinions as each other. Our information loops have drawn us into real-world partisan cocoons—especially in the US, which physically resembles the partisan segregation that reflects its polarised politics.

We are forced into these bubbles not just by the nature of information we have access to, but also its *volume*. There is simply too much content for us to consume—especially when looking for important information, like, 'Hey, what is this whole coronavirus thingy about?' The proliferation of news sites, blogs, videos, memes, tweets—you name it—has two key effects: it means we call more on our brains to apply cognitive biases rather than sort the wheat from the chaff, and it also hands more power to the platform algorithms to decide what we see for us. In the broadcast era, editors decided what information we would consume. Now that decision is made by a computer equation not bound by any of the same journalistic or ethical standards.

The Vortex

It is not just the decision of what appears at the top of your news feed that draws you into these bubbles—there is also a premium for social media platforms to keep you on their site for as long as possible. To do this, they will always recommend what to do and watch next, or another group to join. As soon as your Netflix show finishes, there it is with its algorithmically chosen recommendation on what you, personally, should watch next.

This is the rabbit hole they want you to fall down.

In 2019, Caleb Cain, an unemployed college dropout from West Virginia, handed over the logs of his entire YouTube watch history—more than 12,000 videos and 2,500 search queries dating back years—to a reporter from the *New York Times*.

Using those logs, the newspaper was able to chart the course of how, over a period of years, the young man had been innocuously dragged from harmless self-help videos to the conspiracy-laden far-right fringe—one recommended YouTube video at a time.

They traced his radicalisation back to a decision made by YouTube in 2012, when the algorithm was updated to switch from maximising views (which creators could easily game to get more clicks) to give more weight to 'watch time'. This gave a leg-up to long and engaging videos (like ranting conspiracy diatribes, for example). Then in 2015, YouTube engineers began using a form of artificial intelligence in their algorithm that mimicked the way the human brain works, using 'neural networks' to give recommendations for similar videos to the one just watched. But there was one problem: the videos it recommended were *too* similar. Users got bored.

The genius solution was a spectacular feat of computer engineering: a new algorithm that incorporated a different type of AI to predict which videos would *expand* its users' interests. They even called the algorithm, without any hint of irony, 'Reinforce'. It was heralded as a great success, with one YouTube executive even boasting, 'We can really lead the users toward a different state, versus recommending content that is familiar.'

That 'state' many users were led to was often the supposed deep state: conspiracies, far-right radicalisation, extremism.

In Caleb's own words, as documented by the *Times*' podcast about him, aptly titled 'Rabbit Hole', 'I just kept falling deeper and deeper into this, and it appealed to me because it made me feel a sense of belonging. I was brainwashed.'

We all were. The 2018 election was the first to be held after the shell shock of Donald Trump's ascendancy through widespread social media disinformation. As a consequence, radars were keenly tuned to detect foreign interference in America's feeds.

But it felt like a bit of a fizzer. None of the expected hacking occurred. One NBC journalist tweeted on election night, 'Gotta hand it to Twitter . . . this website had a LOT less bullshit on it in the last 48 hours than it did on Election Day and Eve 2016.'

It wasn't the platforms that had changed—it was our perceptions. Disinformation was imperceptible not because it had been suppressed, but because by 2018 it had become mainstream. The perfect storm had been realised.

It wasn't the bots or the Russian FSB that people had to be worried about—it was the fact that to effectively engage people in this new environment all politicians had to game the same algorithms to compete for our attention. Like mainstream news migrating to clickbait, all political discourse migrated onto platforms where, to be effective, it had to appeal to the worst parts of our nature. Consensus politics was dead.

As computational propaganda researcher Renee DiResta put it, 'We've democratized propaganda, made gaming distribution the key skill required to reach and influence people.'

In the new online attention economy, I fear to think how even a campaign as recent as 2008 would have fared—Barack Obama's 'Yes we can' was fit for the optimism of the early days of the internet, but could not compete against the fear and division reward system of the more recent algorithms.

As DiResta told *BuzzFeed News* in the aftermath of the 2018 mid-term election, 'Our political conversations are now happening on an infrastructure built for viral advertising, on platforms that are purpose-built to generate engagement and amplify sensational content.'

Facebook were fully aware of the contribution their algorithms made to this problem. A leaked presentation in 2018 included a slide admitting, 'Our algorithms exploit the human brain's attraction to divisiveness,' and that 'If left unchecked,' Facebook would be complicit by feeding users 'more and more divisive content in an effort to gain user attention and increase time on the platform'.

Facebook had asked itself the honest question of whether its platform contributed to the growing tribal polarisation in society through its role in spreading disinformation, and then gave itself an answer: yes it had.

But rather than acting on it, insiders told the *Wall Street Journal* that Facebook 'shelved the research' due to concerns that 'proposed changes would have disproportionately affected conservative users and publishers at a time when the company faced accusations from the right of political bias'.

Those who could deceive and inflame most effectively would be the winners in the new attention economy, and there was one type of politician who profited above all others: the one who would be least beholden to antiquated political discourse norms like telling the truth.

Hannah Arendt saw it coming as early as the 1960s:

> It seems significant, and rather odd, that in the long debate about
> this antagonism of truth and politics, from Plato to Hobbes, no
> one, apparently, ever believed that organized lying . . . could be an
> adequate weapon against truth.

As we discovered previously, philosophers always saw ignorance and irrationality as the enemies of truth and reason, and debated them at length. They never predicted the deliberate and collective falsification of facts as part of the human condition—despite our predilection for it, as discussed already in our history of lying.

Yes, people lied all the time, Arendt conceded, but 'it was never meant to deceive literally everybody'. Falsehoods were not a tool to contest 'facts' but a tool to deceive a person about the existence of that fact.

Arendt didn't even have to deal with the algorithmical dumpster fire of the spread of disinformation on social media when she was describing 'organised lying' in her theories. But she was spookily prescient.

It seems that Arendt saw the Trump campaign coming:

> Seen from the viewpoint of politics, truth has a despotic character.
> It is therefore hated by tyrants, who rightly fear the competition of
> a coercive force they cannot monopolize . . . Unwelcome opinion
> can be argued with, rejected, or compromised upon, but unwelcome
> facts possess an infuriating stubbornness that nothing can move
> except plain lies.

Once these theories found the fertile fields of social media decades later, and those fields took over our political discourse, Arendt's fears were realised: the political weaponisation of organised lying.

Enter the disinformation ecosystem.

Part Two
The Disinformation
Ecosystem

J.R Cliff #Trump2020
@CopJrCliff

Husband, Father, and Vet #Trump2020

◎ Philly   ▦ Joined February 2017

79 Following   **24.4K** Followers

Follow

I want to introduce you to J.R. Cliff—an African-American police officer from the swing state of Pennsylvania. A husband, a father and a military veteran.

He took to Twitter after the Black Lives Matter protests during the American summer of 2020 to express his unexpected support for Donald Trump.

'YES IM BLACK AND IM VOTING FOR TRUMP!!!' he yelled at us in all caps, as people who are angry on the internet are wont to do.

There's only one problem: he doesn't exist.

Perhaps he was created out of whole cloth by a fan of the 1980s hit TV show *Dallas*—his name appears to be a mashup of the two central characters in the highest-ever rating TV episode (at the time) 'Who Shot J.R.?': J.R. Ewing and his archrival Cliff Barnes. More than one in every three Americans—83 million of a population of 226 million—tuned in to that episode, including, perhaps, the mystery person behind our friend J.R. Cliff. Or was *Dallas* big in Russia, I wonder? Maybe it was required viewing for Cold War spies to learn about American culture.

Despite tweeting only eight times, J.R. Cliff has an impressive 24,000 followers. One tweet even garnered over 75,000 likes.

So where did J.R. come from? Or to put it another way, 'Who Shot J.R. to Internet Fame?'

The ancient Romans had a simple question to identify suspects of a crime: *Cui bono?* ('Who benefits?') In this case, there is a direct political benefit for a candidate in an election.

J.R. Cliff is one of scores of similar fake African-American accounts which sprung up in the lead-up to the 2020 US presidential election, all denouncing the Black Lives Matter protests and declaring their undying support for Donald Trump. African Americans were a key voter demographic in that election, whose turnout for Joe Biden ultimately proved decisive in the swing states that swung. Without convincing Black voters to either vote for him, or simply not vote for Biden, Trump could never hope to win re-election.

The messages these fake accounts would post were eerily similar; in fact they were often identical. That means they were coordinated. In this case, was it a foreign government trying to get Trump re-elected and hence further cement the decline of the American Empire? Was it the Trump campaign itself—another tool in its drawer of dirty digital tricks? Or was it a grassroots gaggle of enthusiastic supporters taking their inspiration, but not direction, from their falsehood-driven candidate?

Some accounts showed traces of foreign interference, such as Cyrillic characters or one that promoted a Turkish escort service, but these efforts can just as easily be coordinated by anyone domestically.

It doesn't take a bunker full of sophisticated espionage equipment; rows of computers with bespectacled hackers in headsets at keyboards. All it takes is a computer, an internet connection and a disruptive motivation to disinform. Let us explore now the disinformation ecosystem where these, and countless other, efforts take place.

8 / Types of Disinformation

> 'The historian knows how vulnerable is the whole
> texture of facts in which we spend our daily life; it is
> always in danger of being perforated by single lies or
> torn to shreds by the organized lying of groups.'
> —Hannah Arendt

Our disinformation has its roots in the clash of communism and capitalism, and the Cold War espionage that fought to control hearts and minds through deceptive propaganda. This book is not a history of disinformation. For that you should read Thomas Rid's *Active Measures*. But the key takeaway from that history is the inordinate amount of resources thrown at developing disinformation techniques over the last hundred years, before we even had an internet to make it ridiculously cheap and easy for anyone to do without the backing of state power. Disinformation has been democratised through these new technologies.

It would fill volumes if we set out to describe in detail all of the various ways bad actors deceive on the internet. Instead, it is worth outlining the various different forms, and then going into detail on a few key ones to help aid our understanding of the phenomena and make us more likely to be able to spot these attempts when they happen in our own feed.

We should probably start by defining what 'disinformation' means in the first place.

You may have already been thinking to yourself, 'Why does he say disinformation sometimes and misinformation other times?' As mentioned in the introduction, the two are not one and the same—even though much of the discussion we are having relates equally to the two.

*Mis*information is simply information that is wrong or misleading. It might be communicated unintentionally—an article that misstates the number of something and then issues a correction, for example.

*Dis*information, on the other hand, is information that is *deliberately* wrong or misleading, with the intent of deceiving someone.

THREE CATEGORIES OF INFORMATION DISORDER

FALSENESS **INTENT TO HARM**

MISINFORMATION
UNINTENTIONAL MISTAKES SUCH AS INACCURATE CAPTIONS, DATES, STATISTICS OR TRANSLATIONS OR WHEN SATIRE IS TAKEN SERIOUSLY

DISINFORMATION
FABRICATED OR DELIBERATELY MANIPULATED CONTENT, INTENTIONALLY CREATED CONSPIRACY THEORIES OR RUMOURS

MALINFORMATION
DELIBERATE PUBLICATION OF PRIVATE INFORMATION, SUCH AS REVENGE PORN. DELIBERATE CHANGE OF CONTEXT, DATE OR TIME OF GENUINE CONTENT

From Claire Wardle's 'Misinformation Has Created a New World Disorder'.

Claire Wardle, one of the leading experts on disinformation, has documented how, as our algorithms and platforms have gotten better at detecting disinformation, so has the disinformation itself gotten better at avoiding detection.

The best way to avoid an algorithm that is designed to detect falseness is to use information that is true. Just change the context. It's one of the reasons 'fake news' as a term is often inadequate to describe disinformation, as it is regularly found in forms that are neither fake nor news.

Instead, much of the disinformation we see is content presented in a misleading way. This can be as simple as taking a photo or video of one event and claiming it represents another. This happened in the 2016 US election when the Trump campaign used *real* footage of migrants in Morocco but pretended it was at the US–Mexico border. Likewise, *real* footage of ballot stuffing in Russia was circulated saying it was in Pennsylvania.

83

No algorithm will pick up this disinformation, for the same reason our minds will have trouble: we are wired to assume truthfulness. When told the context, we have no reason to suspect (especially if it conforms to what we already believe), and so we will willingly gobble it up—and even share it. Once we share it, it takes on an added layer of truthfulness for our friends, who are hardwired to believe information from their peers.

Wardle calls this the 'atomisation' of misinformation:

> . . . social networks allow 'atoms' of propaganda to be directly
> targeted at users who are more likely to accept and share a particular
> message. Once they inadvertently share a misleading or fabricated
> article, image, video or meme, the next person who sees it in their
> social feed probably trusts the original poster, and goes on to share
> it themselves. These 'atoms' then rocket through the information
> ecosystem at high speed powered by trusted peer-to-peer networks.

She categorises our current 'information disorder' into seven helpful categories of mis- and disinformation:

Fabricated content

Something completely made up and designed for the purposes of deceiving someone. Example: an entirely computer-generated image of a fictitious crowd in Washington DC watching Donald Trump's inauguration.

Manipulated content

Similar to the above, but something existing changed into something deceptive. Example: an actual photo of Trump's crowd size at inauguration, photoshopped with a few thousand more people in it.

Misleading content

Something we do all the time (and I would definitely be guilty of in political and advocacy campaigns): cherry-picking statistics, or selectively quoting something to make it align with our arguments. Example:

taking a quote from someone who said 'Trump had a big crowd, though it was much smaller than Obama's,' and cutting everything after 'crowd.'

Imposter content

Putting a logo on something to make it look official, like a post pretending to be from your political opponent or a fake tweet from the government. Example: a fake article with the CNN logo and strapline: 'Record crowd for Trump inauguration.'

False context

Something real, but changing the context to give it a different meaning. Example: a photo of Obama's inauguration crowd but saying it is Trump's inauguration.

False connection

Real content, but presented disingenuously. Clickbait headlines are the perfect example, where the headline is designed to catch our attention but the article might be different from what is suggested. Example: a news article accurately covering Trump's inauguration, but accompanied by a photo of Melania's nude GQ shoot, with the headline 'Trump Exposed in DC Inauguration'.

Satire or parody

Fake and designed to deliberately deceive the audience, but only for the purposes of entertainment, not a nefarious political motive. (Satire is being used now, however, to seed some serious disinformation narratives. It also is not always clear to the audience—a parody site of Joe Biden's campaign was mistaken for his real one.) Example: a *Betoota Advocate* article headlined 'White House Press Sec Insists Trump Inauguration Had Bigger Crowd Than Auckland 9s'.

Wardle then found that the motivations behind disinformation conveniently all started with the letter 'P': Poor Journalism, Parody, to

Provoke or 'Punk', Passion, Partisanship, Profit, Political Influence or Power, and Propaganda.

When most people think about disinformation, they envisage it on platforms like Twitter, Facebook and YouTube. But there are plenty of other places it exists, including other social media and discussion platforms like Instagram, TikTok, Snapchat, Reddit and 4chan; messaging apps like WhatsApp, Telegram (current favourite of the covid conspiracists), Signal and iMessage; or on their own dedicated disinformation sites like Infowars.

I won't bore you, dear reader, with their 23-step *Freedom of Expression Assessment Framework for Disinformation Responses*, but the UN body responsible for addressing disinformation has identified three useful main categories disinformation comes in: false claims and narratives (often with elements of truth); fabricated images and video (or altered or decontextualised); and fake websites and datasets.

These different disinformation types are typically harnessed through a range of potentially harmful practices, which are not always political. The same UN report lists those practices:

1. State-sponsored disinformation campaigns
2. (Anti-)Government /Other political propaganda
3. Political leaders generating and amplifying false and misleading content
4. Clickbait
5. False or misleading advertisements
6. Impersonation of media, fact-checking organisations, people, governments
7. Astroturfing campaigns
8. Fake products and reviews
9. Anti-vaccine, coronavirus, and other health and well-being misinformation
10. Gaslighting
11. Inauthentic identities and behaviours

The proliferation of these categories and motivations is marked by one startling example of just how perverse our information landscape has become: political disinformation is now so popular and so engaging with audiences online (particularly conservative audiences) that political disinformation is also being used for revenue-generating clickbait. It is making it incredibly difficult to identify the sources behind disinformation because everyone now does it to make money.

In other words, there is an underbelly of the internet that takes something popular (usually celebrity gossip or nudes) and generates traffic and therefore makes advertising revenue off it. What did these 'content farms' use to make money in 2016 and 2020? US political disinformation. It generated more clicks than the usual hot topics of internet buzz.

Technology is also making disinformation easier to make and harder to detect. 'Deep fake' videos, which can now be created at home on your laptop, can put a public figure's face on your body and have them do whatever the hell you want. In February 2021, the Belgian user 'TikTok Tom' made a video of 'Tom Cruise' announcing his campaign for president. It's been viewed over 15 million times and is indistinguishable from the real Tom Cruise. The ABC reported the video was so disturbingly believable it 'set off "terror" in the heart of Washington DC' at the thought of how this technology could be abused.

We have established that disinformation is now such a problem it has spurred long and complicated lists from UN agencies. There are many categories. That's significant because it shows not only that the problem is proliferating, but also that the solutions to address it won't be so neat they will fit onto the back of a napkin.

There are, however, particular types of disinformation that we will break down in greater detail, both because they aid in our understanding of the problem, but also because doing so will help us arrive at a solution.

9 / The Fake Account

'We ask for the simple record of unadulterated
fact; we look, and nowhere do we find the object
of our search, but in its stead we see the divergent
accounts of a host of jarring witnesses, a chaos of
disjoined and discrepant narrations.'
—F.H. Bradley, 1874

If disinformation had a famous poster child it would be the fake social media account.

It's the type of disinformation that often grabs the headlines: the warehouse full of Russian operatives at keyboards, pretending to be patriotic American voters and sowing discord from afar; the Macedonian students in their bedrooms clacking out salacious rumours about world leaders.

But it is much more common than most people think, and it is usually not the work of a shadowy government agency. It could be coming from your neighbour's home office.

The social media platforms even have an acronym for this type of disinformation: CIB. It somewhat euphemistically stands for Coordinated Inauthentic Behaviour. They definitely wouldn't want you calling it what it is in plain English: a group of people on their platform working together to mislead others by pretending to be someone else.

It's the preferred tool of coordinated disinformation campaigns for foreign agents, who will invest in operations that create fake accounts and weaponise them to construct false narratives, exacerbate existing divisions and sow doubt in institutions.

One researcher I spoke to, Nina Jankowicz, detailed a Russian-run 'bot farm' in Ukraine with 40,000 different SIM cards, paying Ukrainians $100 per month to rent out their social media accounts to trump any efforts to identify fake accounts ahead of the 2020 US election.

But it can also be coordinated domestically, at the behest of any influence group, from a party or candidate to an industry group or lobby. It can even be done by an individual at home with a grudge or a barrow to push. It is near impossible to tell the difference.

Twitter tracked 5000 fake accounts emanating from the Middle East all praising the Saudi leadership; 8500 in the Balkans promoting the Serbian ruling party; and more than 3000 on a single internet server in Honduras enthusiastically retweeting the Honduran president's account. 'We removed 3,104 accounts when it became clear a staffer created the fake accounts on the government's behalf,' they said at the time.

Creating fake accounts is relatively easy to do at scale, and very difficult to track.

One tweet by itself can't do much to change the conversation. But within powerful echo chambers these fake accounts play an effective role. By reinforcing the same message across several accounts, real accounts are likely to see and begin to echo the same message. The inauthentic accounts cross into the real world and the manufactured messages take on a life of their own.

The J.R. Cliff account was ultimately suspended by Twitter once some keen observers pointed out the profile image was actually a Portland police officer at a press conference, not a rabid Pennsylvanian Trump convert. But in the six days it existed it garnered 24,000 followers. That is the power of inauthentic accounts when *coordinated* together.

These 'CIBs' are a cheap and easy way to control the conversation. Trump's election victory in 2016 was due in part to the successful suppression of African-American voters through tactics such as these, as we will look at in more detail later. But it doesn't take the resources and coordination of the Russian security agencies or Trump's 'Death

Star' (as he ominously called his digital campaign operation) to create coordinated fake account campaigns.

Anyone, on their own volition, can start a handful of Twitter accounts and begin tweeting the same hashtag, over and over again, until it might turn into a damaging narrative.

You could easily put down this book and your coffee right now, pick up your phone, and within an hour have a salacious rumour about your boss and his pet goat trending nationwide. Twitter users all over the country would help, inadvertently amplifying your rumour by innocently asking, 'Does anyone know why #BillBlowsGoats is trending on Twitter?'

That's how social media platforms work: they look for trends in conversations, for people starting to say the same thing, then they artificially inflate the visibility of those messages. How do you game this system? Easy: pretend to be lots of people, all saying the same thing at the same time.

In 2018 the *New York Times* took a simple three-word slogan from the US midterm elections ('Jobs Not Mobs') and mapped its use to show how a message can move from the fringe to mainstream, until it is picked up everywhere, including by the president himself.

They described what is in essence a feedback loop:

> Since President Trump's election, his loyalists online have provided
> him with a steady stream of provocative posts and shareable memes,
> often filtered up from platforms like Reddit through media channels
> like Fox News. In return, Mr Trump has championed many of their
> messages as his own, amplifying them back to his larger base.

A brand new Twitter account—with no other tweets or followers— first tweeted the 'Jobs Not Mobs' slogan with a very slick accompanying video (produced in a fancy edit suite, not by a Twitter novice at home).

Less than two weeks later, #JobsNotMobs had spread to the centre of the Trump ecosystem, picked up by celebrity endorsers, right-wing pundits and repeatedly by Trump.

These simple hashtag slogans can begin innocuously before they spread like wildfire, and thanks to their simplicity and power can dominate a narrative in the political mainstream.

Are these being created and seeded by political operatives who know how to spark the wildfire with fake or inauthentic accounts? Usually we only have clues. The platforms themselves have more detail (such as whether other accounts are created from the same device using the same internet connection) which they use to proactively identify and suspend suspicious accounts. But they don't make this information public.

Making it more difficult still, the tools of sophisticated hackers and statecraft are now available to all. The types of high-tech 'DDoS' attacks that bring down government infrastructure can now be hired out for as little as $20 a week. 'Botnet' services for hire can have you trending in minutes without you needing to leave the comfort of your lockdown.

Too Close to Home

As you sit transfixed on events happening overseas, you may wonder, *Can you imagine if this sort of dark deception ever happened in Australia?*

It may surprise you to know it already does.

What we saw in Victoria during the covid lockdowns closely mirrors a common playbook from the Trump campaign or the Russian agencies.

The long Victorian lockdown in mid-2020, as covid tore through Melbourne, saw an explosion of tweets critical of Premier Daniel Andrews. Suddenly Andrews, who had been riding high in the polls, seemed like a dead man walking, crushed under the weight of digital vitriol and ruthlessly framed insults.

But all was not what it seemed.

Many of those critical tweets trace their origins to inauthentic accounts. Were these coordinated by the opposition party, another group, a foreign agent or simply a few motivated individuals angry at the lockdown? It is very hard to tell the difference.

Take the curious case of Ben Wyatt.

His account was set up in July 2020 to criticise the Victorian lockdown. The only tweets are replies to other lockdown-related tweets, and it only follows two other accounts (both pro-Armenian in their war with Azerbaijan).

Here are the other clues:

Ben Wyatt @BenWyat16342682 · Sep 25
Replying to @Timothyjgraham
a lot of people who have never used twitter have only started using it in 2020

No original tweets, only replies

○ 5   ⭤   ♡ 11   ▽   ↥

Socially Distant @PMixtress · Sep 25

No profile image or cover image   (Follow)

Ben Wyatt
@BenWyat16342682 ←——— String of numbers in handle
🗓 Joined July 2020 ←——— Recently joined Twitter
1 Following 1 Follower ←——— No followers

Not followed by anyone you're following

Tweets   Tweets & replies   Media   Likes

It is entirely possible (though far from likely) that Ben Wyatt is a real Armenian Australian named Ben Wyatt who just discovered Twitter and is also highly motivated by the discussion of the Victorian government's response to covid. Or (more likely) the account could be one of many set up by another person with a grudge, acting independently to foment criticism of the lockdown policy. It could be (even more likely) one of many inauthentic accounts manually set up by a political opponent of the Victorian government to inflict political damage. It could also be (most likely) an account set up on behalf of a political opponent of the Victorian government using software to create and run inauthentic accounts like this in a coordinated attack that automatically replies to certain lockdown-related keywords.

On its own, it would not be so concerning—just another keyboard warrior bored at night, hiding behind an anonymous profile. But let's look at just how much Trump's playbook of fake accounts is being replicated to chilling effect in Australia.

Dr Timothy Graham, a researcher at the Queensland University of Technology and a leading expert on tracking inauthentic accounts in Australia, created a dataset to track the viral spread of certain terms on Twitter. Using this, he examined the origins of one of the most popular and damaging hashtags used against Dan Andrews: #DanLiedPeopleDied.

It is a variation of the covid conspiracy theory #ChinaLiedPeople-Died, which had already been doing laps around the right-wing echo chamber overseas. Were the two hashtags connected by coordination, coincidence or copycats?

When a hashtag like that comes to the media's attention, it's because it is already trending. They see the interactions and report them as legitimately held widespread beliefs, as by the time they see it actual human accounts are indeed jumping on the bandwagon.

'Melbourne Residents React with Shock and Fury to Lockdown Extension' thundered one News Corp headline, before rattling off examples from Victorians' Twitter feeds. 'Daniel Andrews Has Broken Victorians' Hearts' ran another in *The Age*.

But Graham's study shows the origins of that hashtag and its spread are more suspect. The data shows these Twitter attacks in Victoria were driven by a small number of inauthentic accounts vigorously tweeting over and over again until the topics trended.

The #DanLiedPeopleDied hashtag began with a few very suspect accounts that do not appear to be genuine (brand new, don't have followers and don't tweet about anything else).

Once these suspect accounts created this initial head of steam, genuine accounts (including some far-right 'influencers' with a large number of followers) joined in a deliberate effort to get it to trend, amplified by the retweeting of several very new accounts. These hyper-partisan accounts will be explicit in their efforts: 'let's get this trending' or 'RT [retweet] to keep it going'.

Graham tracked one account that kept posting and reposting the hashtag more than 200 times in seven hours—approximately once every two minutes.

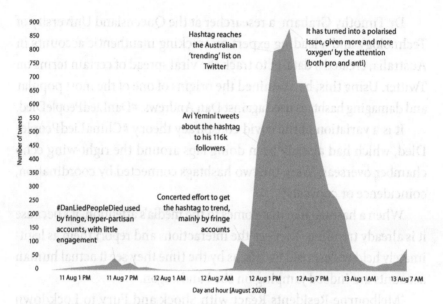

Tim Graham's timeline showing the number of #DanLiedPeopleDied tweets per hour.

And just like that, it was a trending hashtag in Australia, and so comes to the attention of everyone following the top conversations on Twitter.

A disproportionate number of new accounts using the #DanLied-PeopleDied hashtag were created in 2020. This was the same for a similar trending hashtag, #SackDanAndrews. One out of every four accounts tweeting that hashtag was created in 2020. Just twenty profiles accounted for a quarter of all #SackDanAndrews tweets (a massively trending term that saturated Twitter and dominated political discussion at the time).

The first ever use of the #DanLiedPeopleDied hashtag traces back to a now suspended account which only tweeted to either criticise the Victorian government or the Chinese Communist Party. Before February 2020, it only tweeted about Egyptian politics in Arabic. Egypt is a known inauthentic account hub.

Now, similar to our Armenian Australian friend Ben Wyatt, it is *possible* the user behind that account is an Arabophone fan of Barry Humphries (his profile picture was of Sir Les Patterson) who is highly passionate about an odd collection of political topics: China, Egypt and the Victorian state government's response to lockdown challenges.

But if you think that is the most *likely* explanation then I have some land to sell you . . .

It's all too familiar. It suggests that a political operator, or at least an organised group, is engaging large-scale disinformation technology to disrupt a domestic political opponent right here in Australia. We'll meet them again in a later chapter when Dan Andrews takes a tumble down some stairs.

Controlling the Conversation

We know for sure that Australian politicians understand the value in fake accounts boosting their content and informing the political dis-cussion—because several have hilariously been caught doing it.

Government minister Angus Taylor forgot to switch to his fake account before congratulating himself on funding a local car park. 'Fantastic. Great move. Well done Angus' he told himself in third person.

His colleague Senator Amanda Stoker does the same under her Facebook nom de plume 'Mandy Jane' (her nickname plus her middle name—come on Mandy, first rule of disinformation club is to make up a less obvious name). Mandy Jane came to the defence of Mandy Stoker on Facebook, saying 'You'll find that few Senators reject identity politics more than she does.' Identity politics, yes. Facebook identities, not so much.

Angus Taylor MP
4 hrs · 🌐

1000 extra carparks for rail commuters right across the north of Hume!

1000 MORE RWY CARPARKS

Chick Olsson
Brilliant 😊2
2h   Like   Reply

Andrew Thorn
Fantastic 👍1
4h   Like   Reply

Angus Taylor MP ✓
Fantastic. Great move. Well done Angus
Just now   Like   Reply

Mandy Jane

███████████

Another Senator denied formality to the motion – it wasn't Stoker. Ms Hanson needed special leave from the Senate to make her motion, and only one person needed to object to stop it.
I suspect you have been told a less than complete version of how these matters unfolded.
You'll find that few Senators reject identity politics more consistently than she does.

14h   Like   Reply   👍2

Both Andrew Laming MP and Craig Kelly MP, colleagues of Angus and Mandy, have likewise been busted creating fake community groups in their electorates to spruik themselves and control the online conversation. Zali Steggall, an Independent MP, has exposed fake Facebook community groups set up to do the opposite: criticise her. All of these efforts are tacit endorsement of the idea that political discourse is now determined by social media commentary. Hence the creation of fake accounts as a blunt political instrument.

Perhaps not to be outdone, former US presidential candidate Herman Cain tweeted a full month *after* he had died about the virus that had just killed him. 'It looks like the virus is not as deadly as the mainstream media first made it out to be' @THEHermanCain reached out from the grave to tell us about the deadly virus that had put him in there weeks earlier. It was the inauthentic account version of telling us covid was 'just a flesh wound'.

This is not just happening with hashtags on Twitter. These sorts of fake accounts are common on Facebook and Instagram too. In a matter of minutes you can go online and use simple software to create a fake profile (or dozens of them) and program it to automatically respond to something that happens on social media.

The technology is usually innocuous; it is created for marketing purposes—'*Hi, it looks like you're trying to book a train ticket, let me help you with that!*' followed by sophisticated algorithms to allow the programmed 'bot' to respond to your queries in a way that closely mimics how a human would ('*Sure! Where would you like to go?*').

But it is just as easily programmed to sow fear and division, and to spread attack campaigns. Every time someone tweets 'I stand with Dan' you can program it to respond 'How about the 800 people who can't stand anymore because #DanLiedPeopleDied.' Every time someone posts about the covid vaccine, you can automatically send them a link to a fake article about made-up risks.

Did you wonder where all those people spreading arson rumours about the bushfires suddenly came from during the Black Summer of 2019/2020? Many were these same programmed bots, ready to insert themselves into any conversation taking place online. The arson rumours rose to national headlines.

Professor Ryan Ko, the University of Queensland Chair of Cybersecurity, has likewise been tracking this in Australia. He wrote about his research in *The Conversation*:

> . . . bots latch onto official government feeds and news sites to
> sow discord. They retweet alarming tweets or add false comments
> and information in a bid to stoke fear and anger among users. It's
> common to see bots talking about a 'frustrating event', or some
> social injustice faced by their 'loved ones'.

This was in evidence in Victoria in relation to the pandemic, and also elsewhere in Australia. Anywhere that covid raised its head, Professor Ko tracked a bot army that had set up there to sow contention:

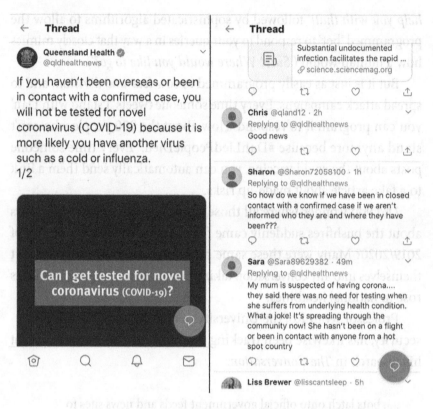

'Sara' and 'Sharon' trying to confuse the health advice early in the pandemic.

Both Sara and Sharon in this example are bots, though to the untrained eye seem legitimate.

The significance of this goes much further than mere annoyance at being spammed or trolled. This is how media narratives are created these days, which in turn influence political decision making.

Social media hype is reported as if it represents an authentic 'finger on the pulse' of the community and their attitudes (recall our examination of shrinking newsrooms stretched thin). Dominate that conversation and you dominate the news. Start a few accounts all accusing the Victorian Premier of something, and pretty soon the headlines will start to read the same. The evidence these articles then present? A bunch of angry tweets.

That's why a handful of unidentified humans created a bunch of Twitter accounts that did no more than tweet, over and over and over again, '#DanLiedPeopleDied'.

The effect these sorts of digital propaganda campaigns have were described by a couple of Oxford University academics looking at the aftermath of Trump's election victory off the back of similar tactics:

> ... bots affect information flows in two key ways: 1) by
> 'manufacturing consensus', or giving the illusion of significant
> online popularity in order to build real political support, and
> 2) by democratizing propaganda through enabling nearly anyone
> to amplify online interactions for partisan ends.

In their analysis, they confirmed that bots reached positions of measurable influence during the 2016 US election. In other words: thank a bot for the Muslim ban and border wall.

It is a familiar pattern worldwide, deployed with ease by savvy political operators. In 2019, Canadian Prime Minister Justin Trudeau criticised Donald Trump's racist attacks on four sitting Congresswomen (Trump told them—three of whom were born in the US—to 'go back where they came from'). Within hours the hashtag #TrudeauMustGo started trending on Twitter.

At its peak, the hashtag was being used 2100 times an hour. Caroline Orr, writing for the *National Observer*, found 'much of the activity surrounding the hashtag was actually driven by accounts tweeting at non-human rates, including about two dozen accounts created in the past 48 hours. For example, @tcanuckchik tweeted more than 230 times within 24 hours of creating an account.'

Then, in response to media coverage of that fact, the retort was a trending hashtag '#NotABot', which analysis again showed was, in fact, a bot.

Only a few weeks later, another hashtag targeted Trudeau: '#Trudeau-Corruption'. Once again researchers found an extensive network of inauthentic accounts were gaming Twitter to get the hashtag to trend, and ultimately 'manufacture consensus'.

Same playbook, different country—though in the Canadian example, it is likely the efforts were MAGA-led out of the US. They may also be for hire. If you trace the activity from disinformation campaign to disinformation campaign, many of the same bots reappear in different campaigns. Many of the accounts actively amplifying Trump in 2016 subsequently amplified the French #MacronLeaks disinformation, though they had little activity in between.

These accounts can keep on disinforming ad nauseam once programmed to do so. The worst offending fake Twitter accounts set up to influence the 2016 US election were still publishing over a million tweets a day ahead of the 2020 election. Despite Twitter claims of a crackdown, more than eight in ten of the inauthentic Twitter accounts responsible for spreading the majority of disinformation in 2016 were still active in June 2021. In the time it has taken you to read this chapter, those accounts have published approximately another 7000 tweets.

What are we to make of the Australian example in Victoria's lockdown, far away from any criticism of Trump and his supporters?

There are two scenarios: the first is that this was genuine—that a small number of Twitter users were legitimately fired up about the Victorian lockdowns and took to Twitter to vent their rage.

That is problematic because if true, it shows how a small number of people can dominate a political discussion in a way that is not reflective of the genuinely held views of the public (this is borne out by the lack of impact the first lockdowns had on Andrews' favourability in the opinion polls).

The second scenario is that this is orchestrated and manufactured by somebody with political motivations. This is obviously even more problematic.

Using common sense, these Australian examples walk, talk and quack like coordinated inauthentic account attacks taking place right here in Australia, in the same way we are so fascinated by it as outside observers when it happens in Russia or Iran targeting the US.

10 / The Fake Article

> 'Now the world is aware that Lean Finely Textured
> Beef is actually an alias for Ammonia-Soaked
> Centrifuge Separated Byproduct Paste.'
> —Jon Stewart, *The Daily Show*

Want to win an election through disinformation? You only need one ingredient: pink slime.

In 2012, a conservative businessman named Brian Timpone was busted when a whistleblower admitted that false quotes, fake by-lines and plagiarised articles were written for Timpone's media company Journatic (a portmanteau word—which really should have given the game away—of 'journalism' and 'automatic').

The whistleblower, who had applied for his job thinking it was a legitimate journalist's gig, told Sarah Koenig from *This American Life* (and later of *Serial* podcast fame) how articles were outsourced to writers in the Philippines who were paid 35 cents a story, then an Anglo-sounding name (some more plausible than others, like 'Jimmy Finkle') would be slapped on them, before being syndicated out to respected newspapers like the *Chicago Tribune*.

It all stemmed from the same business model failings we outlined earlier. In an effort to capture local advertising dollars, the *Chicago Tribune* had launched more than 90 local websites for towns around Chicago and hired reporters to staff them. But they couldn't get the model to work. Reporters weren't writing enough stories to generate enough revenue from the traffic to the sites. Instead, the *Tribune* turned to Brian Timpone and his network of Filipino, Eastern European, Brazilian and African writing farms.

The exposé spelled the end for that particular business model for Timpone, but it spurred something even worse to replace it: if Timpone couldn't sell his automated news to legitimate news outlets then he may as well drop the whole pretence of legitimacy and just start his own partisan local outlets, and get paid to write articles spruiking a conservative worldview by those with a vested interest in them.

The whistleblower, Ryan Smith, summoning his dormant skills for actual writing for the first time since he was hired by Journatic, put it beautifully at the time:

> People didn't think much about the beef they were eating until someone exposed the practice of putting so-called 'pink slime' into ground beef. Once it came out, the food industry moved quickly to change it. I feel like companies like Journatic are providing the public 'pink slime' journalism.

'Pink slime', as the industry has now come to embrace his term, is a key feature of our disinformation ecosystem.

Pink Slime

Just like the US presidential election way back in 1800, when election campaigns were fought on the pages of partisan newspapers, modern election campaigns still jostle for that all-important real estate in news articles—despite the news' decline, as we explored earlier.

There is a very good reason why.

In a time of great distrust in public institutions, and after a precipitous decline in trust of mass media after Donald Trump's attacks on them, a Gallup poll in 2019 still found that 85 per cent of Americans trusted their local newspaper.

At the same time, a Pew survey found 64 per cent of Americans found it hard to tell what is true when listening to elected officials. The number drops to only 41 per cent when asked about cable television news. This helps explain America's trouble responding to a crisis when their elected leaders say one thing and Fox News says another—they are predisposed to trust Fox News more.

So even though local newspapers and legitimate quality journalism are endangered species, and even though their decline explains how disinformation campaigns have been allowed to flourish, there is one very important point to make clear: to be successful, these disinformation campaigns must still dress their falsehoods up in the most effective wrapping—the look and feel of the real news article they have supplanted.

To invent your own reality, and to convince other people of it, you need to put it where it will have the most impact. That is best done by co-opting the architecture of a news article.

The best way to tell the public a story about anything is to find an article saying the same thing. We won't believe a political candidate when they tell us their policies are good for the economy, but we are predisposed to believe it if we read it in the paper. It's more convincing coming from a neutral journalist at *The Age* than it is coming from your own mouth. But lightning doesn't always strike. What if there is no article telling your side of the story?

Conservative parties have it much easier in Australia—for years now they have had an effective way to give this 'neutral' third party validation: a Murdoch media empire with broadsheets, cable news and websites to pump party lines to the masses.

But to make sure there is always a steady diet of just the right stories, for years the Republicans in the US have created their own partisan 'pink slime' news sites full of fake news. These are the source of almost *all* disinformation in that country.

The Knight Foundation conducted a study that looked at more than 10 million tweets containing fake news in the lead-up to the 2016 election, from 700,000 Twitter accounts that linked to more than 600 fake and conspiracy news sites.

Incredibly, they found that 80 per cent of the millions of offending tweets linked to just 3 per cent of the fake news sites—just 24 out of the 600 conspiracy websites the study looked at were responsible for almost all the disinformation. Much of the activity that linked to them looked suspiciously like automated bot accounts all tweeting in unison.

This is nothing new on the Republican side of the digital ecosystem. GOP-connected Political Action Committees ('PACs') have been setting up partisan local news websites for years as prime vehicles for disinformation.

The Tea Party (remember them?) set up media companies controlling these 'news' sites all over the country, and dressed them up in local news clothes to mask their purpose—all timed to take advantage of the extinction events in local news outlets.

From the *Tennessee Star* to the *Minnesota Sun*, all constellations were covered.

Ahead of the 2020 election, Columbia University's Tow Center for Digital Journalism found more than 450 news websites in a network, each distributing thousands of algorithmically generated articles and a smaller number of reported stories. The *New York Times* found one network—Timpone's—with more than 1300 websites covering all 50 states, filling the void left by local news with 'propaganda ordered up by dozens of conservative think tanks, political operatives, corporate executives and public-relations professionals'.

Many of these publications sit under the umbrella of a few media companies—Metric Media, Locality Labs (the rebranded successor to Journatic), Franklin Archer, the Record Inc. All of them are in some way connected back to Brian Timpone.

In Michigan—one of the key swing states to decide the 2020 election—the *Michigan Daily* (an actual newspaper over 130 years old) counted 40 new local news websites that popped up in the months before the election, all of them with a pro-Trump bent.

> The different websites are nearly indistinguishable, sharing identical stories and using regional titles such as the *Ann Arbor Times*, *Grand Rapids Reporter* and *Lansing Sun* . . . Articles featured on the websites include a summary of a report by the conservative think-tank Heritage Foundation, a story about the failure of U.S. Rep. Rashida Tlaib to rally a crowd at a pro-impeachment event and a front-page piece about Michigan Republicans supporting President Donald Trump. Each site has an identical 'About Us' page.

Election disclosures show the Republican candidates who benefit from glowing coverage also coincidentally paid large sums to the media companies owning these websites. Right around the same time Jeanne Ives, a Republican candidate for an Illinois seat, paid $2000 to the company that owned the *DuPage Policy Journal*, headlines started appearing on articles like 'Jeanne Ives is Good for Business' and 'Republicans Are All in For Jeanne Ives'.

In Arizona, Senate candidate Kelli Ward touted a glowing endorsement from a fake outlet, the *Arizona Monitor*, that she furiously denied having set up herself—despite every article spruiking her and denigrating her opponents.

It's a no-brainer in today's election campaigning. Pity the candidate trying to get press the good old way, convincing real journalists that they are fair dinkum.

In 2020, the Democrats finally began to acknowledge this reality, with some pink slime of their own (albeit all transparently declared and factual).

Motivated by the death of local news outlets and the rise of social media, the Democrat-aligned organisation Acronym raised tens of millions to start local news websites in key swing states and to staff them with editorial staff and journalists.

As they outlined in their pitch memo to donors:

> The GOP and the far right . . . media properties are influencing the opinions and behaviours of key audiences, especially audiences who live in 'narrative deserts'. Meanwhile Democratic organizations and campaigns continue to rely heavily on cycle-driven paid advertising programs to inform and mobilize voters.

This is the approach that also got Trump elected in 2016, filling the non-partisan void left by the collapse of local news with partisan content from ideologically driven digital media properties. Acronym's was one of many efforts to help fill it instead with year-round progressive narratives. What else could they have done? The narrative vacuum would have otherwise had only one side filling it.

These sites were then weaponised for the election, with political messages, voting information and confidence in the mail-in voting system that was crucial to Democrat success.

But let's now drop the whole pretence of legitimacy to go another level deeper into the fake article industry.

Pinker Slime

In the wild, wild west of the internet, there is a pretty low bar for reasons to create a fake news website—it's even now the preferred method for scammers. In May 2021, ASIC (the Australian finance regulator) warned Australians to be on the lookout for fake articles purporting to be from the ABC or *The Guardian* singing the praises of cryptocurrencies. In reality they were traps that scammers used to lure unsuspecting investors

The Copper Courier
YOUR SOURCE FOR ARIZONA NEWS   ISSUES ⌄   SUBMIT A STORY   SIGN UP FOR OUR NEWSLETTER   Q

LOCAL

This UN Climate Advisor Worked on Global Policy. Now She Wants to Help Phoenix.

Written By
Alicia Barrón

Originally Published
November 12,
2020 10:00 am
MST

f   SHARE

🔗   LINK

Yassamin Ansari is running to represent Phoenix District 7.
Photo courtesy of Yassamin Ansari campaign.

"Our work now will ensure that future generations can still live here in safety and in good health."

Phoenix City Council candidate Yassamin Ansari is ready.

Most Popular

ELECTIONS

LIVE: Watch Livestreams of Every Ballot
Counting Center in Arizona

CORONAVIRUS
Arizona Man Dies After Taking Drug
Trump Promoted As Possible
Coronavirus Cure

CRIMINAL JUSTICE
Record Number Of Phoenix Police
Shootings Add Fuel To The Fire Of
Protests

YOUR VOTE 2020
Judges Got You Stumped? Use These
Voter Guides to Help You Finish Filling
Out Your Ballot

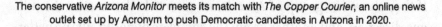

The conservative *Arizona Monitor* meets its match with *The Copper Courier*, an online news outlet set up by Acronym to push Democratic candidates in Arizona in 2020.

in before running away overseas with their money. Scamming, an art as old as currency itself, was forgoing the telephone and the Nigerian prince email in favour of an article looking like legitimate news.

Fake articles are often created for nothing more than mischief. Take the 'World News Daily Report'. Claiming to be written by ex-Mossad agents out of Tel Aviv, it runs articles as enticing as 'Lottery winner shows up naked for his work shift at Walmart store with boss's face tattooed on his ass' and 'Florida teenager lying in critical condition after inserting his genitals inside of a blowfish'. In reality, it is run by two Canadian pranksters.

But getting a lot of clicks can also be very lucrative. That means many of the articles out there are purely clickbait-generating content farms which get a lot of traffic, slap some advertising on them and then collect the revenue. An estimate of World News Daily Report's traffic in 2017 would put their annual advertising revenue at over half a million dollars, before Google began cracking down on ad revenue from fake news sites that year.

Under pressure, Facebook started throttling them too, so the news sites simply copied legitimate news sites. When one of the most prominent fake news sites (the 'National Report') had a hoax story taken down about Ted Cruz saying veterans should start selling cookies to pay for their own healthcare, it simply republished it on a website that spoofed the *USA Today* website, complete with a fake *USA Today* web address (usatodaycom.com). They did the same for another article, creating a 'washingtonpost.com.co' website. Another guy told the actual *Washington Post* he was making US$10,000 a month off the ads on 'abcnews.com.co'.

This practice even has its own name: typosquatting.

Often, the motives are unclear. We know that they may be geopolitical—Russia's foreign intelligence service has built a model of interference where they don't need to be pushing a particular barrow at all. They see value in sowing discord and confusion in whatever form it comes. If they show one group of Americans an article that incites them in one direction, and another group the complete opposite, all the better.

In March 2021, the FSB (the rebranded KGB, sick of all those commie-hating eighties movies giving them a bad name) started pointing their fake news websites, with names like 'News Front' or 'New Eastern Outlook' at attacking the Pfizer and Moderna covid vaccines. It continued a long KGB trend that began with Cold War fake news claiming the AIDS epidemic was unleashed from a US Army biological weapons lab in Maryland (sound familiar, Wuhan?).

Their ploy in that case was to make their articles look as legitimate as possible, not completely outrageous. They selectively quoted or misrepresented real events, as opposed to the bald-face lie—like focusing on how the vaccines could cause Bell's palsy, or how a man in California tested positive for covid after receiving the Pfizer vaccine. These were all events reported in the real media, minus their accompanying contextual explanation.

On the more outrageous end of the spectrum, the February 2020 article 'Vatican confirms Pope Francis and two aides test positive for Coronavirus' appeared on a website called 'MCM News' right as the early wave of covid swept through Italy. Shortly before the domain address was masked, it was bought by a squatter in China. The MCM News site existed pretty much solely to post fake covid news. Was this Chinese state-backed geopolitical mind games, or just a bored kid in their basement?

Early March 2020, when you could alarm people with fake news of covid deaths in the hundreds.

Once MCM News articles were posted, a network of fake accounts would then pump them into Facebook groups. An article, again very early in the covid pandemic days, claimed that 'Tanzania confirms first case of Coronavirus' (you can really place any article in a timeline about the pandemic by which word it uses to name the affliction).

A Facebook user under the name of Elvis Kafui from Accra, Ghana (who had previously also shared the Pope Francis coronavirus hoax article, as well as a false story spreading disinformation about the

Frimp Eunuch shared a link.
March 13 at 4:37 PM · 🌐

BREAKING NEWS

UCRTV.COM

USA Presidential Candidate Joe Biden Tests Positive To Coronavirus - UCR News

👍 Like   ↪ Share

Frimp Eunuch turned off commenting for this post.

Frimp Eunuch loved to post fake news stories into all manner of African Facebook groups.

number of cases in Iran) then started posting the article in 'Buy and Sell' Facebook groups all over Tanzania—from 'Dar es salaam Buy and Sell online' to 'DAR ONLINE MARKET'. His delightfully named friend Frimp Eunuch did the same.

Frimp was also found spreading fake articles from other sites with similar themes—like UCRTV.COM, also registered in China.

Elvis and Frimp posted other MCM News articles into an assortment of Facebook groups. Frimp posted an article falsely claiming soccer star Cristiano Ronaldo's mother was dead in the odd collection of 'Black Business Owners of Atlanta' and 'California Small Business Owner Group', and then a few groups in India like 'Bitcoin India'. India and

China are bitter geopolitical rivals whose tensions would boil over into deadly real-world violence only a few weeks later in Kashmir.

Again we see a network of walking, talking and quacking geopolitical interference ducks, this time from China.

These sorts of websites are incredibly common, and it is often near impossible to attribute motives to them, as the execution of this tactic is perfectly identical whether you are a prankster, a scammer, an entrepreneur or a spy.

What is important to note is their efficacy, especially in the absence of people's ability to tell the difference between fake news and real news. A group of Yale researchers attributed this more to us being lazy than partisan.

But that is not to say partisan fake articles are not also incredibly effective. In addition to any geopolitical or satirical fake news sites, you also have the news sites that represent the evolution of hyper-partisan outrage that Fox News brought to our TVs. In the US it has become more than a cottage industry.

Some of them, you have most likely heard of: Breitbart, Infowars, Daily Caller or The Daily Wire. They have been the beating heart of the Trump-led echo chamber we will discuss in detail.

They have also perfected the art of the fake article as the key artifact of disinformation, in a way that relegated Fox News and its previous outlier gasbags like Sean Hannity to the common-sense middle ground of propaganda-lite.

Collectively, these sites packaged hate and pseudo-patriotism into a commercially viable populist product, creating in the process what one publisher called an 'emergent propaganda state' in the US once Trump was in power. They are filled with conspiracy theories and outright lies, both of which were to form the script for the alternate reality one half of America was to come to live in after Trump's acrimonious defeat and as covid ravaged the country.

Some of the delightful article headlines on Breitbart include: 'Planned Parenthood's Body Count Under Cecile Richards Is Up To

Half A Holocaust', 'Birth Control Makes Women Unattractive and Crazy' and my personal favourite, 'EXCLUSIVE: Donald Trump Plans To Continue GOP Legacy of Leading On Women's, Civil Rights Against Racist, Sexist Democrats'.

I'll leave it to you to decide whether these articles are fact-based or not.

The sum total effect of the fake article, in whatever form it comes, is that a growing number of people are switching off from traditional news sources to get their information only from social media. This is an enormous problem, because for anyone who finds their articles on social media, information is received in a vacuum. In your Facebook feed there is very little to differentiate between the outward appearance of a real article and a fake article. An article from the *New York Times* is given the same real estate, wrapper and authenticity as an article from Infowars or Breitbart.

This takes on an even bigger significance once these bad actors start paying for that real estate.

11 / The Fake Ad

'Advertising is only evil when it advertises evil things.'
—David Ogilvy

In Australia, the law is clear: it is illegal for advertisements to make statements that are incorrect, or even *likely* to create a false impression, regardless of whether or not it was intentional. You can't even make wildly unsubstantiated claims and just add a little asterisk to put the truth in fine print—like saying your chocolate thickshake is 'fat free' and then putting in size-four font on the bottom of the carton 'This product contains fat.' The penalties are harsh. Breach these consumer laws and you could pay as much as $10 million in fines or 10 per cent of your annual turnover.

These laws apply equally to social media advertising. As the ACCC lays out in black and white: 'Consumer protection laws which prohibit businesses from making false, misleading or deceptive claims about their products or services have been in place for decades. These laws apply to social media in the same way they apply to any other marketing or sales channel.'

Now, I know what you're thinking—*Wait a minute, then how come my morning paper is wrapped in yellow-and-black ads from Clive Palmer saying 'James Shipton from ASIC is a vampire'?*

It may surprise you to find out that there is a gaping exception to the rule: it is perfectly legal in Australia to lie in political advertising.

We tried to fix this—it was illegal for a few months in 1983 but then parliament thought better of it, getting all post-structural philosopher on us and deciding that because the truth is hard to define and political advertising consists of 'intangibles' which are 'not capable of being untrue . . . It is not possible to control political advertising by legislation.'

How could regulators ever get to the murky bottom of whether Bill Shorten *did* actually have a death tax in his 2019 policy platform?! We can never know! Surely just reading that policy platform would never clear it up! Maybe The Greens secretly *have* been in power and stopping the back-burning of any bushland! Maybe James Shipton objectively *is* a vampire!

Our legislators in 1984 could not have foreseen the changes in advertising that were to come twenty years later once the internet arrived and became an enormous hoover for all the personal details of our lives and spending habits.

Now that such an age has arrived, political advertising has taken on a new significance.

Whereas it was very easy to tell the content of a political advertisement when a candidate put it on a billboard or on TV, in 2016 it was impossible to know what they were advertising online.

Journalists covering the Australian election that year tried in vain to understand this, instead reporting on whatever appeared in *their* feed as if it represented the sum total of a campaign's efforts. They all boldly declared the Liberal Party the winner of the social media campaign because Malcolm Turnbull had a lot of likes on Facebook, ignorant to the fact that Labor was quietly serving more than 100 million impressions to persuadable voters far under the radar of the media's gaze.

While the media reported on the 'paltry' $776,900 Labor spent on TV ads attacking the Liberals for wanting to privatise Medicare, they missed the fact that swing voters were each getting an average of 45 customised ads in the last eight weeks of the campaign alone—online. It then surprised everyone that in the election results Labor far outperformed expectations and came within a seat of pulling off the most improbable victory.

As Labor's head of digital at the time, Erinn Swan, said, 'Beneath the mainstream media was bubbling away by far the most customised and segmented, engaging advertising campaign by a political party in Australia. What you saw play out with Labor's Medicare campaign for example, and what was visible in the mainstream media was just above-the-line result of a mass scale data-driven campaign going direct to voters.'

I know all this because I was the one serving them those 'Mediscare' ads. Back then, there was no transparency on what we were doing. These ads were only visible to the people targeted by them (spoiler alert: political journalists are not swing voters and didn't get them in their social media feeds).

At around the same time, a company called Cambridge Analytica, which had illicitly harvested the data of up to 87 million Facebook profiles, was pitching the Ted Cruz and Donald Trump campaigns on a simple idea: with what we know about these people on Facebook, we can create psychological profiles of every voter in America and target them with ads designed to appeal specifically to them.

No doubt you've heard of the scandal. But in reality what Cambridge Analytica was talking about was no different from how any advertiser was using the internet in 2016. The 'crime' Cambridge Analytica had committed was in how it had obtained the data, a breach of Facebook's Terms of Service, not in how it had targeted voters with a creepy amount of data on them—that part was routine.

That it became such a scandal spoke more to the surprise most people had that *anyone* had that much data on them, and that companies freely traded in the details of our lives online. It woke the world up to the issue of data privacy, and what rights we had over our own digital lives.

Roy Morgan knows much more about you than Cambridge Analytica does.

This all takes its place in the rich tapestry of disinformation campaigns, because the easiest way to find a target online is not to build groups and profiles aligned with their interests in the hope they come to you—it is to pay to directly go to them, through an ad that appears in their feed.

Trump did just this, and in the process was able to wind up whole sections of the population to be angry about things the rest of the country didn't even know about. It was the first time an election had been fought along completely different parallel lines depending on what you already thought. If you were an African-American swing voter in Michigan, your experience of the election was vastly different from a Texan housewife.

Still, all the Cambridge Analytica data in the world is not much use unless you can find and target those voters, and that's what social media advertising allows us to do.

The transparency has come a long way since then: on Facebook the advertiser must be verified and disclosed, and the ads are available for public view in an 'ad library' for seven years, with some rudimentary details about their demographic and geographic targeting. Facebook banned political advertising altogether in the week before and months after the 2020 US election. But these efforts are much like the tax code: those who want to will look for loopholes to exploit, and the platforms will play catch-up and plug them after the fact.

The rules also allow for a convenient distraction from the real issue. Advertising makes the disinformer's life easier, but it is by no means the main way that disinformation spreads. The social media platforms could remove the keys to their feeds for advertisers completely, and it would do little to prevent the fake account spreading the fake article to invent a fake reality.

It also ignores the enormous scope for disinformation to occur *within the rules*. This is what prompted Elizabeth Warren, during her 2020 campaign, to highlight this by deliberately creating an ad with fake news (that Mark Zuckerberg had just endorsed Donald Trump) in an effort to show it would not be taken down (it wasn't).

For some of the social media platforms, fake political ads just weren't a fight they thought it was worth having. Twitter banned all political advertising in 2020, and TikTok banned political ads and manipulated media which it said 'misleads users by distorting the truth of events in a way that could cause harm'.

It is easy to focus on the platforms and their rules as the cause of and solution to all of the problems surrounding disinformation. But they can be a massive smokescreen.

Yes, they have provided a fertile ground for disinformation to thrive, but they are also expert in using your concerns about disinformation

Elizabeth Warren
Sponsored · Paid for by WARREN FOR PRESIDENT, INC.

Breaking news: Mark Zuckerberg and Facebook just endorsed Donald Trump for re-election.

You're probably shocked, and you might be thinking, "how could this possibly be true?"

Well, it's not. (Sorry.) But what Zuckerberg *has* done is given Donald Trump free rein to lie on his platform -- and then to pay Facebook gobs of money to push out their lies to American voters.

If Trump tries to lie in a TV ad, most networks will refuse to air it. But Facebook just cashes Trump's checks.

Facebook already helped elect Donald Trump once. Now, they're deliberately allowing a candidate to intentionally lie to the American people. It's time to hold Mark Zuckerberg accountable —add your name if you agree.

MY.ELIZABETHWARREN.COM
Mark Zuckerberg just endorsed Donald Trump
It's time to break up our biggest tech companies like Amazon, Google, and Facebook.

Sign Up

Elizabeth Warren tries and fails to have her fake news ad banned by Facebook.

to build their own moat of regulation. That moat outwardly appears to address the problem but in reality just increases the barriers to entry for any commercial competitors to these massive tech behemoths that dominate our online lives. 'Regulate us at your own peril' they dare us.

Removing advertising on the social media platforms, or even removing the platforms entirely, would not change the fact we currently live in a society with massive information disorder. Nor would it remove the people who stand ready to manipulate that.

12 / The Fake Citizen

'Pity the nation divided into fragments, each
fragment deeming itself a nation.'
—Kahlil Gibran, *The Garden of the Prophet*

On an unseasonably humid May afternoon in 2016 in Houston, Texas, the crowd gathered in front of the Islamic Da'wah Center was growing tense. What had been supposed to be a routine opening of a new library at the old mosque and religious centre was turning out to be anything but:

> We got a message from one of our folks that monitored our Twitter page, I think it was, or maybe our Facebook page, it's a bit fuzzy now, that they had reached out and were asking if we wanted to participate in some rally.

On one side of the road, an angry mob—a mix of White supremacists, Texan secessionist cowboys and neo-Nazis—had formed to protest the Islamification of their city at an event advertised on Facebook as 'Stop Islamification of Texas'.

On the other side of the road, a ragtag group of socialists, Antifa and citizens concerned about the growing brazenness of anti-immigration racists, had gathered in counter-protest, coordinated through a Facebook event called 'Save Islamic Knowledge'.

As confederate flags and swastikas waved in the face of peace and protest signs, tensions mounted until conflict erupted, the angry confrontation prompting police to move in.

Journalists in attendance tried in vain to find and interview the protest leaders:

I just basically did what I always do. I just went down the line. So, I'm talking to people: Why are you here? That sort of thing. And what was unusual is I kept asking . . . do you know who's running this . . . who's in charge, and nobody knew who was in charge.

More than a year later it would finally emerge why, when thousands of miles away lawmakers in Washington DC released samples of 3000 Facebook ads purchased by Russian operatives during the 2016 presidential campaign.

Among them were ads from the group who organised the anti-Muslim protest, and ads from the group who organised the counter-protest. Both had in fact been set up by the Internet Research Agency—the Kremlin-backed 'dezinformatsiya' machine. The ads had deftly promoted these conflicting protests for the exact same time and location.

One of the counter-protest organisers was circumspect enough to put their finger on exactly why it worked: 'Apparently somebody there was smart enough to realize that if folks know that there's going to be a racist event, a racist will come out and an antiracist will come out against it.'

For the bargain basement price of US$200 worth of Facebook advertising that brought opposing groups to the concurrent physical events, the Russian agency had successfully sown violent division on the streets of Texas.

Cold War bean counters no doubt rolled in their graves. It's an incredibly cost-effective geopolitical manoeuvre. During the Cold War it would have taken many years and roubles to embed deep-cover operatives in these American groups and have them work their way towards fomenting real-world division and violence.

It was also incredibly well calculated. America was already a country divided against itself; all a foreign saboteur had to do was add the camel's back-breaking straw. After researchers from the University of Texas interviewed those involved, they concluded the tactics could not have worked in a vacuum:

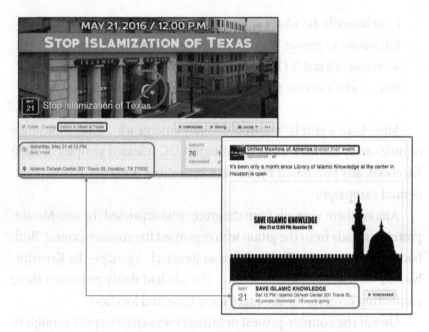

Evidence of the simultaneous protests presented to the Congressional inquiry into Russian interference.

Appealing to divisive issues is a propagandist's strength and a population's weakness. In Houston, the IRA [Internet Research Agency] harnessed anti-Muslim sentiment, racism and xenophobia—homegrown problems of the United States . . . It is clear that the IRA succeeded in holding up a mirror to America, revealing a stark societal chasm, tribalism, and hatred.

The Mueller report (or its less catchy official title, 'Report on the Investigation into Russian Interference in the 2016 Presidential Election') documented in great detail how the Russians understood that to damage the old enemy they would need to find existing cracks to pour their disinformation into.

They sent operatives to travel the Midwest as far back as 2014 to have conversations with middle Americans to gather intelligence in communities marked by a lack of it. On their return to Russia they were able to report on how to defeat America: talk about culture war issues that already divided them, like gun rights and Black Lives Matter.

A senior cybersecurity adviser to Vladimir Putin boasted to the Russian national information security forum that their new-found ability to use social media to disrupt American politics was akin to them developing a new atomic bomb for the disinformation age:

> You think we are living in 2016. No, we are living in 1948. And do you know why? Because in 1949, the Soviet Union had its first atomic bomb test. And if until that moment, the Soviet Union was trying to reach agreement with Truman to ban nuclear weapons, and the Americans were not taking us seriously, in 1949 everything changed and they started talking to us on an equal footing. I'm warning you: We are at the verge of having 'something' in the information arena, which will allow us to talk to the Americans as equals.

That 'something' turned out to be an army of American social media accounts and a trove of hacked emails and salacious rumours to arm them with. The website DCLeaks.com, created in June 2016 by the GRU (the Russian military intelligence agency), began publishing the hacked emails, and had fake American accounts share them.

'Katherine Fulton' was one who posted in stilted English: 'Hey truth seekers! Who can tell me who are #DCLeaks? Some kind of Wikileaks? You should visit their website, it contains confidential information about our leaders such as Hillary Clinton, and others.'

The Russian accounts were expert in reeling Americans in with posts like, 'Like if you believe in Jesus' or a picture of a gun-toting Yosemite Sam on a Confederate flag saying 'Like & share if you grew up watching me on television, have a gun, and haven't shot or killed anyone!'

Half of the Internet Research Agency ads in 2016 mentioned race, and half of those again mentioned it in the context of policing and crime. The Internet Research Agency is one prominent example of a front of

Russian ads placed by the Internet Research
Agency to sow division
Source: US Senate Intelligence Committee

disinformation where state-backed groups harness the same dynamics of our disinformation ecosystem that are used for domestic political gain.

Most of them operate 'troll farms,' creating thousands of fake accounts and putting them to good use overseas. The Internet Research Agency was reported to have had as many as 600 employees and an annual budget of more than US$10 million. It is likely much higher. One Russian agent was caught with financial documents outlining a US$35 million operating budget for one six-month operation alone. Researchers from Clemson University called the Internet Research Agency 'industrial machines in a modern propaganda factory' who advance their agenda through a combination of propaganda, 'sockpuppetry' and 'astroturfing'.

Other famous efforts of the Internet Research Agency include 'digital blackface'—posing as African-American Trump supporters mentioned at the start of this section. Our friend from Dallas J.R. Cliff could well have been Й.Р. Цлифф.

More active than even the Internet Research Agency was the 'Secondary Infektion' campaign: a long-running Russian information operation, encompassing multiple campaigns on social media run by an unknown central entity, still running at least until August 2021 (the time of writing this), whose usual approach is to create forged documents, articles and accounts to provoke tensions between Russia's perceived enemies and smear their opponents.

It's not all about influencing the US—that just gets the most prominent media attention. Secondary Infektion has targeted Ukraine mostly, and its campaigns have been aimed at everything from destabilising Turkey over its proxy war in Syria to discrediting the World Anti-Doping Agency for banning juiced-up Russian sports teams from international competition.

As opposed to placing ads on Facebook like the Internet Research Agency, Secondary Infektion appears to prefer the 'leaked forgery' as its main thrust of disinformation, which may appear on anything from Reddit, Medium or Twitter to Quora, Facebook or YouTube. Like the forged letter on official letterhead from European Union Commissioner

Johannes Hahn to a fellow commissioner, in which he says Russian opposition leader Alexei Navalny should not be awarded a prize as he is an 'odious nationalist'. Classic EU insult.

They will then provoke discussion about it, like the Reddit thread discussing whether German Chancellor Angela Merkel is an alcoholic, based on a forged article in *BuzzFeed*: 'Frau Chancellor is known to enjoy admiration of the political colleagues due to her rare alcohol endurance. Merkel's visits to local pubs during her tours to foreign countries, e.g. Australia, are also no secret.'

Perhaps as odd for Russians as it would be for Australians, alcoholism seems to be the accusation of choice for Secondary Infektion to bring down its opponents. There was strangely even a weird flurry of accusations against Dmitry Medvedev, Russian prime minister at the time, calling him an alcoholic—and worse: Ukraine's preferred candidate for Russian president. Presumably he pissed off the wrong troll.

Sometimes their efforts lacked a little in the execution; Google Translate can't always get it right. Here is a supposed American journalist talking about secret CIA plans he uncovered to assassinate Kim Jong-un (read it in your best Russian accent inner monologue):

> Something rather newsworthy happened during that chat-in. After mentioning the North Korean dictator, one the soldiers who came for lunch approached us and asked whether I was an American. Having a positive reply he energetically told that his brother was one of the 'three thousand' and he came home not long ago for he was granted a furlough.

When Twitter released their investigation into state-backed influence operations during the 2016 US election, there was an unwelcome surprise waiting for Australians. Following the trail left by those Russian troll accounts led right back to our own Australian political discussion, with many of the same tactics of foreign subterfuge happening right under our noses.

Some 70 of the Internet Research Agency Twitter accounts targeting the US election were also active in Australia, possibly in retaliation for the Australian government blaming Russia for the MH17 crash, or for Australia deploying planes to patrol Syrian airspace (both correlate with spikes in activity from these Russian troll accounts mentioning Australia). Or maybe it was simply because the Internet Research Agency loves to mess with all geopolitical rivals and it is incredibly cheap and easy to do so. In any case, in these tweets we see the Russians were attempting to pour salt into the same wounds they did elsewhere: finding divisive issues and using them to drive us apart.

How do you drive a wedge between Australians? The most common hashtags used were topics like '#Nauru', '#Manus', '#letthemstay' and '#refugees'.

The troll accounts then tried to link these to other issues of contention, like '#Isis'. Researchers from the University of Canberra who mapped these accounts told a Senate inquiry into 'Foreign Interference through Social Media' that:

> Troll accounts attempted to influence the direction of discourse
> around the issue of refugees and asylum seekers by inferring that
> refugees being housed on Manus Island are potentially connected to
> Islamic State (and thus a security threat to Australia). This also serves
> to divide Australian society internally along 'us vs them' lines.

The other activity the Internet Research Agency got up to in our Twitter feeds seems more banal, but were likely attempts to lay the groundwork for future interference. Much of it was designed to destabilise from every side, focusing on One Nation from one direction and The Greens from the other: anything to upset the usual balance of power. They also appear heavily in discussions featuring accounts like Andrew Bolt's, Miranda Devine's and others in the Murdoch stable of outlets and personalities, suggesting the Russians were targeting our disruptive fringes. The same researchers told parliament their conclusions as to what the Internet Research Agency was up to:

From our analysis of the dataset, it is apparent that Twitter 'troll' accounts controlled by the Russian Internet Research Agency (IRA) pursued a multi-pronged engagement strategy in Australian social media. These tactics included developing relationships with users to enable future propaganda dissemination; injecting divisive content into existing debates; and attempting to colour online discussions of #Australia with negative content.

This type of foreign interference is not all the Russians, either.

As the pandemic began to rage across the US in March 2020, phones across the country began buzzing with text messages warning of a national lockdown. Security forces traced their spread back to Chinese agents. The agents spread anti-American conspiracies on social media about the virus to mirror those Trump was spreading about China, retreating into the background once real Americans picked up the rumours and gave them their own life.

NSC 45 Archived
@WHNSC45   ...

Text message rumors of a national #quarantine are FAKE. There is no national lockdown. @CDCgov has and will continue to post the latest guidance on #COVID19. #coronavirus

2:48 PM · Mar 16, 2020 · The White House

11.8K Retweets **1,277** Quote Tweets **24.5K** Likes

Nor is it just security agencies. A key civilian inauthentic player in the US context was the pro-Trump Falun Gong disinformation machine 'The Beauty of Life' ('The BL'), from the far-right anti-China newspaper the *Epoch Times* (which Australian readers may even recognise as a free physical newspaper handed out in their neighbourhood). The *Epoch Times* leaders saw Trump as an anti-communist messiah, and so wheeled out an extensive disinformation campaign to get him elected in 2016.

The BL, now banned from Facebook, ran a sophisticated network of hundreds of Facebook pages, first growing their readership through viral clickbait and then promoting Trump campaign ads. The efforts included the mass creation of fake American Facebook profiles, bots to generate fake likes and shares, and faux 'pro-America' groups like 'America Daily' (which alone has more than a million followers) to disseminate the content. The network of disinformation was one of the main engines behind the biggest conspiracy theories around the election, including that Obama spied on the Trump campaign.

The right-wing media company's Facebook footprint now rivals Breitbart in terms of followers, with tens of millions of fans spread across multiple properties related to the *Epoch Times* that led its reporters all the way into Trump's White House press briefings.

Their archenemy, the Chinese Communist Party, more than rivals that ambition, including in Australia where Chinese Australians are fed a steady diet of disinformation through official accounts on the social media app WeChat—now used by almost three million Australians.

Then you have the small town in central North Macedonia, Veles—population 43,000 Macedonians and many more trolls. (You may have missed the memo, but in a conflict that began with Alexander the Great, the Greeks and Macedonians have now settled their irredentist dispute, and what was 'the Former Yugoslav Republic of Macedonia' is now the only slightly less catchy 'North Macedonia'.)

In Veles, fake news is big business and an army of Macedonian millennials are raking in a 'digital gold rush' by getting paid to write clickbait articles on American disinformation websites.

The BBC interviewed one of them:

> Every morning, Tamara would open her laptop to a fresh email with a link to a spreadsheet. This document contained eight stories based on the other side of the world from her, in the US . . . Her job was to churn out semi-plagiarised copies of articles originally published on US extreme right-wing publications, so that her boss could serve

them back to unsuspecting Americans thousands of miles away . . .

'I tried not to think about writing propaganda. My take was that if people are stupid enough to believe these stories, maybe they deserve this. If they think this is the truth, then maybe they deserve this as a way of punishment.'

While the genesis of the fake news factories in Veles linked back to a lawyer with links to Republicans in America, the websites soon took on a life of their own once the Macedonian teenagers realised they could make money off the amount of traffic their sites were generating. While Tamara was only paid €3 a day, the owners of the sites with more than a million followers on Facebook could rake in €1500 a day.

€1500 a day can go a long way in central North Macedonia.

But while these foreign interferers dominate the media coverage of the topic of disinformation, it is important we don't assume the story of disinformation is all about them.

It's a more comfortable narrative to tell ourselves that disinformation is a problem caused by coordinated forces in alien countries, but it masks the truth: the forces of disinformation that tear apart our social fabric are of our own domestic making. They take place well within the social media platforms' terms of service, and are more likely to come from our neighbour than a Russian agent.

By focusing on foreign interference we risk getting distracted by the captivating 'edge cases' and therefore miss the real problem staring us right in the face: your real, human relative inhabiting an entirely different reality from you even if they are physically only metres away.

13 / The Fake Reality

> 'Lies are often much more plausible, more appealing
> to reason, than reality . . . whereas reality has
> the disconcerting habit of confronting us with the
> unexpected, for which we were not prepared.'
> —Hannah Arendt

In 2019, a bored college kid who lived with his parents in California was up late one night scrolling through Facebook.

On a whim, he created a meme—'Storm Area 51, They Can't Stop All of Us'—and a Facebook event to go with it, imploring everyone to meet at the notorious Nevada air base rumoured to house captured aliens, and simultaneously storm the base. The event description read: 'Let's see them aliens'.

Three million people RSVP'd to the event, prompting the Air Force to issue a statement warning people to stay away from the base. Two Nevada counties prepared for a state of emergency, the Federal Aviation Administration closed the nearby airspace and the FBI paid a visit to the college student's home.

No doubt the thousands of people who turned up in Nevada on the day (only 150 actually made it to the gates of the Air Force base, and most just took selfies and went home) were among the 45 per cent of Americans who believe UFOs have visited us on Earth.

In Australia, it's 34 per cent—exactly the same number who believe Adam and Eve is the true story of creation, and slightly less than the number who believe ghosts are real and exert their will on the living.

No doubt it anecdotally seems that these days you are hearing more about crackpot theories than usual. This is because we turn to conspiracy theories in times of global uncertainty, and they in turn are being weaponised in disinformation campaigns. We are in the midst of a twin pandemic of conspiracy-fuelled disinformation.

Seventy-one per cent of Americans have heard of a conspiracy theory circulating online that powerful people intentionally planned the covid outbreak (and 80 per cent among those who get their news mostly from social media). Of those who have heard it, *36 per cent say it is either definitely or probably true.* The same levels of belief have been borne out in other research polls.

Even more (40 per cent) believe it was created in a lab in China. The same number believe there was a 'deep state' cabal working to undermine Donald Trump's presidency. When asked if the statement '*A group of Satan-worshipping elites who run a child sex ring are trying to control our politics and media*' is true or false, almost one in every five people thought it was true. More than a third weren't sure. Less than half were able to correctly say it was false.

Let's just put those numbers in perspective: there are *millions more* people in America who believe in QAnon's child sex ring conspiracy than there are *left-handed* people.

All told, about half of Americans believe at least one disproven conspiracy theory.

Even before the covid pandemic hit, conspiracy thinking was not only on the rise but becoming increasingly weaponised for political purposes. It is not just a social problem—conspiracy theories are a major political problem. Even though many of these conspiracy theories may not seem overtly political in nature (though many also are), they destroy faith in every institution and any party's ability to govern; in the wrong hands they have become a very potent political tool. They are a key mode of disinformation to tackle.

Research into conspiracy theories has found no innate correlation between conspiracy thinking and left or right political orientation (in fact as discussed in Part Four, it could also be rapidly breaking down these traditional ideological groupings). But as Adam Enders, who researches how conspiracy theories affect politics, puts it: 'Conspiratorial thinking can be pulled in one direction or another; it can be harnessed. And that's exactly what we're seeing. Strategic politicians can cue conspiratorial thinking.'

This is borne out in the same Pew poll about powerful people planning covid—of those who got their covid news from Trump and his task force, the number of those believing the conspiracy theory jumps to 56 per cent (by contrast only 22 per cent of people who got their news from national news outlets were likely to believe it).

But one particular conspiracy theory, or rather set of conspiracy theories, is dominating all others. The results have been fatal, and terrorism experts are bracing for worse.

QAnon

When Frank Cali, mafia boss of the notorious Gambino crime family, was gunned down in the driveway of his Staten Island home in 2019, the police were bracing for the worst. There hadn't been a mob killing this high-profile in New York since John Gotti had ordered a hit on 'Big Paulie' Castellano outside Sparks Steak House in order to replace him as head of the Gambino family in 1985.

Now, they worried, another mob war could spill blood onto the streets of New York. Worse, their usually solid intelligence had not picked up on any internal power struggle indicating a move like this was coming. What else had their intelligence missed?

New York crime bosses rarely even travelled with their goons for security anymore, and kept a much lower profile than their flamboyant predecessors. Did this hit represent not only a changing of the guard, but also an escalation of the tactics police had hoped were a thing of the past?

Within a week, the police had tracked down the blue pickup truck caught on surveillance camera and identified its owner as the gunman. Anthony Comello was arrested and charged with murder, but details of the motive were still unclear. How was he connected to the crime families? Was he a foot soldier of a powerful rival, or an enterprising up-and-comer trying to rise through the ranks on his own initiative? Some even suggested it was a romantically inspired hit, with Comello wanting to date Cali's niece.

At his first court appearance it became clear none of the above theories were correct. The truth was much stranger. Comello, in handcuffs and prison greens, held up his hand for the cameras to see—there in his palm in blue biro was unmistakably a hastily scribbled letter 'Q', along with some harder to decipher phrases including 'United we stand' and 'MAGA forever'.

By the time of his next hearing, his lawyer could offer more clarity on his client's defence: the accused gunman had been radicalised by 'hate words from the White House' and online conspiracy theories.

Comello hadn't been cavorting with criminal associates—he'd been in his parents' basement surfing the internet. There, in the deep dark recesses of YouTube and Facebook, he had become convinced that Cali was a member of the 'deep state', a global cabal of child sex traffickers. Comello had gone to Cali's house under 'the protection of President Trump himself' to execute a citizen's arrest. The month before he had unsuccessfully tried to make citizens' arrests on New York Mayor Bill de Blasio and other Democratic lawmakers for the same reason.

The mob boss had been gunned down by a follower of the latest internet craze, QAnon. It wasn't the first time the online cult had spilled into real-world gun violence by crusading foot soldiers, and authorities now label it as one of the key domestic terror threats.

The normalisation of once-fringe conspiracy theories is best seen through the rise of QAnon. In case you are lucky enough to have never heard of QAnon, *The Guardian* describes it like this:

> QAnon is a baseless internet conspiracy theory whose followers
> believe that a cabal of Satan-worshipping Democrats, Hollywood
> celebrities and billionaires runs the world while engaging in
> pedophilia, human trafficking and the harvesting of a supposedly
> life-extending chemical from the blood of abused children. QAnon

followers believe that Donald Trump is waging a secret battle against this cabal and its 'deep state' collaborators to expose the malefactors and send them all to Guantánamo Bay.

But instead of just being the subject of derision and the butt of late-night comics' jokes, nearly one in five Americans believe QAnon's main conspiracy. There are QAnon adherents now found in US Congress, in state legislatures and in city councils—and endorsed by Trump himself, who, like murderous White nationalists and Ku Klux Klansmen, he lauded as 'people that love our country'. He retweeted QAnon followers at least 315 times before Twitter confiscated the keys to his account.

In Australia, one of Scott Morrison's long-time friends is one of Australia's most prominent QAnon acolytes, who supported the violent storming of the Capitol. Far from disavowing him, the prime minister's office hired his wife. Morrison even appeared to use what QAnon followers saw as QAnon language in his apology to victims of institutional sex abuse—calling it 'ritual' abuse, a term adopted by QAnon in their Satanic conspiracy, but not described as such in the Royal Commission report Morrison was speaking to. Nor was it in the twenty-page briefing advising him on which terms to use in his apology. 'No one knows where it came from,' one member of the panel advising the apology's wording told *Crikey*. Morrison's QAnon friend triumphantly texted a fellow follower hours before the apology: 'I think Scott is going to do it!' The prime minister's word choice was met with delight by QAnon adherents who celebrated it online.

Deliberate or no, QAnon supporters will actively seek out these sorts of 'crumbs', or imagine them when they aren't there, to reinforce their beliefs. It can be as simple as a word or a gesture.

It is easy to look at conspiracy theories with a mocking eye and dismiss them as fruit-looped fantasies. (Morrison's buddy coincidentally named his health food business 'Fruit Loop'.) But when viewed through the lenses of group psychology and social media algorithms, they instead appear more as inevitable conclusion than unexpected consequence. Take our evolutionary impulses, sprinkle in some social dynamics and then fan the flames with our new information ecosystem, and you see conspiracy theories are merely the dry kindling of our social media bonfire.

Nowhere is this more applicable than in the case study of QAnon.

Radicalisation experts have looked on in terror at the viral load QAnon possesses; as infectious as measles in its spread and just as deadly among the unvaccinated. The journey to radicalisation to Al Qaeda can take years; to ISIS (they were shocked) could take mere days; QAnon can take just minutes to draw otherwise sane people in.

Its hypnotic power took a mild-mannered 51-year-old father of three from Colorado and had him dragging a police officer down the steps of the Capitol and mercilessly beating the cop with his own baton. It convinced a 32-year-old man from Nevada to arm himself to the teeth and block the Hoover Dam with a heavily armoured vehicle, all to demand an independent government investigator complete an administrative process. It made a 33-year-old woman from Kentucky murder a man for not helping her kidnap her own children to save them from a government plot. These are just a sample of the rising number of kidnappings, murders and political violence stemming from QAnon followers.

It is an intoxicating spell of disinformation, and it is scarily effective.

It reads like a Hollywood script: a nefarious set of powerful villains hiding in plain sight, a vulnerable and innocent set of victims, and in true American style—the ultimate anti-hero riding in to save the day just when everybody least expects it. Trump, in this narrative, is a hero of uniquely American proportions. The rough-edged vulgarity of *Die Hard*'s John McClane fused with the idealised yesteryear values of John Wayne, behind a public cover as perfectly unlikely as Clark Kent's alter ego to his Superman.

Our brains love a good story, as later chapters will explain. There's a need as old as cavepeople to fit a complex world into a simple yarn, and that's what we see happening with phenomena such as QAnon. It's a compelling and virtuous adventure in a confusing world.

In October 2017, Donald Trump caused a bit of consternation doing what he always does: talking off the cuff. After hosting his senior military commanders and their spouses to a dinner in the State Room, he assembled the last stragglers of the press corps still working late on their deadlines to an impromptu photo op. While the shutters snapped, he offered a concerning throwaway line.

Journalists from the *New York Times* who were in the room reported on the strange exchange they had witnessed the next day:

Gesturing to his guests, he said, 'You guys know what this represents? Maybe it's the calm before the storm.'

'What's the storm?' asked one reporter.

'Could be the calm before the storm,' Mr Trump repeated, stretching out the phrase, a sly smile playing across his face.

'From Iran?' ventured another reporter. 'On ISIS? On what?'

'What storm, Mr President?' asked a third journalist, a hint of impatience creeping into her voice.

As the generals shifted from foot to foot, Mr Trump brought the game of 20 Questions to an end. He praised his be-ribboned guests as the 'world's great military people' and excused the stymied reporters, who returned to their workstations to start another round of: *What was the president talking about?*

Unbeknownst to them, they had witnessed the birth of QAnon.

As the media grappled to make sense of the cryptic comments that sounded to them like the US president was planning some kind of military attack, an anonymous poster on the crackpot-magnet online message board 4chan claimed to have the answer. They said they possessed the high-level security clearance ('Q' level) that gave them insight into the recruitment of Donald Trump by military intelligence in 2016, who had urged him to run for president in order to stage an undercover takedown of a powerful cabal of paedophiles.

Obviously the intelligence services couldn't come right out and tell the public about this secret plan, so they had recruited 'Q' to leave crumbs of information for the public to work it out for themselves.

Trump supporters already held other 'truths' that laid fertile ground for this rumour to take root and germinate. First, they already suspected the deep state was working against their president, evidenced by the Russia-gate 'hoax,' where the intelligence agencies were (in supporters' minds) promoting a conspiracy theory of their own: that the Russians had colluded with the Trump campaign to get Trump elected through widespread disinformation.

While to other observers this merely looked like the intelligence agencies gathering evidence of foreign interference in their election processes, to Trump supporters this was a deliberate 'deep state' effort to bring down the president before he could expose criminal wrongdoers.

Second, many already believed high-profile Democrats were involved in running paedophile rings (which is what you get for hanging out in international waters with Jeffrey Epstein—every good conspiracy theory has a kernel of truth). When WikiLeaks published the emails of Hillary Clinton's campaign manager during the 2016 election, internet sleuths deduced that every time John Podesta emailed someone about 'pizza', he really was using a code word for 'paedophile'. The next logical conclusion was that 'cheese pizza' was in fact code for 'child porn'.

SUBJECT: Walnut sauce?

2015-04-11 17:45

FROM: Jim Steyer

TO: John Podesta and Mary Podesta

Hey John,

We know you're a true master of cuisine and we have appreciated that for years . . .

But walnut sauce for the pasta? Mary, plz tell us the straight story, was the sauce actually very tasty?

Love to all the Podestas from the Steyers! Cheers,

Jim

2015-04-11 19:51
FROM: John Podesta
TO: Jim Steyer and Mary Podesta

It's an amazing Ligurian dish made with crushed walnuts made into a paste. So stop being so California.

JP

The apparent translation: 'pasta' = 'little boy,' 'walnut' = 'person of colour'. The email, its bourgeois banter completely alien to the everyday parlance of internet conspiracists, was viewed as an inquiry about providing the sexual services of an African American boy.

Keen amateur detectives combed WikiLeaks for clues then connected with each other to discuss their findings. Imaginations ran with ease, fuelled by the gamification of gossip.

This led to a very confused and disappointed 'patriot' driving all the way from his home in North Carolina and firing his assault weapons into Comet Ping Pong pizza restaurant in Washington DC in an effort to free all the kidnapped children locked in its basement. He surrendered to police once he searched the restaurant and discovered it didn't even have a basement, let alone any child-trafficking victims.

Into this already unhinged reality that a deep state was protecting a secret cabal entered Q and his access to the *truth*. (See, there it is again—even the most irrational actors need to dress their falsehoods up in the protective cloak of reason: '*I did my research.*')

In their reality, Trump was sent to 'clean up' the US government. It accorded with his campaign platform of 'draining the swamp' and his outsider candidacy. 'The storm' that Trump hinted at in his photo op is the imminent mass arrest of the Clintons, Obama, Podesta and all the others connected to the cabal, and their imprisonment in Guantánamo Bay.

Q Clearance Patriot

My fellow Americans, over the course of the next several days you will undoubtedly realize that we are taking back our great country (the land of the free) from the evil tyrants that wish to do us harm and destroy the last remaining refuge of shining light. On POTUS' order, we have initiated certain fail-safes that shall safeguard the public from the primary fallout which is slated to occur 11.3 upon the arrest announcement of Mr Podesta (actionable 11.4) . . . On POTUS' order, a state of temporary military control will be actioned and special ops carried out. False leaks have been made to retain several within the confines of the United States to prevent extradition and special operator necessity . . . We will be initiating the Emergency Broadcast System (EMS) during this time in an effort to provide a direct message (avoiding the fake news) to all citizens . . . POTUS will be well insulated/protected on AF1 and abroad (specific locations classified) while these operations are conducted due to the nature of the entrenchment. It is time to take back our country and make America great again. Let us salute and pray for the brave men and women in uniform who will undertake this assignment to bring forth peace, unity, and return power to the people.

God bless my fellow Americans.
4,10,20

This message was posted by Q in November 2017. You and any other keen observers reading this will note that there was, in fact, no mass uprising and arrest of political leaders on sex-trafficking charges in the US in November 2017. But to think that would deter QAnon supporters in their fervent beliefs is to misunderstand the way 'facts' and beliefs work (as we will discuss in great detail later).

With every passing deadline for Trump to out himself as the great saviour in disguise, and the obvious impediment of him losing the presidency, QAnon has only strengthened its support. Part of the reason behind this is the 'catch-all' nature of QAnon. It quickly became a big tent for all conspiracy theories. It covers everything from JFK's assassination, 9/11 and extra-terrestrials, to covid and 5G concerns. It is a beacon for all conspiratorial thinking in the Trump and post-Trump eras. It has broadened its reach outside the US to encompass global conspiracies from Japan to Germany. It is very popular in Australia, fourth only behind the US, the UK and Canada in terms of QAnon activity.

The QAnon movement led the 'stop the steal' narrative after the 2020 election loss and was one of the main forces behind the Capitol insurrection that followed. They duly stood by and awaited Inauguration Day, when they believed Trump would refuse to leave office and trigger 'The Storm' by declaring martial law instead of handing power to Joe Biden.

Imagine their disappointment when Trump instead boarded a plane to his Florida golf course.

There are many theories as to why QAnon has such appeal. That it has become such a broad and versatile church for all conspiracy theories indicates we are seeing something deeper than just one particularly nutty set of beliefs—it's a microcosm of all that this book discusses: the deep human need to make sense of complexity, the desire to form groups with others who share our beliefs, the hostility to all information that contradicts those beliefs, the political utility of such groupthink, and the technology that allows the beliefs to spread.

Some have theorised that QAnon became the catch-all for these phenomena because it had all the elements that make video games so popular.

It definitely resembles many of the features of what online gamers call a MMORPG (that's a 'massively multiplayer online role-playing game' to you), where you link up with other players to go on adventures that usually involve attacking someone (like outspoken swimsuit model Chrissy Teigen, in QAnon's case). Adrian Hon is a video game designer who specialises in 'alternate reality games' which often resemble a treasure hunt you play with others. He recognised his work at play in QAnon adherents. Hon put it to a journalist like this:

> What caught my eye is that almost everyone who discovers QAnon uses a phrase like, 'I did my research.' I kept hearing that and I couldn't get it out of my head. This research is, basically, typing things into Google but when they do, they go down the rabbit hole. They open a fascinating fantasy world of secret wars and cabals and Hillary Clinton controlling things, and it offers convenient explanations for things that feel inexplicable or wrong about the world. It reminded me specifically of how people get to alternate reality games . . .
>
> Sometimes as a designer you will change something in the game on the fly based on how people are playing it. Sometimes their instincts and suggestions add depth to the game and so you quickly rewrite. You can see that happen with QAnon. New theories and tangents appear at dead ends . . . It's a collaborative fiction built on wild speculation that hardens into reality.

Games have appeal because we like problem solving. Problem solving with others adds a social element. Scavenger hunts are fun because we like challenges and discovery. Layer on top of that a rich Hollywood narrative and you have some of the ingredients that make QAnon such a juggernaut that blends reality and fantasy. It's more than a theory, it's a community.

Others have likened it to a church, in the way it connects people in an effort to give higher meaning to their lives. Whatever the reason, it is scarily effective at recruiting, convincing and connecting people in a way that is not rooted in any fidelity to truth or reason.

In the US at least, and increasingly overseas, QAnon is no longer a fringe movement. It started in fringe platforms and was able to quickly enter the mainstream through the big social media platforms like Twitter, Facebook and YouTube, built to encourage users to be drawn down into rabbit holes. Nothing says 'rabbit hole' like a wide-ranging conspiracy theory masquerading as a networked celebrity scavenger hunt.

While the facts were unable to dissuade people from following QAnon, the platforms were able to put a massive dent in the movement by simply removing QAnon accounts. In the wake of the 2021 Capitol insurrection and its roots in QAnon, social media platforms Twitter, Facebook and YouTube removed thousands of accounts that promoted QAnon theories.

This pushed many QAnon adherents back to the obscure corners of the internet they had come from, like the message board '8kun', favoured platform of mass-murderous fringe radicals. It also had another curious effect: the number of Twitter followers of senior Republicans plummeted. In the weeks after the riots, Trump ally Lindsey Graham lost 112,000 followers, Mitch McConnell lost 45,000. Seventy-five per cent of all Senate Republicans lost followers.

In Australia, when Twitter purged tens of thousands of the worst QAnon-supporting accounts in the wake of the insurrection, Pauline Hanson lost 4 per cent of her followers.

As mentioned above, nearly 20 per cent of Americans (more than 55 million people) believe in the QAnon conspiracy. You're twice as likely to meet a QAnon believer in America than a Greens voter in Australia. We can't simply explain it away by likening it to similar fantasies of global cabals pulling unseen strings or making up moon landings. Instead we need to unpack the reasons why people have embraced it and other conspiracy theories dominating our lives, as if we have entered yet another historical era once again governed more by superstition than science.

The psychological reasons for which people embrace conspiracy theories are explored in more detail in Chapter 24—but the fundamental feature of the *weaponisation* of conspiracy must be rooted in our understanding of how conservatives dominate online engagement. Conspiracy theories are very engaging.

Anti-Vaxxers

'We're not just fighting an epidemic; we're fighting an infodemic.'

—Tedros Adhanom Ghebreyesus, World Health Organization

When Ann Davis sprouted horns in 1806, the anti-vaxxer movement was born.

The covid pandemic woke the world up to a reality that had been long forgotten: living under the constant threat of deadly communicable disease. Parents who kept their young children at home during lockdown had long forgotten their forebears who would invent excuses to get out of a playdate for fear of polio. Political leaders who scrambled to save their populations had long forgotten that the last words of a dying Roman Emperor Marcus Aurelius were, 'Weep not for me; think rather of the pestilence and the deaths of so many others.' (Side note: Marcus Aurelius was also a noted Stoic philosopher, one who argued the plague that had killed a third of his subjects was less deadly than misinformation—'For a far greater plague is the corruption of the mind, than any certain change and distemper of the common air can be.')

In eighteenth-century Britain, smallpox was a sober reality of life— one in every five deaths was as a result of the disease. One historian estimated that up to 'one-half of the population was visibly marked in some way by smallpox prior to 1800'. One in every three people who got smallpox died; survivors were often horribly deformed, blind or infertile.

So you'd think that people would have rushed to embrace a miraculous medical breakthrough that could prevent its transmission: the invention of the vaccine.

Medical research was a bit more rudimentary back then, and when country doctor Edward Jenner realised his milkmaids never seemed to get smallpox, he had the notion (squeamish readers look away) to inject the fluid from a milkmaid's cowpox pustule into the unwilling arm of his gardener's young son. Next he infected him with smallpox. A lifetime of PTSD for the kid; great news for us: it worked.

Jenner had unknowingly invented immunology. They might not have known *how* it worked, but they were certain it did. He named his process after the cows ('vacca' in Latin) donating their pox: 'vaccination'.

Come vaccination; cue anti-vaccination.

I mean in their defence, it does sound pretty whack—even for the medical standards of the day. Inject healthy people with cow pus? The detractors had a pretty easy job, and began printing pamphlets suggesting people who received the vaccination would start growing cow parts—like Ann Davis, who anti-vaccination campaigners claimed had grown cow horns after receiving the smallpox shot.

The Cow-Pock _ or _ the Wonderful Effects of the New Inoculation! _ Vide. the Publications of y Anti-Vaccine Society.

An Anti-Vaccine Society pamphlet from 1802 showing patients developing cow parts after their small pox vaccinations (not pictured: Pete Evans).

The objections to the lifesaving treatment would be familiar to us. Some were religious ('The Creator stamped on man the divine image, but Jenner placed on him the mark of the beast'—many anti-covid vaccine posts on social media still warn of 'the mark of the beast'); some questioned its efficacy; most decried made-up side effects (like hoofs and horns).

But whereas misinformation may be born of fear or ignorance, disinformation always has a motive. The fiercest critics of Jenner's bovine jab, like William Rowley and Benjamin Moseley, made their money from variolation—the altogether more dangerous practice of giving people a small dose of smallpox itself. Many, including King George III's son, would die from the variolation dose, as would those treating them.

Ah the good old profit motive. It rears its head at each miraculous milestone on our vaccination story.

Americans in the 1950s had long forgotten the fear of smallpox, despite its brutally effective use against the Indigenous population in one of the earliest examples of biological warfare.

Their fever dream was instead filled with another affliction: the fear their children would die or be paralysed by polio. A national poll found it ranked second only to fear of the atomic bomb—and this was at the peak of the Cold War.

Read this description in *Scientific American* of life under the threat of polio in the 1950s by biologist Sean B. Carroll. Does it sound familiar to your more recent covid pandemic experience?

> . . . parents watched anxiously for any sign of infection, often keeping them away from swimming pools, movie theaters, bowling alleys, anywhere where there were crowds and the dreaded microbe might lurk. Travel and business were sometimes curtailed between places with outbreaks, and public health authorities imposed quarantines on healthy people who may have been exposed, in order to halt the spread of the disease.

People wept in the streets when it was announced that Jonas Salk's vaccine trial had been successful in 1955. Parades were held in his honour. Church bells rang.

But there was one group who weren't applauding.

Prior to the vaccine, a popular treatment against polio had been chiropractic adjustments. It made chiropractic treatment big business in an America racked by tens of thousands of cases of polio each year.

Chiropractors and their professional bodies waged a campaign against the new vaccine, which continued even as polio cases were miraculously disappearing (due, in the chiropractors' explanation, to natural cycles of ebb and flow—sound familiar, climate science?).

The National Chiropractic Association published a booklet, 'The Prevention of Poliomyelitis', which had its own alternative treatment:

> There is much that can be done. Get the patient to bed, isolate him, begin the application of hot packs to the spine, if you understand their application. In any case, apply heat. Remember, time is of the essence in these cases . . . You may save your own child from life-long misery.

In March 1959, the *Journal of the National Chiropractic Association* ran an article stating 'The test tube fight against polio has failed . . . the death rate has increased among the children who have been vaccinated.'

When the Colorado State Board of Health sent letters to churches throughout the state to encourage congregations to take the Salk vaccination before the upcoming polio season of 1956, the Colorado Chiropractic Association responded with a letter of their own to the same churches, its message little different from the anti-Jenner pamphlets of the 1800s:

> Your thoughtful consideration should be given to the fact that contamination of the human body through the injection of diseased animal cells must be abhorrent to the Creator who equipped us with cell life peculiarly our own, and is not miscible with that of animals.

Dr Stephen Barrett, founder of the US National Council Against Health Fraud, has tracked how anti-vaccination attitudes *still* prevail among chiropractors, even decades later. In 1992, a third of all chiropractors still said 'there is no scientific proof that immunization prevents infectious disease' and a further 23 per cent said they were uncertain. In 1999, a chiropractic magazine surveyed readers and found 42 per cent had given their children no vaccinations and 22 per cent only some vaccinations. A 2004 study in Canada found 27 per cent of chiropractors still advising their patients against vaccinations and 70 per cent stressing the freedom of choice. In 2016 our own health authorities ordered the Chiropractic Board of Australia to instruct all their members to stop giving anti-vaccination advice and stick to cracking backs. If a patient asked for vaccination advice, the directive said, they were to refer them to 'an appropriately qualified health professional' (i.e. not a chiropractor).

As covid reared its head and attention quickly turned to the race for a vaccine, who came out against a 2020 Connecticut law that mandated vaccinations? The Connecticut Chiropractic Council.

The opposition to vaccines is nothing new. The arguments made today against the covid vaccines are strikingly similar to the arguments that were made against the smallpox vaccine by the variolationists and the polio vaccine by the chiropractors.

Nor is disinformation in an epidemic new either. The fight against Ebola in West Africa was dogged by it. Eight health educators were killed when they visited a village in Guinea to educate the population about how to prevent the disease, because rumours had arrived before them that the health workers were actually there to spread Ebola.

Anti-vaccination narratives are successfully eroding trust in a vital global health outcome that has the potential to save millions of lives— just as we did against smallpox and polio. But is the disinformation ecosystem making these public health efforts harder than they were in 1800 and 1950?

In modern anti-vaxxer campaigns before covid, like the oft-reported lies about the MMR (measles, mumps and rubella) vaccine, the focus has been on safety. But covid vaccines narratives are as likely to focus on the political intrigue behind the vaccines as the vaccine itself.

This time, it's not Ann Davis but Bill Gates who has horns.

It has been an ill-fated meeting between those who were already steadfastly anti-vaccination and those who were disruptively anti-covid response. It's an unholy marriage between New Age hippies and QAnon adherents. Now they have both met the playbook for disinformation campaigns, the results are a disaster of tragically epic proportions.

The first recipients of the covid vaccines, like 90-year-old Margaret Keenan in the UK, received much media fanfare. As soon as they did, disinformation began appearing that these people were already dead. The little old lady on TV was a 'crisis actor'—a well-trodden conspiracy whenever anything goes against someone's worldview is that the victims are just 'actors'—an accusation sickeningly levelled against the parents of Sandy Hook Elementary victims and the kids from Parkland, Florida, who survived their school shooting.

This type of disinformation may seem ridiculous to your brain, but it actually works. A study found the number of people who would 'definitely' accept the vaccine dropped by 6.2 per cent in the UK and 6.4 per cent in the US after they were exposed to conspiracy-laden disinformation—like that Bill Gates was secretly trying to reduce over-population through the vaccine causing infertility. The more like science the disinformation looked, the more effective it was.

In May 2020, the world had an unexpected hit film: *Plandemic*. The film, which 'exposes the truth' about covid (read: spreads lies about covid) went viral. A closer inspection of the accounts that seeded its spread, however, tells a familiar story: thousands of newly created Twitter accounts with no followers helped it gain the attention of the QAnon networks, who in turn seeded it within Trump supporter groups. By that stage its spread could gain a life of its own thanks to the algorithms with their antennas trained to spot virality.

The filmmakers even planned for their own takedown. They built a disinformation campaign to encourage viewers to download the film and then upload it and post from their own accounts (as opposed to sharing the video the filmmakers posted, as usually happens). This counterintuitive instruction helped ensure any 'ban' on the film could not outpace its spread through smaller accounts. While the platforms are tuned to spot a handful of accounts sharing disinformation to millions of followers, *Plandemic* inverted this. It tried to spread through millions of followers sharing it to a handful of their own friends. As predicted, the platforms removed the film within days, but, like a snake-headed hydra, millions of views were racked up across different uploads.

When Facebook looked at their own data about vaccine hesitancy they found an enormous overlap between communities who were sceptical about the covid vaccine and those affiliated with QAnon. They also found that most of the vaccine content was coming from just a handful of accounts—in the most vaccine-hesitant population group they found, incredibly, just 111 accounts were responsible for 50 per cent of all vaccine hesitancy content. They are actually the most damaging covid 'superspreaders'.

One of the problems identified was that much of this conversation was taking place within private Facebook groups, not in any publicly viewable feed, which reinforces the echo chamber.

A report by advocacy group Avaaz found health disinformation–spreading networks spanning at least five countries generated 3.8 billion views on Facebook in 2020, peaking just as the global pandemic was escalating around the world. Content from the top ten health dis-information websites (like 'RealFarmacy') had four times as many views as the ten leading health institution websites' content (like the World Health Organization).

It always helps when the politics are on side. In the first few months of the pandemic, Donald Trump claimed 38 times that covid would 'go away' and declared it a 'new hoax'. Scientists call these 'elite cues': our brains are wired to take our opinions from hints our leaders give. One study tracked the gap between Democrats' and Republicans' trust in science agencies for information about covid. Between March and July 2020 they were shocked to see the gap grow from ten points to a staggering 64 points—the increase coinciding with 'a sharp reversal

20 Minutes ✓
March 16 · 🌐

[ALERTE INFO]

20MINUTES.FR
🔴 La France suspend la vaccination par AstraZeneca
L'annonce du président de la République fait suite à la décision de l'Allemagne de suspendr...

👍❤️😮 13K   6.4K Comments 11K Shares

👍 Like   💬 Comment   ↗ Share   📣 ▾

Rekor Jaeger
Le problème avec les complotistes, c'est qu'ils ont raison mais trop tôt 😄
Like · Reply · 25w   👍❤️😮 1.5K

'The problem with conspiracy theorists, is that they are right but too soon' —
top comment on French article on France suspending AstraZeneca vaccine.

of attitudes toward the [Centers for Disease Control and Prevention] expressed by President Donald Trump'. It was hardly surprising then when his supporters were less than enthusiastic about wearing masks and taking jabs—their pre-built disinformation echo chambers pointed their weapons at the vaccines when they arrived.

It follows that in the US, opposition to the covid vaccine was much greater among Trump supporters than others. It was also greater among those who were drawn to conspiracy theories. If you already think 5G spreads covid, vaccine opposition is not far around the bend. At time of writing, 99 per cent of the people dying of covid in the US were unvaccinated.

Now I know what you smart cookies are thinking: *Hang about a tick, this isn't disinformation this is just misinformation—the genuinely held beliefs of idiots doomed to suffer at the thin end of Darwin's natural selection wedge.* Not so fast—these anti-covid vaccination efforts are deliberate campaigns designed to deceive.

Just as it was in 1800 with the variolation practitioners and in 1950 with the chiropractors, today we have to look no further than the good old profit motive to see the real driving forces behind vaccine disinformation. Being an anti-vaxxer is big business.

In 2021, the Center for Countering Digital Hate very conservatively estimated that the top twelve anti-vaxxer 'Disinformation Dozen' were raking in US$36 million a year. As an audience, 62 million anti-vax social media followers could be worth up to US$1.1 billion.

The quack doctor Joe Mercola, who conveniently peddles both health disinformation and alternative covid supplements (his latest book title: *The Truth About COVID-19: Exposing the Great Reset, Lockdowns, Vaccine Passports, and the New Normal*) was estimated to have raked in more than US$7 million during the pandemic alone, by tearing down good public health advice and then selling his own. His net worth is US$100 million. Mercola and others get rich from advertising revenue, books, and spruiking their own remedies to people who are susceptible to suspicion and fear. Greed is a powerful ideology.

Anti-vaccination campaigns have changed remarkably little over the 225-year history of vaccines, ever since the first lanced cow boil was injected into the first gardener's son. The stakes were high then, as they are now—though our expectations about living without the constant fear of fatal disease are uniquely new.

Covid has both given rise to that ancient fear we had forgotten, but also to a pandemic of disinformation. It has also helped us realise just how important it is to re-establish ways to get factual information to the masses when our lives depend on it.

We are always precariously placed between suppression of these diseases through collective health action and the disease having the upper hand. Despite decades of near-blanket vaccination against measles, all it takes is one group to get a bit hesitant (like the Orthodox Jewish population in Brooklyn did in 2019, with the Mayor having to declare a city-wide public health emergency) and the disease gets ahead of those efforts to defeat it.

Just a little bit of doubt creeping in can collapse the whole immunological house of cards. Social media disinformation allows for a floodgate of doubt-inducing disinformation to be opened, just as people go looking for answers to new problems like a new disease and its cure. It's our perfect storm, plus a perfectly suited lightning rod.

14 / The MAGAphone

'The multitudes remained plunged in ignorance . . .
and the leaders, seeking their votes, did not dare to
undeceive them.'
—Winston Churchill, *The Gathering Storm*

When I started working in politics I had a novel tool up my sleeve that my conservative opponents had not woken up to: the internet.

With it, I was able to do things that were antithetical to my conservative opponents. I could eschew traditional fundraising's dependence on a handful of big corporate donors by asking for a little bit of money from a lot of people. I could bypass the expensive traditional avenues for broadcasting a message, like TV and radio, by getting supporters to pass messages on to their friends by email—or, later, on social media networks. I could even level the playing field by recruiting people to knock on doors and make phone calls in great numbers without the expensive machinery of the established players.

Within a few years these ideas were brought to a wide audience by Barack Obama's upstart campaign for president, where a rank outsider could harness the actions of many people online to build an enormous grassroots political movement. Ideas like 'hope' spread like wildfire on the email and social media networks more and more people were newly embracing.

'The sooner our politicians see the internet as a vehicle for two-way communication, not a new medium for old static press statements, the sooner the inclusive, democratic and liberating power of online engagement will be harnessed in the same way Obama did—to such a transformative effect,' I optimistically told the *Sydney Morning Herald* in 2009, in an article about how the last election 'saw both Kevin Rudd and John Howard dabbling with new web technologies like MySpace'.

In the same article, one of the guys who directed Obama's online strategy boasted, 'The conservative parties tend to be much more top-down and less open to new ideas.'

Progressives always had the top hand in online politics, engaging and mobilising freely by embracing these liberating technologies while conservatives clung to their top-down hierarchies and centralised controls. But then something changed. As the decisions about what would be in our information diets became less organic and more governed by the platform engineers, ideas like 'hope' could not compete with ideas like 'hate'.

Conservatives now *dominate* online. It is the progressive parties playing catch-up, scrambling to recreate a model that is way outside their comfort zone and instincts for policy-driven consensus campaigns. For the first time since the embrace of the internet for political engagement and mobilisation, progressives are at a disadvantage and are struggling to make sense of why.

Conservatives have the advantage of what I call the 'MAGAphone': a machinery into which they can put disinformation and it will be amplified. It's a hyperconnected army of commentators, content farms, cable news, private groups, conspiracy websites and shock jocks. In its totality, it is capable of ignoring reality to create its own parallel information universe that is impenetrable by outside facts.

It is how in the face of an irrefutable tally of evidence to the contrary, for example, Hillary Clinton is responsible for the deaths in Benghazi, but Mueller's investigation into Trump and Russia is a 'witch hunt'. They are narratives created in a Breitbart production meeting, injected into willing social media streams, reinforced by the echo chamber and then enter the permanent lexicon of a Trump supporter's vocabulary and neurology.

The following list is not taken from any special day—just a typical day on the internet in the aftermath of the 2020 election when we hit peak online-Trump. It looks the same as this, day in, day out (with the exception of Trump himself, who at time of writing is banned from Facebook until 2023):

Facebook's Top 10 ...
@FacebooksTop10

The top-performing link posts by U.S. Facebook pages in the last 24 hours are from:

1. Donald J. Trump ◄————————————— Trump
2. Donald J. Trump ◄————————————— Trump
3. Dan Bongino ◄————————————— Pro-Trump InfoWars/Fox
4. Donald J. Trump ◄————————————— Trump
5. CNN ◄- News
6. The Pioneer Woman - Ree Drummond◄- - Thanksgiving eggnog recipe
7. Franklin Graham ◄————————————— Pro-Trump evangelical
8. ForAmerica ◄————————————— Pro-Trump meme factory
9. Ben Shapiro ◄————————————— Pro-Trump Daily Wire/Breitbart
10. Team Trump ◄————————————— Trump campaign

3:17 AM · Nov 19, 2020 · Twitter Web App

(The Thanksgiving eggnog was delicious, by the way. My wife, like all Americans, can take something as intuitively stomach-churning as an alcoholic milk punch and make you somehow go back for thirds. But I digress.)

These sorts of realisations from the researchers monitoring social media led the *New York Times* to ask in mid-2020 in the title of an article 'What if Facebook is the Real "Silent Majority"?':

> Listen, liberals. If you don't think Donald Trump can get re-elected in November, you need to spend more time on Facebook.

Now that the algorithm reigns supreme, the political right are enormously better at recruiting, engaging and messaging online than their opponents.

The way conservatives view and describe the world and issues is a natural fit for the algorithms of social media platforms that favour controversy, conspiracy and emotional engagement.

Nuance, balance and detailed policy discussions are the domain of the left, and are a natural fit for the opinion pages of a printed newspaper or a think tank Zoom webinar.

Understanding this is key to grasping the forces at play that drive digital disinformation.

During the 2020 election, Donald Trump would routinely consume 90 per cent of Facebook's 'share of voice' (the number of interactions), while Joe Biden and the other candidates languished in single digits.

Given that a growing number of voters were at the same time switching off from traditional news sources to *only* get their information from social media, this posed an enormous problem. For these voters, disinformation was imperceptible from factual information.

In this ecosystem, disinformation reigns supreme. Political content producers can write their own realities without constraint, and those realities can permeate the real world through the large-scale uptake they receive through their primed digital audiences (often without even a need for fake accounts to seed them).

The day after the 2020 election in the US, the top two posts on all of Facebook—both from Donald Trump—contained disinformation about the election results. That disinformation became his supporters' reality.

Donald J. Trump ✓
November 5, 2020 · 🌐

Last night I was leading, often solidly, in many key States, in almost all instances Democrat run & controlled. Then, one by one, they started to magically disappear as surprise ballot dumps were counted. VERY STRANGE, and the "pollsters" got it completely & historically wrong!

👍😮 817K   230K Comments 74K Shares

👍 Like   💬 Comment   ↪ Share   💬 ▾

Donald J. Trump ✓
November 5, 2020 · 🌐

We have claimed, for Electoral Vote purposes, the Commonwealth of Pennsylvania (which won't allow legal observers) the State of Georgia, and the State of North Carolina, each one of which has a BIG Trump lead. Additionally, we hereby claim the State of Michigan if, in fact, there was a large number of secretly dumped ballots as has been widely reported!

👍😮 847K   208K Comments 69K Shares

The Illusion of Balance

Facebook has even admitted—to an extent—the dominance of the MAGAphone. After the 2016 US election put an unwelcome spotlight on their platform, and pressure to remove disinformation mounted, one of their senior executives pushed back against any such removal with what was to become the prevailing attitude within the company: 'We can't remove all of it [the disinformation] because it will disproportionately affect conservatives.'

It reminds me of the old adage that 'reality has a well-known left wing bias' every time I hear this false equivalency between 'left' opinion and 'right' opinion. Culture warriors trot this equivalency out every time they seek 'balance' or 'not politicising' something—like Mark Latham crying politics when schools in New South Wales wanted to teach kids about discrimination, as if not being a racist was a feature of political ideology not universal decency. We see it every time climate change is treated as a 50/50 split between those in favour and those against—if we put a 'balance' filter on removing climate change misinformation then the majority of junk science would remain. If we put a 'truth' filter on it instead, then yes, unfortunately, the removals would overwhelmingly and disproportionately affect conservatives. As Thomas Mann said, 'A balanced treatment of an unbalanced phenomenon distorts reality.'

We saw this to the extreme whenever the political pundits after the 2020 US election would wax lyrical about how having a QAnon member, Marjorie Taylor Greene, on the Congressional backbench somehow gave symmetry to Alexandria Ocasio-Cortez on the other side of the aisle, as if we can equate some kind of moral equivalency to 'poor people should have healthcare' and 'Jewish space lasers started the California bushfires'.

Facebook walked into this trap by viewing any removal of political disinformation, or even incendiary and violent extremism, as compromising their 'political neutrality'. Hence in the name of 'diversity' they even included Breitbart in their tab for 'quality news' and the White nationalist outlet Daily Caller as a—pause for dramatic effect—fact-checking partner.

I've worked for Silicon Valley companies, and for me it reeks of the weird culture that emanates from that tech bubble which is far removed from the norms of broader society. They all worship on the altar of open-source freedoms: provide an open platform for all and the best ideas will rise to the top and the bad ones will be weeded out. It's a technocapitalist utopian's free market wet dream.

But just ask anyone who has conducted an online poll what happens when you let the internet decide anything: Mountain Dew tried to open-source a new flavour and got 'Hitler Did Nothing Wrong'; VH1 asked for a Taylor Swift concert location and got a school for the deaf; a British science agency let the public name their latest research vessel and famously ended up with 'Boaty McBoatface'. Remember, after all, that the people in Silicon Valley are so far removed from normal society that they thought people would wear Google Glasses.

But what if Facebook is *not* actually the silent majority? What if the information ecosystem we operate in is actually the *driving force* behind this conservative dominance, rather than a mirror to reveal it? The Biden–Harris campaign had a saying to remind them of this (in this instance to shield them from a loss of true perspective against the loudest opinions): 'Twitter is not real life.'

This question of the role social media and its algorithms play in amplifying conservative voices was put to the test in 2021 when an unwitting experiment was conducted: Would Donald Trump's ranting and raving be as popular in a neutral setting?

Trump and his team thought so. When banned from Facebook and Twitter, and firmly believing his own Messianic hype, he started a blog. *Let them come to me!* he thought, sure that what had originally attracted his millions of followers had been a deliberate and rational decision-making process of their own, rather than the outsourced thinking of an algorithm designed to draw them in subconsciously. In May 2021 he hit 'publish' on his blog, 'From the Desk of Donald J. Trump'. The messages were largely the same as the ones he had posted on social media before he was banished to the internet's naughty corner.

Trump's blog lasted 29 days.

On 3 June the Trump team put the blog out of its misery, taking it down due to a sad lack of visitors. The entire website, including his merchandising and fundraising along with his ill-fated blog, had attracted fewer visitors than the pet adoption service Petfinder.

Trump's ability to draw a crowd—real or online—had always been his claim to legitimacy and power. It was how he could circumvent the mainstream media's criticism and fact-checking to reach and connect to his supporters directly, without filter. But whereas on the social media platforms Trump had consistently been the most shared and discussed figure, once removed from their algorithmical advantage he was left looking more like the sad loner pundits had first projected he would be before his meteoric rise had confounded them. Within an ecosystem that rewarded disinformation and division, Trump's content was boosted. In the real world, it floundered.

Remove the artificial amplification of a MAGAphone and you just get a shouty old guy. The angry emperor had no clothes.

The Enemy of the People

Banning Trump from social media didn't shut off the MAGAphone, however. It just left it to others to tell his narratives while they were still artificially boosted by the same forces. That was done by a network of nefarious news sites—the real 'enemy of the people' Trump had labelled the legitimate media—who carry on the work of this disinformation ecosystem, running with the fervour of a decapitated chook even after the axe has swung.

In the same week 'From the Desk of Donald J. Trump' was switched off, nine of the top ten most engaged-with political stories on social media were still From the Brain of Donald J. Trump, if not directly from his desk.

The top story was from foxnews.com, entitled 'Florida's DeSantis signs law prohibiting transgender athletes from competing in female sports', then numbers two through six (and number nine) were all from the Daily Wire, with titles like 'Oklahoma Lawmakers Rename Stretch Of Highway After Donald Trump'. Seven and eight were from similar Trump-supporting websites, one praising him for supporting

WEBSITE	HEADLINE	ENGAGE-MENTS
foxnews.com	Florida's DeSantis signs law prohibiting transgender athletes from competing in female sports	653,872
dailywire.com	Lawmakers Introduce Bill to Ban Black Lives Matter Flags From Being Flown Over U.S. Embassies	518,493
dailywire.com	DeSantis Signs Bill Protecting Girls From Competing Against Biological Males On First Day Of Pride Month	368,376
dailywire.com	DeSantis On NCAA Threat To Pull Events From States That Protect Girl Sports: 'To Hell' With Your 'Events'	330,219
dailywire.com	Oklahoma Lawmakers Rename Stretch Of Highway After Donald Trump	328,368
dailywire.com	Court Rules Recall Effort Against Michigan Gov Gretchen Whitmer Can Move Forward	315,952
washingtontimes.com	Trump pays tribute to 'fallen heroes' on Memorial Day	292,528
rumble.com	AOC Says America Should Stop Building Jails In Order To Reduce Violent Crime	277,058
dailywire.com	'We Are Going To Expose You': Vets Crenshaw, Cotton Create Whistleblower Doc To Combat 'Woke' Efforts In U.S. Military	273,054
washingtonpost.com	Texas Senate approves stringent voting restrictions after all-night debate	254,671

Most engaged-with political stories in the week after Trump's blog shut down.

the troops and the other criticising Alexandria Ocasio-Cortez for some nonsense or other.

Of the ten, only the tenth most engaged-with article was not from the MAGAphone ecosystem: an article from the *Washington Post* about Texas passing laws to stop people from voting (so conceivably also still shared mostly within the MAGAphone networks). The following week, the top seven articles engaged with on Facebook were all from the Daily Wire, with only the sad news of the Bidens' beloved dog Champ dying preventing them from a clean sweep.

The line between conservative opinion and disinformation on these websites is often imperceptible. That's because they get it: politics is now a competition for eyeballs. And the playing field is not level—it is grossly tipped towards disinformation. The more fanciful and emotive a story the better it will do online. Like a septic tank, the more full of shit something is, the more likely it is to rise to the top.

Infowars, famous for starting conspiracies like that the mass shooting murder of twenty kindergartners in Sandy Hook Elementary was a hoax and their grieving parents merely actors—a theory they later defended in court as merely 'rhetorical hyperbole'—is a factory for disinformation. The FBI even investigated them and Breitbart to see if the websites were complicit in the Russian interference with the 2016 election. Meanwhile during the investigation Breitbart's Facebook page was racking up more likes, comments and shares than the *New York Times*, *Washington Post*, *Wall Street Journal* and *USA Today* combined.

The conservative media is not just wildly successful at getting traffic to their websites, it is also incredibly good at keeping them there. On one website, PJ Media (with its catchy headlines like 'Here's Why I Won't Be Using Your Preferred Pronouns' and 'If the Woke Fascists Decide to Target and Destroy You, They'll Target and Destroy You'), the average time a website visitor spent there was more than half an hour. For comparison, CNN's average was four minutes.

In April 2021, of all the publishers on Facebook the far-right wing disinformation mill the Daily Wire dwarfed all others, generating nearly double the amount of engagement than the next closest competitor, and triple the amount of CNN (despite posting only a quarter of the number of posts). On top of its website, its podcast was the second most popular in America.

As a case study that demonstrates the MAGAphone in action, it's worth breaking down how the Daily Wire is able to game the algorithm to generate so much engagement on Facebook.

Ben Shapiro was an editor at Breitbart before he left to become a right-wing megastar in his own right, helped by a conservative Hollywood executive who recognised the market opportunity in the culture wars and created Shapiro's new personal brand to cater to it. Funded by Texas oil money (shock, horror: the site also publishes climate change

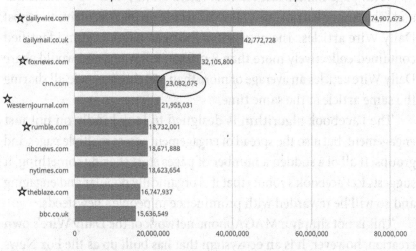

Top Web Publishers on Facebook: April 2021

Publisher	Value
☆ dailywire.com	74,907,673
dailymail.co.uk	42,772,728
☆ foxnews.com	32,105,800
cnn.com	23,082,075
☆ westernjournal.com	21,955,031
☆ rumble.com	18,732,001
nbcnews.com	18,671,888
nytimes.com	18,623,654
☆ theblaze.com	16,747,937
bbc.co.uk	15,636,549

Star indicates part of the MAGAphone ecosystem.

disinformation) Shapiro started the Daily Wire at the same time Donald Trump's presidential primary campaign was in the ascendancy.

To call the Daily Wire 'news' or even an 'outlet' would be like calling dumpster diving behind a supermarket 'fine dining'. I'm not even going to italicise it, as the convention would be for an established publication—it's a toxic aggregation of unoriginal race-baiting, misogyny and conspiracy-laden bullshit. Media Matters more politely called it 'a cesspool of bigotry and hatred', but I think that was too generous to them and too harsh on pools of cess.

As well as frequently publishing false and misleading information on all manner of topics, the Daily Wire built its sizeable audience by simultaneously fuelling and riding the culture war waves against the usual slew of topics like gender-neutral bathrooms, Black Lives Matter protests and immigration.

But it's what happens after the Daily Wire publishes their stories that is instructive in how the MAGAphone works. That dominance is not all what it seems. Judd Legum, the founder of *ThinkProgress*, was able to identify a network of Facebook pages that were simultaneously sharing Daily Wire content to their conservative audiences.

With page names like 'Conservative News', 'Fed Up Americans' and 'The Angry Patriot', this network would go into overdrive to repost Daily Wire articles. The network of fourteen pages Legum identified contained collectively more than 8 million followers, and would share Daily Wire articles an average of more than 300 times a week: all sharing the same article at the same time.

The Facebook algorithm is designed to look kindly on not just engagement, but also the spread of engagement across multiple pages and groups. If all of a sudden a number of pages start sharing something, it suggests to Facebook's robots that it is organically popular and engaging and so will be rewarded with prominence in people's newsfeeds.

This is not simply a MAGAphone network of the Daily Wire's own creation, however. It is an ecosystem that has built up as the Fox News set began migrating online, where they would be rewarded with the splintering into ever more extreme voices no longer bound by the limited restraints of TV regulation and advertiser appetite.

The pages that promote the Daily Wire content had grown their own audiences by trawling through the news archives, finding the most racist stories they could, and then republishing them as if they had happened at the time of publishing. The reason is simple: these are the stories that elicit the most emotional reaction from their intended audience, and that emotional reaction is what the Facebook algorithm is geared to spot and then reward.

One of the main pages that shares Daily Wire content is 'Mad World News', with more than 2.1 million followers. In their own words, it started with Corey and Christy Pepple, 'an ordinary American couple in Pennsylvania who wanted to share their thoughts on current issues through their worldview as Christian Conservatives'. Once they noticed their blog (really just republishing others' articles and adding Christian Conservative commentary) was bringing in more ad revenue in a month than their day jobs did in a year, they quit to do it full-time.

Unlike Mad World News, the Bible is mostly silent on whether Bill Gates conspired with Anthony Fauci to sinisterly set up Donald Trump with a global pandemic.

The net result of all this posting and reposting, as well as the nature of the content, is that Daily Wire articles generate an absurd amount of engagement: shares, likes—and especially comments, which the algorithm loves. In May 2020 the average number of engagements per article of the Daily Wire was more than 50,000. The *New York Times* was less than 4000.

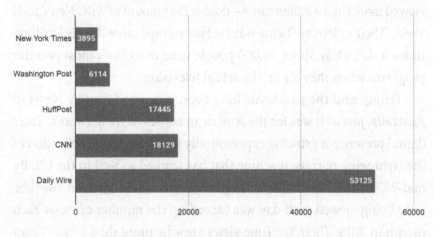

Facebook engagement per article (May 2020).

Sky's the Limit

Lest we think this dominance of conservative content is a uniquely American problem, here in Australia conservatives rule online too, through the same ecosystem. The same kind of highly partisan conservative disinformation content is sneaking around under the radar, much of it unnoticed and unreported. These networks are global (a lot of Infowars' traffic comes from outside the US, from places like Australia), but more importantly the blueprint is the same. We should be aware of how it is being replicated in our own backyard.

While in Australia we obsess about traditional TV ratings and mock Sky News Australia and its contributors for having such a small television viewing audience (it averages about 3 per cent of the total audience share), those same Sky News pundits are dominating somewhere else: social media.

On the internet, Sky News Australia is number one, with daylight second and every other Australian news brand even further behind.

They are easily number one on YouTube, and easily the number one most engaged-with Australian media brand on Facebook.

Sky News' videos on their Australian YouTube channel have been viewed more than *a billion times*—double the amount of ABC News' total views. Their videos are being watched on average more than 3.7 million times *a day*. Only about 70,000 people tune in to Sky's most popular programs when they air on the actual television.

Trump and the pandemic have been very good for Sky News in Australia, just as it was for the American conservative networks. Their digital presence is growing exponentially thanks to their replication of the right-wing outrage machine that has worked so well in the US. By mid-2020, the number of times Sky News Australia's videos on YouTube were being viewed each day was exceeding the number of views each month in 2019. Their YouTube views grew by more than 600 per cent and their Facebook engagements by 300 per cent over the same period. Three out of every four people watching Sky News Australia are now doing so on social media and other digital platforms.

In the month before journalist Cam Wilson wrote in 2020 about Sky News' exploding numbers, there had been a total of 1.6 million Facebook shares across all of Australia's major broadcast television news' Facebook pages. Sky News accounted for almost 900,000 of them:

> Facebook posts from their Page had more total interactions last month than the ABC News, SBS News, 7News Australia, 9 News and 10 News First Pages—and they've had more shares than all of them combined.

Sky News is firmly planted in the digital ecosystem of the right-wing culture wars, largely unnoticed as most media observers have yet to catch up with a non-traditional media landscape.

Alan Jones even said as much out loud, when kicked off his *Daily Telegraph* column in the face of sponsor backlash: 'Have a look at Sky News YouTube, Sky News Facebook and Alan Jones Facebook and you can see. The same column that I write for the *Tele* goes up on my Facebook page. The public can check it for themselves.'

Each month, 3.3 million Australians watch the Sky News Australia YouTube channel. When sane people hailed their week-long ban from uploading new YouTube videos due to spreading 'content that denies the existence of Covid-19' in August 2021, the premature celebrations forgot one thing: 'banning' is a red badge of courage within these ecosystems (side note: it should be a disturbing wake-up call about media regulations when the social media platforms have a hairier trigger for removing lies than the actual media regulators themselves). We will talk about this in later chapters, but being put in the internet naughty corner achieves little more than riling up the base and reinforcing their worldview that the elites are censoring the 'truth'. In the seven days *after* their seven day ban, Sky News Australia's covid-related videos had over 4.2 million views on YouTube. In an average week, only 1.4 million people watch their TV channel.

What is the secret to their staggering success? The same formula that worked so well for the right-wing echo chamber in America that they were emulating: hyperpartisan disinformation, plus incitement.

The same kind of online networks exist in Australia, led by the standard bearers who you will accordingly also find on Sky News regularly: Craig Kelly, Pauline Hanson, Mark Latham, George Christensen and Clive Palmer. They understand instinctively that their breed of anti-woke outrage hits a note that resonates far and wide with their base, who are hyperconnected through social media. As Christensen, admitted: 'I can be derided, Pauline and Trump can be derided. Yet all we're doing is listening to people, then repeating what they tell us they want.'

While Trump was dominating the online share of voice in the States, could you hazard a guess what the post with the most interactions on

Facebook in Australia *in all of 2020* was? Out of *every single post* in the entire country for a year we mostly spent on social media?

'Clive Palmer Diggs Deep to support Australians during the COVID-19 crisis.' His post begins, 'I will do what it takes to get 1 million doses of Hydroxychloroquine for Australians to fight the COVID-19 pandemic...'

Clive Palmer ✓
March 24, 2020 · 🌐

I will do what it takes to get 1 million doses of Hydroxychloroquine for Australians to fight the COVID-19 pandemic. Whilst the trials are ongoing, we need stockpiles ready to use here and capability to manufacture in Australia to protect all Australians as soon as possible.

We need to do this to help make a difference for all Australians and protect our future for our people.

#COVID-19 #CORONAVIRUSAUS

L COVERAGE   SPECIAL COVERAGE   SPECIAL COVERAGE   SPECIAL COV
MALARIA DRUG TO FIGHT COVID-19 sunrise
Small number of patients helped by Hydroxychloroquine **LIVE**
WATCH MORE VIDEOS ⟩ sunrise.com.au

WWW.UNITEDAUSTRALIAPARTY.ORG.AU
Clive Palmer Diggs Deep to support Australians during the   Learn More
COVID-19 crisis.

👍❤ 84K   18K Comments 28K Shares

This video, from the biggest Facebook post in Australia in 2020, had over 11.5 million views.

On some days, 40 per cent of all the interactions across every single Australian politician's Facebook pages would be on posts by Craig Kelly. Pauline Hanson's posts would dominate on other days. As the mainstream Australian media would scratch their heads as to why Craig Kelly busied himself so much with the conspiracy theories of another country 10,000 miles away, his online audience would grow larger and larger. Craig Kelly may not quite be the moron we assumed, but actually just the earliest Australian politician to embrace the new realities of effective political engagement, just as Sky News has done.

> **auspol_posts**
> @auspol_posts   ...
>
> 44.6% of all interactions on Australian politician Facebook pages yesterday were on posts by Craig Kelly.

The Echoing Cocoon

To see the echo chamber as merely a connected set of news-ish websites is to miss an enormous part of how the MAGAphone works.

The digital infrastructure that allows the most extreme right-wing fringes to dominate the conversation has three pillars: high-profile individuals with large megaphones and audiences, digital media properties where the fake news articles can live, and large groups of connected supporters who can easily share content between them (both public and private).

On top of this, the research shows that people perceive messages from multiple sources to be more credible than those from just one source. In other words, disinformation within this echo chamber infrastructure, where people hear the same thing from many different people and groups, makes the disinformation more likely to be accepted as true.

It is a recipe for a disinformation bonfire.

Groups on social media with names like 'THE TRUMP TRAIN' or 'Donald Trump For President 2020!!!!!!' (count those exclamation marks: six), with none of the page transparency rules for candidates, organisations or publications, abound.

These do not compete with official party channels, but amplify them, often in a closed feedback loop that enables information to go unchecked and unscrutinised. It is in these loops that disinformation narratives are born.

The importance of this is also underlined by another key fact: paid advertising is not how the majority of disinformation is spread online. This means that when campaign media budgets dry up or political ads are arbitrarily banned by platforms like Facebook (as they were in the US in the aftermath of the election fraud disinformation), without their equivalent echo chamber Democrats or other progressive groups have no recourse or lever to counter the disinformation gaining traction online.

The key feature of these groups, and the experience of those who inhabit them, is that it creates a 'filter bubble' effect where no outside information (read: facts) can penetrate the reality of those who are in a self-reinforcing cocoon of dangerous insularity.

For the informed reader, no doubt the reality of the Trump presidency reads something like this: An administration mired with ties to foreign influence begins with a series of prosecutions for illegal activity from high-ranking officials, which turns up volumes of concerning evidence including that even the conservative intelligence agencies were deeply concerned. One scandal leads to successful impeachment as the president demonstrably enlists a foreign power to bring down a political opponent. Meanwhile the economy is suffering unnecessarily under a trade war that only harms American farmers, businesses and consumers. All of this pales into insignificance once a pandemic hits that is so grossly mismanaged hundreds of thousands of Americans die unnecessarily. A resounding election defeat ensues.

That is an objective reading of fact. How do I know? I discovered it through meticulously researched, fact-checked and corroborated accounts of these events from respected journalists writing for trusted news publishers, peer-reviewed research and convincing informed commentary.

That is not the reality an enormous number of Americans (and many Australians) live with. In their reality: An administration embarked on an ambitious program of reform, and in response to Trump's crackdown on corruption, a complicit media saturated the country with negative coverage while ignoring good news stories of economic gains; a vested cabal of Silicon Valley technocrats amplified this with algorithms to suppress conservatives; a Democratic opposition pulled every lever available to advance their hoaxes; and the 'deep state' security agencies tried to bring down the president from the inside. The investigation cleared Trump of all wrongdoing and a fake news impeachment coup was defeated. When a pandemic hit, Trump then stared down attempts to ruin the economy with fearful overreaction. The Democrats finally achieved their coup through massive mail-in voter fraud. (This is to say nothing of the other reality for a smaller group, where Trump was heaven-sent to destroy a Satanic paedophile ring who harvest children's glands for anti-aging tonics.)

For these Americans, their reality feels just as objective and fact-based. Why? If you ask them, it is grounded in meticulously researched, fact-based journalism. How do they know? 'I did my own research. Google it' is a common refrain.

> # I did[1] my own[2] research[3]
>
> [1] *watched*
> [2] *someone else's*
> [3] *shitty YouTube video*

Sometimes memes say it better.
Provenance unknown

One journalist from *The Atlantic* described her efforts to understand this phenomenon by creating a Facebook account that followed Trump-supporting pages:

> There were days when I would watch, live on TV, an impeachment hearing filled with damning testimony about the president's conduct, only to look at my phone later and find a slickly edited video— served up by the Trump campaign—that used out-of-context clips to recast the same testimony as an exoneration. *Wait,* I caught myself wondering more than once, *is that what happened today?*

I spoke to other researchers who spent so much time studying anti-vaxxer disinformation they found themselves questioning the safety and efficacy of vaccines, even though they had mentally prepared themselves for the risk of this happening.

These filter bubbles occur when someone is only exposed to information and opinions they agree with, while being sheltered from opposing perspectives.

As one Republican digital strategist put it, 'We live in two different countries right now. Facebook's media ecosystem is a huge blind spot for people who are up to speed on what's on the front page of the *New York Times* and what's leading the hour on CNN.'

These bubbles are a natural conclusion of our new social media–driven connections to each other, but they are being weaponised to great effect. After the 2016 election, as the focus on foreign interference dominated the post-election fallout, rather than examine strategies of how to prevent foreign interference, Trump and his allies began to adopt them.

The Atlantic went on to describe how autocrats around the world take advantage of this noise:

> These leaders have learned to harness the democratizing power of social media for their own purposes—jamming the signals, sowing confusion. They no longer need to silence the dissident shouting in the streets; they can use a megaphone to drown him out. Scholars have a name for this: censorship through noise.

The whistleblower research director at Cambridge Analytica outlined how 'with the right kind of nudges, people who exhibited certain psychological characteristics could be pushed into ever more extreme beliefs and conspiratorial thinking. We were essentially seeding an insurgency in the United States.'

In 2016, researcher Johnathan Albright was one of the first to map this ecosystem. He took hundreds of fake news sites active in the US election that year and found an organism 'capturing people and then keeping them on an emotional leash'. He couldn't believe what he found. He told Carole Cadwalladr of *The Guardian*:

> They have created a web that is bleeding through on to our web. This isn't a conspiracy. There isn't one person who's created this. It's a vast system of hundreds of different sites that are using all the same tricks that all websites use. They're sending out thousands of links to other sites and together this has created a vast satellite system of right-wing news and propaganda that has completely surrounded the mainstream media system . . . This is a propaganda machine. It's targeting people individually to recruit them to an idea. It's a level of social engineering that I've never seen before.

They were ably assisted by the platforms' algorithms. Facebook's own research in 2016 found two-thirds of people who joined extremist groups did so because they were recommended by a suggestion from the platform.

We have already outlined how YouTube's 'recommended videos' algorithm can radicalise individuals by sending them down a rabbit hole of fervent misinformation and hyperpartisanship, and how the internet is in reality a personal information ecosystem specific only to you. The feedback loop you create with your browsing and behaviour on websites and social media platforms makes this a constant process of them refining and understanding your own preferences.

Layer on this the deliberate creation of an alternate political reality and you have the partisan ingredients for disaster and disinformation. In 2016 the Trump campaign's digital operation had more than 3000 data points on every voter in the country. It mercilessly rolled out content to micro-target the right message to the right audience.

It was all backed by the industrious landscape of the MAGAphone.

One successful circuit-breaker for these harmful bubbles has been to kick them off the established social media platforms entirely. But while this is very successful in suppressing their spread, it can give rise to entirely new platforms within the same bubble. Parler, Gab and GETTR are examples of new networks set up to welcome the hordes of disinformers fleeing Facebook and Twitter. MyPillow founder and Trump election fraud backer Mike Lindell pumped US$10 million of his own money into 'Frank', a YouTube competitor built expressly to spread election lies videos around the ecosystem.

When faced with disinformation in this context, we have little hope of penetrating that noise to reach through and correct a disinformation perceived as reality.

Not only is the bubble difficult to pierce, it is even more difficult to see it when it bleeds into our normal lives, like it did in Australia with the issue of a bizarre political press release.

We can see this bubble ecosystem in Australia, and its symbiosis with its political masters and the trail of 'crumbs' they leave below the surface for the internet's fringes, if we revisit the hate Dan Andrews gets on Twitter.

The cabal of inauthentic accounts that had given rise to the '#DanLied PeopleDied' narrative in 2020 did the same the next year, after Dan Andrews had taken a tumble down a set of stairs: an online con-spiracist's dream.

For most of us, the first time we were alerted to the conspiracy was when the Victorian Liberal shadow treasurer Louise Staley issued an official press release with a weird set of questions she demanded the premier answer, months after the fall, like, 'Who owns the property?', 'Who was in the house at the time the incident occurred?', 'What ambulance station was the ambulance dispatched from?' and 'Did the police attend?'

To the press gallery it was a press release unlike any they had ever received. In a vacuum, it made no sense—but it made sense to an audience who heard the subtext loud and clear: Australia's own MAGAphone ecosystem.

For them, it was vindication of a reality they had been pushing since not long after the fall itself, the fantasy that the Victorian premier didn't fall but was 'bashed' because of child sexual assault (the QAnons had long been pushing their disinformation narrative that Andrews kept abused kids locked in tunnels under Melbourne in order to harvest adrenochrome from their glands).

The origins of the 'Dan Andrews was bashed because he slept with Lindsay Fox's seventeen-year-old granddaughter' disinformation campaign had its roots in exactly the same ecosystem we have been mapping. Originating in one of the encrypted messaging app groups many conspiracists have retreated into, one of the earliest traces of the story was found on a fake news site like the ones we examined earlier, which in turn quoted comments it found from unnamed 'Facebookers'.

The 'Cairns News' alerts its readers to the most pressing issues of the day, like underreported studies that 'Doctors prove face masks are useless' and videos waking Australia up to some hard QAnon realities: 'Names and locations of thousands of kids captured for Adrenalin harvesting worldwide. This data dump video is not for the fainthearted. Big business, big money, government purchases and is very sickening.'

The site is part of a network of conspiracy-laden sites that have taken steps to mask the identity of those behind them. The ecosystem of sites, with names like 'Australian Loyal Resistance' and 'Australian Patriot Radio' are all pro–North Queensland politician Bob Katter and contain the expected vomit of anti-government and pro-Trump nonsense, and a litany of conspiracies on topics from covid to Port Arthur.

We can rule out anyone who has ever studied website design. The look and feel puts it somewhere between Lyndon LaRouche's Citizens Electoral Council and your crazy great-aunt's Comic Sans email newsletters.

But the look and feel was 'news-ish' enough for those on Twitter looking for something tangible to fill the barrow they wanted to push. On social media, the 'Cairns News' is afforded the same real estate as the *Courier-Mail*.

Accounts like 'Wayne Scott' suddenly popped up to spread the story, bearing the avatar of a Seinfeld character and the usual string of numbers in its handle, along with hundreds of responses to any tweet mentioning

'#COVID19Vic'. This snippet of his activity contains an impressive range of racism, violence and homophobia for such a small sample:

Waynescott @Waynesc50182402 · Jun 5 ···
oh the left are going to be a little torn when the truth on andrews comes out. #askmrfox #COVID19Vic

♡ 1   ↺   ♡   ☒   ↥

Waynescott @Waynesc50182402 · Jun 5 ···
oh mr andrews what have you done? #sexualassualtnotok #COVID19Vic

♡   ↺   ♡   ☒   ↥

Waynescott @Waynesc50182402 · Jun 5 ···
8 cases. wow. get ready for lockdown extension . #COVID19Vic

♡ 3   ↺   ♡   ☒   ↥

Waynescott @Waynesc50182402 · Jun 4 ···
dear indians. stay in your own country. thanks. from everyone. #COVID19Vic

♡   ↺   ♡   ☒   ↥

Waynescott @Waynesc50182402 · Jun 4 ···
i heard that brett sutton was a poof #COVID19Vic

♡   ↺   ♡   ☒   ↥

Waynescott @Waynesc50182402 · Jun 4 ···
i wpuld love to punch anyone that still follows dan and brett. maybe a corky. absolutely deserve something #COVID19Vic

Joining the dots you see a familiar pattern: his tweets are liked by other accounts that don't have any other activity other than liking porn and cryptocurrency tweets in a range of languages, including Indonesian. Wayne is one of hundreds of other accounts, many of them inauthentic, which in their totality create a disinformation narrative amplified by the Australian MAGAphone.

But this was one of the first times it crossed over into the political mainstream, in a way it has within the Trump ecosystem in the US. The relationship between the two is important to understand, and very disturbing. In Staley, Australia found their political disinformation collaborator; our very own Trump-like 'elite cue' link to complete the disinformation loop.

In reply to anyone who tweeted about Louise Staley's bizarre press release, Wayne was there like his batman alter ego's namesake:

Waynescott
@Waynesc50182402   ...

Replying to @AmandaBresnan1

what andrews has done is vile and he deserved what he got. it will come out soon

8:20 PM · Jun 7, 2021 · Twitter for Android

Louise Staley clearly knew her audience was not the media when she issued her conspiratorial press release—it was the army of online conspiracy theorists she obviously knew would hear its dog whistle. She didn't have to accuse Andrews of harvesting adrenochrome herself—she just had to leave a breadcrumb for a keen troll army to pick up. As in the US, the two work in symbiosis, as discussed in Chapter 18.

The predictable clarifications from the authorities (as the Victorian ambulance and police services dutifully did) and the oxygenation from the media who unwittingly played along by duly reporting the asking of the questions and whether they have been answered (The police never interviewed Andrews? How suspicious!) round out the impact of Staley's complicity in the deliberate manufacture of a disinformation campaign against the Australian public.

It both legitimises and fuels the disinformation. It enables crackpot conspiracists to be embraced into mainstream political realities, and places them on your front pages. Collaboration from politicians like Staley is the necessary link in a chain to move disinformation from a rogue fringe bubble to the dominant political ecosystem. Every Australian should be supremely concerned we have made that leap, for now we are one massive step closer to Trump's MAGAphone ecosystem.

Complicit political actors like Staley know they don't have to start these disinformation narratives, they just have to lay the foundations for them to flourish. It's a vintage move from Trump's playbook, who often picked up on organic disinformation to exploit for his own political ends and realities. As inauthentic account expert Tim Graham put it to me, in terms of Australian disinformation the open complicity of a publicly elected official 'is a turning point. It's a lot more out in the open—we're not in Kansas anymore.'

Part Three
Game Time: The US Elections

15 / Hail to the Chief

'The party told you to reject the evidence of your
eyes and ears. It was their final, most essential
command.'
—George Orwell, *1984*

If at times it seems this book focuses heavily on events in America, there
are some very good reasons for that other than your author's personal
connection to having both lived through and worked to combat the
events in question. The experience of the US since 2016 tells the story
of our disinformation age and the disinfodemic that defines it. The 2016
and 2020 campaigns, and the bookends either side of them, are the gold
medal winners in our disinformation Olympics.

More so, the phenomenon of Donald Trump and his campaign
represents something at the heart of this entire thesis: in the age-old
struggle between reason and emotion, both within people and between
people, Trump personifies the emotive forces.

His appeal demarcates the parts of us that respond to emotive
triggers, and it demarcates the parts of society that preference belonging
over knowing.

The story of his improbable election, and then the bisection of
America into two parallel realities after his defeat, tells us all we need
to know about both the risks and the rewards of our new information
ecosystem that so many have been so slow to grasp we are living in.

It is a cautionary tale, and at the same time one we all have to live
with. His election and defeat in the US cast pebbles that rippled to disturb
every corner of the oceans—including in Australia, where those who

hitched their political wagon to his ride then had to navigate a political world defined by his rejection.

And yet Donald Trump is the cause of nothing. He is the symptom of our malaise; more a creation of the forces we are examining than their progenitor.

We collectively allowed our baser parts to embrace resentment, and our safety net of truth to be rotted away by a news model that relied on stoking that resentment rather than defeating it with the disinfecting sunlight of investigation. President Trump was the result.

As Trump's star waxed and waned, it was the perfect weathervane for the ascent or descent of truth and reason. The manner in which it happened was the measure of our willingness to accept falseness as a virtue and to let it chip away at institutions long thought sacred. The result of that experiment was stark: much of what we thought was chiselled in stone was in fact mere plaster which crumbled away at the slightest nudge.

We thought the story began simply: that, like the dog that beyond all expectation caught the bird it was chasing, Russia set out to merely disrupt America by driving small wedges into the cracks they saw, and instead sparked its decline. But Russia was a distraction. Their actions were the catalyst for something already happening without their assistance: the reorganisation of society around new ways of relating to each other and to our world.

The timing of the 2016 and 2020 US elections saw twin crises that helped make disinformation central: in 2016 the Brexit campaign in the UK honed its disinformation efforts in tandem with the Trump campaign, and in 2020 the spread of covid took disinformation into the stratosphere.

16 / 2016

> 'Bad publicity is sometimes better than no publicity at all.
> Controversy, in short, sells.'
> —Donald J. Trump, *The Art of the Deal*

In 2016, independent fact checkers determined 70 per cent of Trump's statements were false or mostly false. His ascent is critical for us to examine, because it was the realisation of a terrible experiment that no researcher would have ever been able to get funding for: what happens when disinformation reaches the apex of our institutions?

The TV President

Two days after his 69th birthday, Donald Trump took a long golden escalator ride down into the annals of world history.

The world's eager media gathered, frothing at the prospect of a walking headline adding some spice to a contest that otherwise looked to be dominated by a Wisconsin governor who couldn't even be drawn on whether he thought Obama loved America, and yet another, less interesting, Bush.

It was never supposed to amount to much. Reuters sent their intern. The world had seen this all before, after all.

But as soon as Trump opened his mouth to begin the next chapter of our lives, we should have known what was coming. The times had changed to suit him.

In what would come to define not just his campaign and not just his presidency, but the entire trajectory of the late twenty-teens, the first words he uttered to announce his candidacy to the world were a lie—the first disinformation of many to come:

'Wow. Woah. That is some group of people. Thousands!' he said to a room full of a few dozen people who had each been paid US$50 to show up.

The Extra Mile Casting agency had sent an email to their list of acting extras: 'Looking to cast people for the event to wear t-shirts and carry signs and help cheer him in support of his announcement. We understand this is not a traditional "background job," but we believe acting comes in all forms and this is inclusive of that school of thought.'

Trump's campaign announcement speech got a lot of attention for what would come to be familiar: an off-script rambling stream of consciousness containing an incoherent litany of falsehoods, from calling Mexicans 'rapists' to his infamous declaration 'nobody builds walls better than me, believe me . . . I will build a great, great wall on our southern border and I'll have Mexico pay for that wall.'

And how we did mock and titter.

Collectively, the political world in 2016 believed in a few inalienable principles: that voters were rationally self-interested; that 'trustworthiness' was a virtue and so they would punish a candidate who peddled in lies; that a ruling class was an unlikeable but necessary evil; that they held deep affiliations to their parties of choice; and that they would expect consequences for those who violated these rules.

Trump destroyed all of these illusions.

Yet the lasting truth that Trump would expose above all others was that the truth mattered at all—not just in politics or media, but to our collective social experiment.

Trump intuited that in reality we are governed by our emotions, not our rationalisations, and he found his brand of uncouth dissatisfaction with the status quo struck a chord with parts of our psyche not usually activated by the conventional political campaign.

Politically, Trump had variously been a registered Democrat, Republican and Independent, but it was another role he played that fed more into Americans' perceptions: the corporate deity figure in *The Apprentice*.

Americans not only knew Trump, they had seen him in the role of benevolent overlord with the power to fire deferential celebrities as they grovelled in the celebrity version of the show. Celebrities in America are worshipped—to see them hired and fired at the whim of Trump, who would float in and look pensive while they plead their case before he made his rulings, was powerful. The optics of someone looking very presidential in the TV boardroom aren't far from picturing them in the Oval Office.

But this in itself was another lie.

The Trump who Americans knew from TV was in fact a fictional character created by producer Mark Burnett. Burnett had created the most successful reality TV franchise in history, *Survivor*, and was looking to create a spin-off set this time in the urban jungle of corporate America.

There was one sticking point, however: he couldn't find any successful titans of corporate America who were willing to lower themselves to the base level of reality TV and assume the role of judge, jury and corporate executioner. So he created one from whole cloth, a decisive tycoon, and cast Donald Trump—a tabloid fixture—to play him.

It was a wild success—the first season's finale drew in more than 28 million viewers. As the show grew, Trump grew richer off it than his other business ventures. He'd been on the verge of bankruptcy before Burnett had reached out and offered him a lifeline. Years later, as he was on the cusp of clinching the Republican nomination, Trump ran into Jeff Zucker, the former head of NBC who had greenlit the show, in a bathroom. 'You think any of this would have happened without *The Apprentice*?' Trump asked. 'Nope,' Zucker was said to have replied.

Even before it began, Trump's presidential campaign was built on an elaborate fabrication fed to America through the mass-marketed lens of prime-time reality TV. It's no wonder he turned out to be the prime-time reality-TV president.

Trump's campaign would not have been successful in another era, one without the ability for us to retreat into our closed networks of emotive hyperpartisanship or without the 24/7 news cycle's insatiable demand for telegenic outrage.

Trump existed in symbiosis with the 'lamestream' media he derided. The *New York Times* was in dire financial straits and had just been forced to sell off a large chunk of the paper to Mexican billionaire Carlos Slim to repay loans, then 'Trump Derangement Syndrome' fuelled a massive spike in new subscriptions and a successful transition to a revenue model centred on a closed intellectual network of its own. It similarly saved CNN, who before Trump arrived on the scene was struggling to fill 24 hours with ratings-worthy content.

CNN, MSNBC and the other cable news networks obsessed around the clock with each shocking Trump scandal, wilfully ignorant to the fact their obsession had oxygenated his upstart campaign in the first place. 'Why is he so popular?!' they thundered into their 417th straight hour of blanket coverage of him and his campaign.

Over the course of the 2016 election it was estimated Trump received US$5.8 billion worth of free media (how much this airtime would have cost him if he paid for it). By comparison, Trump spent US$398 million on his *entire* campaign, all advertising included. It pays to be controversial.

The Lit Match

To understand the relationship between Trump's successful 2016 presidential campaign and the disinformation ecosystem, you have to first peel back a few of the narratives that we have come to know the campaign by in hindsight.

The first is that Trump was elected thanks to Russian disinformation sown from afar, and the second is that he was elected thanks to his own brand of domestic disinformation.

There are elements of truth in both, but neither wholly explain the relationship. Trump was elected because his campaign was timed to ride the perfect storm of many factors—the 'perfect storm' of Chapter 6.

He didn't create these factors but was merely a product of the forces that gave rise to them: cheap, sensational news that looked more like reality TV; an audience disconnected from actual reality; and algorithms that would connect them.

Disinformation didn't deliver us Donald Trump—it just greased the wheels for his arrival. A fake news story about a caravan of Guatemalans approaching the southern US border doesn't make a voter racist—it fuels their existing feelings about immigration and capitalises on their pre-existing intolerance. It incites them to vote with their racist parts and suppress their kinder notions. It helps them connect with other like-minded voters and firm their existing suspicions, but it does not create them.

The backdrop for Trump's election was a stack of dry kindling and his disinformation campaign was the lit match. He merely hit us at a nadir in the age-old battle over reason.

Many have tried to lay the blame at the feet of others: the Russians, Facebook, angry White men, Hillary Clinton. Instead this book tries to place it all in its much larger context.

There were a lot of column inches dedicated in the aftermath of Trump's 2016 victory (itself a 'Post-Trump Stress Disorder'–inducing event for those in the Democrat filter bubble) debating whether the election result was due to the manipulation of Facebook with fake news. This misses the point because it presumes that the contest was one between competing sides' version of the truth, as if the winner would be the one judged to have most successfully prosecuted their 'truth'. Facebook didn't swing the election. Instead, one side successfully capitalised on having eroded the idea of trustworthiness to the point where the truth no longer mattered.

One Facebook executive who was in charge of advertising during 2016 weighed into the debate in a leaked memo to his own staff:

> Was Facebook responsible for Donald Trump getting elected?
> I think the answer is yes, but not for the reasons anyone thinks. He
> didn't get elected because of Russia or misinformation or Cambridge
> Analytica. He got elected because he ran the single best digital ad
> campaign I've ever seen from any advertiser. Period.

Likewise, the much-reported Russian interference certainly didn't hurt his election chances. The Mueller report outlined in great detail how the Internet Research Agency had operated coordinated disinformation campaigns on platforms like Facebook and Twitter by setting up fake accounts that recruited audiences and promoted political content by purchasing targeted advertisements. That always helps.

Expert opinion is divided on whether they did so mainly to support Donald Trump's chances and harm Hillary Clinton's, or whether they did it just to sow general discord across the ideological spectrum, but neither view is totally right nor totally wrong. The truth is that you can have both: how do you sow the maximum amount of discord across the ideological spectrum? You elect Donald Trump as president. The results spoke for themselves; America has not been so divided since there was literally a Mason–Dixon dividing line separating the two warring sides of the Civil War.

The volume of disinformation is certainly not under dispute. Stanford researchers counted 30 million shares of fabricated stories favouring Donald Trump; the reality is probably even higher. One study looked at 171 million tweets from 2.2 million twitterers, and found that 25 per cent of the tweets that linked to news articles spread either fake or extremely biased news, largely influencing Trump supporters' activity. Another estimated that 20 per cent of the entire Twitter conversation about the election was not from humans. Oxford University researchers examined 25,000 messages shared on social media in Michigan during the campaign and found that nearly half of them were 'unverified WikiLeaks content, and Russian-origin news stories' that could be considered propaganda. Fewer than 10,000 Michigan votes stood between Hillary Clinton and the White House.

It takes a lot to move a voter's intention; even more so in America where voting can be an enormously taxing commitment and so relies on an abundance of motivation. Chances are that if you were the type of American who believed Hillary Clinton ran a cabal of paedophile pizza shops then you were not too likely to vote for her before being exposed to disinformation suggesting that conspiracy. But our perceptions are a patchwork quilt made up of many different data points over time, and while no one square of material is definitive they each comprise the whole.

If you receive such disinformation in the absence of any other information then its persuasiveness increases. If your peers embrace it then its persuasiveness is even more pronounced. Eventually there is a volume of disinformation that will prove persuasive for anyone—even for you, dear informed reader.

There is a psychological phenomenon we will explore later that shows how repeated exposure to a piece of disinformation increases our belief in it. One study was even able to replicate this using actual fake news headlines from the 2016 campaign, presented as they were seen on Facebook. It found that even a single exposure increased subsequent perceptions of its accuracy 'despite a low level of overall believability and even when the stories are labelled as "contested" by fact checkers *or are inconsistent with the reader's political ideology'*.

The Death Star

Perhaps the place where disinformation was most effective for the Trump campaign in 2016 was not in its efforts to convince anyone how wonderful Trump was and to vote for him, but in its efforts to convince people *not* to vote at all.

On 24 October 2016, the Trump campaign—still the subject of incredulous derision, and only weeks out from an election every pundit and poll predicted they would lose handsomely—began running a series of ads featuring a South Park animation of Hillary Clinton with the text: 'Hillary Thinks African Americans are Super Predators.'

Unless you were in that very narrowly targeted group—African American swing voters in swing states—you would have never seen it. It was part of a sophisticated 'dark post' campaign to suppress the votes of certain demographics by targeting them with Facebook ads visible only to them.

As Brad Parscale, then Trump's digital director and later his 2020 campaign manager, said at the time, it was part of a major effort to prevent Black voters from showing up at the polls and voting for Clinton. One campaign official admitted, 'We know because we've modelled this. It will dramatically affect her ability to turn these people out.' When Britain's Channel 4 got their hands on five terabytes of leaked data on 200 million American voters from Trump's 2016 campaign, they found 3.5 million Black voters profiled and categorised as 'Deterrence'. The label referred to the fact they were voters the Trump campaign wanted to stay home on election day—and so they set out to 'deter' them from voting.

The 'super predator' ads ran heavily in Michigan, where Black turnout was decidedly lower on election day than the previous election. Other voters got ads telling them election day was a week later than it actually was.

The ads were brutally effective. The 2016 election was the first US election this century that saw a decline in the African American vote. A study by researchers at Ohio State University (OSU) found that about 4 per cent of President Barack Obama's 2012 supporters defected from voting for Clinton in 2016 because of their belief in fake news stories. In Michigan alone that's roughly 100,000 votes, according to a *Washington Post* hypothetical rerun of the election using the OSU data.

Hillary lost Michigan by only 10,000 votes, and this handed Trump the electoral college votes and the keys to the White House. If African Americans in Michigan had turned out in the same numbers they had in 2012, President Hillary Clinton would have been running the Centers for Disease Control and Prevention when the coronavirus hit in 2020. It's a tragic historical 'what if'.

This microtargeted digital campaigning is a useful example of something the Trump campaign successfully executed that was anti-thetical to the way the Clintons had campaigned for decades.

Clinton had a great digital team at the top of their game, brilliantly led by Jenna Lowenstein, but under Clinton's traditional campaign structure the digital team was complementary to the campaign strategy rather than the beating heart of it. Trump's campaign was digital-first. It used the internet as a crude instrument to bludgeon American voters with thousands of videos, memes, articles, photos—whatever—and force their way into the attention economy regardless of what the candidate did, said or rambled—and without any inconvenient regard for the truth.

It had its roots in corporate marketing, whereas Clinton's had its roots in prime-time network news–led analogue political campaigning that had changed little since her husband first ran for office in 1974 and had learned little from Obama's victory over her in the 2008 primary.

The corporate world, however, had long moved on from the analogue. It used audience data and obsessed about the psychodemographic profiles of its customers. It was happy for its message to be led by the whims of those buying its product rather than trying to convince them they would be better off with a product that would on balance be better for everyone.

Parscale was just a guy who had built the Trump corporation a couple of company websites and was now trying his hand at politics using the same principles. By his own account, it was his background in advertising and marketing that helped. In his eyes, Trump was a 'great product' and the task at hand was simply selling him to the American people:

> I think I had come from a consumer world for a long time and
> America was moving, eyeballs were moving to social media in huge
> numbers, into your mobile phones and your devices. And when
> Donald Trump asked me to work on the campaign I also knew I had
> a great piece of product that would resonate with Americans.

Hannah Arendt had already presciently warned us about the application of consumer marketing to politics, as far back as the 1960s. She called it 'Madison Avenue gimmickry'—a tip of the hat to the then new class of advertising and public relations spinners made famous in *Mad Men*, who she considered to be particularly pernicious.

By 2020 Parscale had a name for the digital advertising operation assembled around the Trump constellations: the 'Death Star', apparently never having seen the end of *Star Wars*, when the forces of good under Luke Skywalker blow the evil emperor's murderous machine to smithereens.

For all the media fawning of Parscale's 'genius', it was all fairly rudimentary marketing for the time. What he did do, in his own words, was to turn the Republican Party 'into one of the largest data-gathering operations in United States history'. Unlike other political campaigns, Trump kept his campaign running year-round—it never stopped campaigning between 2016 and 2020. It amassed more than 3000 data points on every voter in the country. Over the course of the 2016 campaign they then served those voters six million different versions of highly targeted messages.

When it came to naming things, Parscale had as little grasp on history as he did *Star Wars*; his data operation he called 'Project Alamo'—referencing another crushing defeat, this time for the Americans who had invaded Mexico to steal Texas before they even knew it had any oil under it.

It's impossible to know how much disinformation was served in those six million pieces of content, for at the time Facebook ads were completely 'dark'. It was these efforts by the Trump campaign and its proxies that led to Facebook's subsequent transparency rules.

What we can know about the content Project Alamo served to unsuspecting Americans is the overarching campaign narratives that those six million ads fit into, and themes from the organic echo chamber networks that reinforced them.

To be successful in the campaign, first the Trump campaign needed to manufacture fear, then it had to undermine the credibility of its opponent, and lastly it needed to frame its candidate as the solution.

All of these things are best done by emotive narratives served by disinformation. From the fear of illegal immigration and the crimes the immigrants supposedly cause once they get there, to the high crimes and misdemeanours of Clinton (many and varied, all served by a trove of WikiLeaks, from ISIS supporter to #Pizzagate), to the apocryphal stories of Trump ferrying wounded marines in his private jet or offering broad platitudes to 'drain the swamp': these were all disinformation's bread and butter.

The right-wing echo chamber thrived in this environment; their outrage-inducing content custom made for the task at hand.

The major elements that marked the success of the 2016 campaign, especially that very same echo chamber, we have examined in detail in our study of the 'MAGAphone'. The disinformation narratives they seeded and spread, sometimes helped along by an interfering foreign hand, were willingly embraced by their candidate. At other times he seeded them himself. The sum total of their emotive parts was a remaking of the modern American political state.

While the established political commentary and coverage struggled to make sense of our first truly postmodern political campaign, it surged to victory past their gaping jaws.

They had less than four years to catch up if they were to prevent a repeat.

17 / 2020

There's a popular post you may have missed from **Donald J. Trump**: "I WON THE ELECTION!".

1h

•••

If in 2016 the world was taken by surprise by disinformation, in 2020 it was ready.

Only it was ready for the wrong thing. The prevailing narrative emerging from 2016 was that it was shadowy and sophisticated foreign hackers and state-backed saboteurs that had interfered with the American democratic process.

In 2020, it would be the Americans themselves who would interfere with their own democratic process.

Election observers didn't need to switch on their carefully calibrated disinformation detection machines scanning the dark web for coordinated efforts to subvert American democracy and steal the election—they just had to turn on their TVs.

Having spent the intervening years readying the country for foreign activity, the 2020 election turned out nothing like the experts predicted—because shadowy foreign interference was rendered null and void by the brazen disinformation emanating from the White House and the candidate themselves in broad daylight. Disinformation freely broadcast from the White House podium and from verified political Twitter accounts with blue check marks.

There were certainly the anticipated outside attempts to influence and disrupt, but a combination of factors made this more difficult for foreign disruptors to achieve. The cybersecurity agencies were mobilised

to expect and detect these threats, and spent years planning their miti-
gation strategies, and the campaigns likewise beefed up their security
to prevent hacking and phishing. The social media platforms were also
focused heavily on preventing this type of foreign interference and
conducted massive waves of proactive fake account sweeps, which in turn
made the foreign interference much more costly and time consuming
for the foreign state actors, who had to hire real American people to
conduct this as opposed to the cheap labour of Macedonian teenagers.

But by far the most significant reason this threat was overblown
in the 2020 election was the fact that organic domestic right-wing disinformation happened at such scale it crowded out the social media real
estate available to foreign state actors, and also obviated the need for
them to confect manufactured conspiracies to fracture the country in the
first place. America was doing a perfectly good job of that themselves.

The foreign interference campaigns to stir trouble in the US were
rendered null and void by the hyperactive trouble-stirring of actual
Americans, who needed no help to bring the country to its knees with
fanciful narratives of conspiracy, deliberate efforts to undermine democracy
and coordinated campaigns to sow doubt in crucial public information.

The potential ramifications of this were brought home when America
realised twin worst-case scenarios: a violent uprising to overthrow the
democratically elected government and overturn the election results,
and the deaths of hundreds of thousands from polluted public health
information—both because of deliberate disinformation campaigns.

It was a pyrrhic post–Cold War victory for the Americans over the
Russians: the Russians could never have dreamed of being as successful
at dividing America as it was itself.

The Election Integrity Partnership, a collaboration set up to monitor
election disinformation in real time during the election, grouped what they
found into four categories: 'procedural interference', tricking people into
not voting or voting incorrectly; 'participation interference', intimidating
or deterring people from voting; 'fraud', disinformation encouraging
people to cast illegal ballots or destroy them; and 'delegitimisation of
election results', disinformation to dispute the results after the fact.

All four occurred on a massive scale both throughout the campaign and after it. The partnership made their conclusions after the election that 'false claims and narratives coalesced into the metanarrative of a "stolen election", which later propelled the January 6 insurrection'.

Not only that, they also found a lot of it started from accounts with 'blue check' verification marks—the partisan media outlets, social media influencers and political figures (including Trump and his family) who the platforms signified were worth listening to, amplifying and turning often honest misunderstandings into a cohesive story that found fraud at every turn.

I'll break down a few of the key disinformation themes that dominated the 2020 election, to demonstrate the pervasiveness of the information disorder that swept the US and then tried to bring down its government.

The Reverse Campaign

In 2020, what had worked so well for the Trump campaign in 2016 was rolled out again.

The voter suppression efforts continued, again with a particular focus on African American voters—who the campaign knew (and as it eventuated) would be essential to Joe Biden's win.

We've already discussed the example of one way this was executed: the mass appearance of fake profiles purporting to be Black supporters of Trump, like J.R. Cliff.

This had been one of the favourite methods of foreign state actors to exacerbate divisions in the US. An Iranian disinformation campaign taken down by Facebook in 2019 used a phony website called BLMnews. com, claiming to be a 'Source of African American News all around the world', to push manipulative content. The Russian Internet Research Agency urged Black voters to skip the 2018 mid-term election, with a Facebook ad targeting those who had an interest in the topics of 'civil rights' and 'MLK Jr'.

The Trump campaign in 2020 adopted the same playbook. This fake account 'I Went Democrat to Republican' gathered 39,000 likes on one tweet in less than a day before the account was removed by Twitter.

I Went Democrat to Republican ✳ Follow ⌄
@WentDemtoRep

I've been a Democrat my whole life. I joined the BLM protests months ago when they began. They opened my eyes wide! I didn't realize I became a Marxist. It happened without me even knowing it. I'm done with this trash. I will be registering Republican. Giving Twitter a shot!

4:44 PM - 23 Aug 2020

11,359 Retweets **38,785** Likes

As you can see by searching Twitter for the same text, these same tweets also show more of the coordinated inauthentic behaviour we have come to expect on Twitter: the same message appearing verbatim from other fake users in reply to other tweets, to create an echo that trends and is favoured by the algorithm to then build its own momentum.

The Trump campaign voter suppression efforts against African Americans extended to both before and after the election. The ballots his legal challenges focused on in the immediate aftermath of the count were in cities with the largest Black populations, an effort to invalidate the large number of Black votes Biden won in key states. It was even the subject of a lawsuit making that specific civil rights charge.

Before the election, the disinformation was targeted at preventing them from casting their ballots in the first place, as it was in 2016. In Michigan and Pennsylvania, Black voters received robocalls falsely warning them that mail-in voting would result in the harvesting of their private information to be sold to debt collectors. Others said the police would be on hand to enforce outstanding warrants. Latino robocalls focused on stoking fears that immigration status would be monitored.

Technology was harnessed to do this effectively, with robots scraping social media posts to then reflect back to the person it targeted the messages, language and nuance of the language those targeted use themselves.

danny @overlywierder · Aug 26, 2020 · · ·
Replying to @JamesFallows and @BetteMidler
I've been a Democrat my whole life. I joined the BLM protests months
ago when they began. They opened my eyes wide! I didn't realize I became a
Marxist. It happened without me even knowing it. I'm done with this trash. I
will be registering **Republican**. Giving Twitter a shot! ••

◯ 1   ⟲   ♡   ▽   ⬆

stinkfist 🚬 👽 ♦ ♦ ♦ 👤 @WallyPoncho · Aug 26, 2020 · · ·
Replying to @JackPosobiec @Malcolm_fleX48 and @sirhottest
I've been a Democrat my whole life. I joined the BLM protests months
ago when they began. They opened my eyes wide! I didn't realize I became a
Marxist. It happened without me even knowing it. I'm done with this trash. I
will be registering **Republican**. Giving Twitter a shot!

◯ 4   ⟲ 1   ♡   ▽   ⬆

JoshWah @SirJoshWah · Aug 26, 2020 · · ·
Replying to @RyanAFournier
I've been a Democrat my whole life. I joined the BLM protests months
ago when they began. They opened my eyes wide! I didn't realize I became a
Marxist. It happened without me even knowing it. I'm done with this trash. I
will be registering **Republican**. Giving Twitter a shot!

◯ 2   ⟲ 2   ♡ 2   ▽   ⬆

stinkfist 🚬 👽 ♦ ♦ ♦ 👤 @WallyPoncho · Aug 26, 2020 · · ·
Replying to @Americanpride94
I've been a Democrat my whole life. I joined the BLM protests months
ago when they began. They opened my eyes wide! I didn't realize I became a
Marxist. It happened without me even knowing it. I'm done with this trash. I
will be registering **Republican**. Giving Twitter a shot!

◯ 1   ⟲   ♡   ▽   ⬆

please go touch grass @peristera_deo · Aug 26, 2020 · · ·
Replying to @Letoll8 and @LogicalLIberal5
I've been a Democrat my whole life. I joined the BLM protests months
ago when they began. They opened my eyes wide! I didn't realize I became a
Marxist. It happened without me even knowing it. I'm done with this trash. I
will be registering **Republican**. Giving Twitter a shot!

Sometimes these voter suppression efforts did not have to enlist bots
or fake Twitter accounts to achieve their end. The 'Protect My Vote'
campaign, which spent massively on Facebook ads, outwardly looked
like a neutral website to give voters information about enrolment and
absentee ballots.

The reality, however, was far darker. It was created by Freedom-
Works (which originated from the Koch brothers and gave us the Tea

Party) and targeted mostly Black voters to undermine their confidence in mail-in ballots. One ad even went so far as to doctor a LeBron James clip to make it look like he was condemning mail-in ballots as 'systemic racism' (he was in fact doing the opposite).

There are of course even more significant efforts that suppress the minority vote in America, before disinformation even enters into it: voter ID laws, gerrymandering, purging of the rolls and of course making it incredibly difficult to actually cast your vote. In 2021, Georgia—where voters in Black districts can be in line for ten hours or more—made it a crime to give water to people waiting to vote. God bless America, bastion of democracy.

The Socialist Campaign

A lot of the post-election coverage was dedicated to one demographic group that surprisingly swung *away* from the Democrats and towards the GOP—Latinos (and Latinas—linguist pedants please note I am not anti-semantic: there is an unresolved debate on the most inclusive term for Latins of all genders, from Latine to Latinx). This would not have been surprising to the teams on both campaigns able to monitor in real time the efforts to persuade a growing demographic that with each election becomes a larger chunk of the American whole.

To the outside observer this swing would seem strange: a group of people the candidate has variously described as rapists, illegals and drug dealers switching their support to him. But this is to ignore the power of a digital disinformation narrative.

The one the Trump campaign deployed so successfully to Latino voters was that Biden was a socialist—a very dirty, loaded term in America—knowing that particularly in Florida and Texas a large number of Latino voters had fled socialist autocrats in Cuba and Venezuela.

It worked.

A massive disinformation campaign primarily focused on those states was deployed. The digital rapid response director for the Democrats went on to say the Trump campaign 'shamelessly embraced disinformation as a central pillar in their 2020 campaign strategy targeting Latino voters'.

Like all good disinformation, it was bespoke to the target community.

It ranged from exaggerated claims that Biden embraced Fidel Castro-style socialism, to more outlandish ones—like, for instance, that Biden supported abortion minutes before a child's birth or that he orchestrated a caravan of Cuban immigrants to infiltrate the US southern border and disrupt the election process.

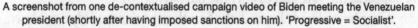

A screenshot from one de-contextualised campaign video of Biden meeting the Venezuelan president (shortly after having imposed sanctions on him). 'Progressive = Socialist'.

Particularly disturbing was that, while this campaign took place on social media like Facebook, it also occurred in closed messaging services like WhatsApp and Telegram, which are near impossible to monitor.

Content posted to WhatsApp (which Latinos used more than any demographic) is only viewable to members of the group it's posted in, so authorities have great difficulty gauging the spread of disinformation on the app.

Only by asking people in those groups to tell you what they see can you know what's going on within them. When advocacy group Avaaz asked members to submit examples they saw in Spain, they received 2461 forwarded messages. Disinformation circulates within these many large, closed groups simultaneously with no oversight.

Additionally, often algorithms are only programmed to detect misinformation in English, with Spanish language content mostly passing through undetected.

Disinformation was also widely circulated among Latino communities that aimed to play them off against African American communities, and specifically the Black Lives Matter movement.

A post-election report by EquisLabs found a nationwide Latino swing towards Trump, as pronounced as 20 per cent in some areas of Miami and as much as 14 per cent in Texas.

The Malarkey Factory

If 2016 saw the Clinton campaign caught off guard by the deliberate disinformation campaigns waged against them, the 2020 Biden campaign was determined not to be caught napping. They expected an unprecedented level of targeted disinformation and mobilised in advance to head it off and inoculate its targets against its effect.

The lessons of 2016 saw two main concerns emerge in advance for the Biden campaign: the threat from the outside (deliberate foreign state actors), and the threat from the inside (Trump campaign efforts to suppress the vote and distort the narrative).

As we have already learned, the first threat was massively overblown.

The major concern from the second threat was a repeat of the successful efforts to suppress the turnout of key voters which happened to such dramatic effect in 2016, handing Trump the presidency.

The spectre of the 'super predator' efforts was fresh in the Biden campaign's minds—not just institutional knowledge, many of Biden's staff including his digital director Rob Flaherty were staffers on Clinton's campaign and the result still stung severely.

The Biden campaign could not hope to win in 2020 if it did not win the digital narratives circulating on social media platforms that in 2016 had delivered Trump the White House.

They built a campaign machine to combat Trump's disinformation, then called it something that only the campaign of a 77-year-old curmudgeon could get away with: 'The Malarkey Factory'.

'Malarkey' is an American term for insincere nonsense; a 2015 analysis concluded Biden had said the word malarkey on the floor of Congress more than anyone since the nineteenth century, when it was much more in fashion.

The Malarkey Factory was shorthand for an effort to mobilise the resources, technology and content to specifically focus on combating damaging false narratives pushed online by the conservative echo chamber and troll armies.

What set The Malarkey Factory apart was that its answer was often doing nothing at all.

As outlined in later chapters, often the correct response to disinformation *is to do nothing*. The task of the campaign, then, becomes identifying when to make an exception to that rule and take disinformation head on. As the Biden campaign put it:

> We need to find and identify the misinformation that is actually moving voters, even if it is a small number of voters, then find who those voters are and see if we can intervene. There's misinformation that inflames a base. There's misinformation that persuades people. And there's misinformation that suppresses a base.

A piece of disinformation could have been generating a lot of attention but not be credible. Likewise, some disinformation could be credible, but not with swing voters (for example, QAnon conspiracy theories that are particularly credible with some voters but do not have a perceptible effect on people not already likely to vote for Trump).

Sometimes the difference is obvious, like the conspiracy theory Trump tweeted that Biden had Navy SEALs killed to cover up the fact they had not actually killed Osama bin Laden. The Biden campaign used research to test these assumptions and monitor the effect of various false lines of attack.

The Malarkey Factory found, for example, that the Trump efforts to target Black voters with Biden's record on criminal justice (he co-authored a deeply punitive and unpopular Crime Bill) were not having the desired effect of suppressing African American support for Biden. Thus creating and posting content to inoculate against this was not a priority.

But the efforts to portray Biden in cognitive decline, however, were— and with the very types of demographics the Biden campaign needed to persuade. This was not pure disinformation: there was no need to doctor clips of Biden to make it look like he was confused and misremembering things (though they still did), as there was plenty of real material showing that happening. Adding to these perceptions was his frequent stumbling for words, with most voters unaware of Biden's lifelong stutter.

In the war for the dominant online narratives, whether your opponent's narratives are false or fair does not change the strategy to defeat them. Here came the rub: The Malarkey Factory did not address the disinformation head on. They instead had a saying: 'Don't treat the hit, treat the wound.'

The disinformation attacks on the Biden campaign over his son Hunter, for example, dominated the attention economy. The right-wing echo chamber was in a frenzy, and an *NY Post* article about rumours of Biden's son smoking crack while engaged in a sex act was making headlines. It would have been tempting for the campaign to panic into a response (like it did with conventional PR: giving comment to correct the record).

Instead, using the threshold for what was actually doing damage where it counted, it was found that while the Hunter Biden story was particularly credible with some voters, it did not translate into a change of vote choice or demotivation for those audiences not already likely to vote for Trump.

'Treating the hit' would have seen the massive attention the story was getting and responded in kind.

'Treating the wound' on the other hand, saw that the blow was not inflicting damage and the decision was made not to respond through the machinery of The Malarkey Factory.

It's a well-established crisis communications principle to not give oxygen to a bad story.

The attacks on Biden's cognitive decline, on the other hand, did not outwardly appear to be a big 'hit'. Trump's MAGA crowds loved it as a line of attack on 'Sleepy Joe', and eagerly shared clips like one manipulated to make it look like he was asleep during a TV interview, but it did not dominate headlines in the way Hunter Biden did.

The Malarkey Factory's research, however, discovered that the 'hit' was causing a significant 'wound': the narrative that Joe Biden was in cognitive decline was breaking through to swing voter audiences, and more importantly changing their attitudes to the candidate negatively.

This prompted a response to reverse the damage it was doing.

The other aspect of 'Don't treat the hit, treat the wound' was the *type* of response. Treating the hit directly is responding to the content of the attack, i.e. 'Joe Biden does not have any cognitive impairment', whereas treating the wound ignores the actual hit to focus on repairing the damage it has done by offering a counter-narrative to replace it.

So instead of talking about cognitive decline head on, they simply showed those audiences clips of Biden talking clearly and articulately about anything at all, to demonstrate a different reality: a working brain.

A working brain: Facebook ads the Biden campaign showed of their candidate using full sentences.

The Biden campaign team estimated that the damage from the mental acuity issue went down by eight points as a result of those clips, and shored up hundreds of thousands of votes for the Biden column.

18 / 'The Big Lie' Lie

'Anyone who thinks my story is anywhere near over
is sadly mistaken.'
—Donald J. Trump

By mid-2020 the election was already lost for Trump despite polling day being months away.

His failed response to the covid crisis had fuelled a desire to return to normalcy that flipped the advantage of covid incumbency demonstrated in other elections around the world held during the pandemic. His campaign could no longer rely on mustering some votes and suppressing others to get the electoral college results needed to remain president. By any count, Trump wouldn't have the votes.

They had to find a new strategy.

This election was like no other, thanks to the pandemic that was surging around them and which by election day was taking more than 1000 lives and adding 100,000 new cases each day.

His campaign instead set about laying the narrative groundwork for a radical alternative to winning the electoral college: contesting the ultimate result.

To aid him in these efforts, Trump had the entire right-wing ecosystem that had been built and then severed from any central fact-based reality. It was the ideal environment to invent a new truth that widespread voter fraud had snuck in under the cover of covid and the remote early voting the pandemic precipitated.

The Red Mirage

Trump's campaign also knew that the covid election would present a different story on election night: votes cast in person on the day of the election would favour Trump (whose supporters would be less likely to heed covid safety measures or trust the vote-by-mail system their candidate had been working overtime to undermine), while early and postal votes would heavily favour Biden. In Pennsylvania for example, a state that proved decisive, Biden won 76 per cent of mail-in absentee votes, while Trump won 65 per cent of the votes cast on election day. That's a whopping 85 point difference.

The result of the byzantine way election results are tabulated would be a 'red mirage'.

On election day, most states start counting in-person votes first, and report those results as they are tabulated. Mail-in and absentee ballots are counted later. The result would make it look early on like Trump was doing much better than he was, with most of his votes reported first (as in-person ballots), and Biden's being reported subsequently (as mail-in ballots). In a normal election this pattern is not decisive, as usually only 6 per cent of votes are cast by absentee. In 2020, due to covid keeping people from in-person voting sites, absentee voting was in excess of 45 per cent. A further 26 per cent voted early. Only 28 per cent of all votes were actually cast on election day itself.

You might remember this if you watched the results live in November 2020. 'Champagne corks remain unpopped at Australian election watch parties today,' I wrote in the *Australian Financial Review* the next day, 'as people rush to familiarise themselves with labyrinthine US election counting procedures.' Dissatisfied election party–goers went to bed without a result, and then spent the rest of the week becoming armchair experts in American state and county administrative law.

Right next door to my opinion column was 'The AFR View', the newspaper's editorial for the day. And hook, line and sinker you could see the red mirage in full effect: 'Donald Trump's high-energy barn-storming performance around America's swing states has humiliated the opinion pollsters and conventional wisdom once again. The cautious centrist Joe Biden has failed to trump the unashamedly crowd-pleasing populist.' It was the modern-day Australian equivalent of the famous 'Dewey Defeats Truman!' headline.

The red mirage itself was even part of a deliberate Republican strategy. Knowing the vote counts would follow this pattern, they mobilised in the states in which they controlled the legislatures to rush through rules to make sure Trump votes were counted first. Efforts to count early votes as they came in were resisted at all costs. (Trump himself, always on-brand, never believed he would lose—and likely still believes he didn't, partly fuelled by the red mirage he witnessed on TV on election night.)

Trump began telegraphing this version of reality on Twitter months out from polling day. By priming his audience in advance of a particular reality, once it played out they were halfway into the fallacy. They pre-manufactured a post-election America where Trump had won:

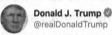

Donald J. Trump ✓
@realDonaldTrump

RIGGED 2020 ELECTION: MILLIONS OF MAIL-IN BALLOTS WILL BE PRINTED BY FOREIGN COUNTRIES, AND OTHERS. IT WILL BE THE SCANDAL OF OUR TIMES!

9:16 PM · Jun 22, 2020 · Twitter for iPhone

89.6K Retweets   **244.8K** Likes

'The Big Lie' (a term Hitler had used to fuel anti-Semitic propaganda after World War I) was that Joe Biden was the beneficiary of millions of fraudulent votes and that in reality Trump had won the election.

At 2.30 am after polls had closed, Trump fronted the world's media to build upon the foundations he'd been laying for months:

This is a fraud on the American public. This is an embarrassment to our country. We were getting ready to win this election—frankly, we

did win this election. We want all voting to stop. We don't want them
to find any ballots at 4 o'clock in the morning and add them to the list.

It was part of a long-term disinformation campaign to firstly undermine
the confidence of people in the election, keep some of them home on
election day while turning others out, and then challenge the validity
of the election results after the votes were cast and counted.

 Donald J. Trump ✔ ⁰⁰⁰
@realDonaldTrump

Some or all of the content shared in this Tweet is disputed and might be
misleading about how to participate in an election or another civic process.
Learn more

Big problems and discrepancies with Mail In Ballots all
over the USA. Must have final total on November 3rd.

10:43 AM · Oct 27, 2020 · Twitter for iPhone

A week before election day, Trump lays more groundwork for the post-election narrative.

The election results played out just as predicted, and the next phase
of the strategy swung into action. Post-election, over half of Republicans
in America believed Trump won the election (with even more—68 per
cent—believing the vote count was rigged to favour Biden).

The Grassroots Mirage

The 'Stop the Steal' disinformation campaign—and the 6 January attack
on the Capitol it resulted in—shows just how these right-wing networks
function to rapidly create sticky narratives and parallel realities.

Kate Starbird, an expert in the spread of disinformation campaigns,
calls this 'participatory disinformation'. In reality they are a feedback
loop between the political 'elites' and their audiences, the latter who
generate their own proof points to reinforce the frames they are fed
from their leaders and influencers. This is the closed feedback loop we
discussed in Chapter 14 when Victorian Liberal Louise Staley decided

to play along in this deadly game. Social media is both the connective tissue and the gratifying reward.

On social media, these narratives outwardly seemed organic, to spread like wildfire out of anyone's control or direction, when in fact there was a heavy hand of control from the top echelons of Trump's campaign and his proxies. The grassroots 'Stop the Steal' movement that broke out into impromptu protests all over the country and dominated social media feeds was in fact largely astroturf—a fake grassroots campaign.

When protesters would turn up outside the offices of petrified county election officials to try to bully them into stopping the vote count, what we saw were the angry spontaneous mobs but not the coordinated forces that turned them out. Anonymous text messages would prompt people with messages like 'ALERT: Radical Liberals & Dems are trying to steal this election from Trump! We need YOU! Show your support at the corner of 12th St. & Arch St. in Philadelphia' which could then be traced back to a company owned by Trump's 2020 campaign digital director.

Roger Stone, the flamboyant political strategist who bears an enormous tattoo of his former boss Richard Nixon on his back, first launched the 'Stop the Steal' website back in 2016 to fundraise ahead of that election. It briefly resurfaced in the 2018 midterms, and then exploded shortly after 2020's election; its Facebook page managed by former staff of Stone and Steve Bannon.

In the lead-up to the 2020 election, right-wing shock jock Ali Alexander said in a video on YouTube, 'I'm thinking about bringing Stop the Steal out of retirement. In the next coming days we are going to build the infrastructure to stop the steal.'

Once the election passed, Stone hit the usual airwaves to promote Stop the Steal, Alex Jones' Infowars among them. As one digital investigator, Ben Decker, put it: 'Stop the Steal is a highly coordinated partisan political operation intent on bringing together conspiracy theorists, militias, hate groups and Trump supporters.'

It shows the level of coordination in rapidly advancing these disinformation narratives, to the point they can incite real-world violence.

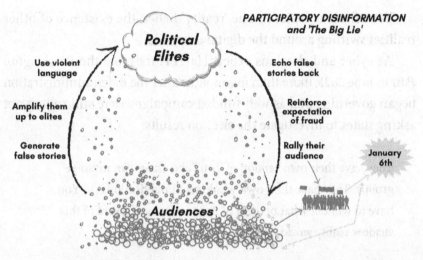

The feedback loop that turned the 2020 election into an uprising.

The Storming of the Castle

Violent mobs have stormed their castles and congresses since they first invented peasants and then gave them pitchforks. The descent of The Big Lie into the 2021 Actual Real-World Attempted Overthrow of the US government is not remarkable for the violent excitements of the mob. Political violence abounds when elections don't go the way you want.

Still, it was remarkable for the United States in the 21st century, and unique among developed democracies who trade in the global currency of free elections and peaceful transitions of power. And it was unique in the participation of members of a government actively participating in their own violent overthrow and attempted assassination. Any country that the US in the past had invaded to install democracy must have been delighting in the irony.

The level-headed sections of society breathed a sigh of relief as reality set in during the weeks after the election. Court cases disputing the results were getting thrown out in one sentence judgments; dead voters were fronting the media to make it clear that rumours of their death were greatly exaggerated; one suitcase of illegal ballots turned out to be a box of camera equipment.

Yet a firming belief in one 'reality' belied the existence of other realities swirling around the digital ecosystem.

As cyber and elections expert Harri Hursti told the *Washington Post* in June 2021, more than five months after the Biden administration began governing and as well-funded campaigns were still rolling out asking states to investigate the election results:

> They have their own version of YouTube, their own message groups. They have their own whole set of publications . . . You have to wonder what percent of America is even aware of this shadow reality world.

Answer Questions ✕

WE THE PEOPLE
🔒 Private group · 2.8K members

Your request is pending
You can finish your request by answering these membership questions. Your answers will make it easier for admins to review your membership.

Do you support our Freedom , Rights, Constitution of the ···
united states And are willing to fight or maybe even Die for
YOUR Country ?
You can choose one option

◯ Yes

◉ No

Are you ok with the government taking your Gunn's ···

Do not enter your password or other
sensitive information here, even if you're   Cancel   Submit
asked to by the WE THE PEOPLE admins.

A pro-Trump Facebook group asking prospective members if they are willing to die for the president before joining.

Pick apart the carcass of the social media conversation leading to the storming of the Capitol and you'll find the corpse littered with the usual detritus: your conservative media outlets like Gateway Pundit, Fox News, *Epoch Times* and *The Federalist*; your partisan outrage pundits like Sean Hannity, Dan Bongino and Dinesh D'Souza; your ragtag bunch of White nationalists, QAnon nuts and Proud Boys; and the 147 Congressional Republicans who had all sworn an oath to uphold the Constitution that outlined the electoral processes they now spurned.

After the event, Democratic congresswoman Zoe Lofgren published a whopping 2000 pages of her colleagues' social media posts that 'aided and abetted the insurrection or incited the attack [that] seriously threatened our democratic government'.

For months before 6 January, groups from Trump supporters to conspiracy theorists to far-right 'Boogaloo' militia all began coalescing on social media over a 'second civil war'.

It had been born in the Tea Party anti-government tradition, fed by the right-wing echo chamber election narratives, fermented during covid lockdown protests and finally burst into our mainstream consciousnesses when it piled over the broken Capitol ramparts. The grand disinformation experiment had produced its results.

The events of 6 January itself were a real-world physical manifestation of the worst elements of what we see in our social media feeds—hence the cartoonish spectacle of equal parts terrifying political violence and sad fancy-dress absurdity. Describing the eclectic images of pro-Trump, alt-right and quasi-militia insurrectionists on the steps of the US Capitol, Starbird called it 'the online caricatures of political partisans come to life . . . wearing and waving the symbols of their social media profiles'.

It was even a bridge too far for Facebook, who had always resisted the moderation of 'political speech' ('Facebook does not believe that it's an appropriate role for us to be the arbiter of truth . . . or to referee political debates and prevent a politician's speech from reaching its audience and being subject to public debate and scrutiny.') An internal report admitted they had been 'outmaneuvered by a powerful network of coordinated accounts' and had failed to stop it from using their platform 'to deligitimize the election, encourage violence and help incite the Capitol riot'. They banned Trump on 7 January, the day after the insurrection.

Yet by then the damage was done. By May that year, after Facebook had decided to extend Trump's ban by two years, 61 per cent of Republicans still believed 'The Big Lie' that the election was stolen from Trump.

The storming of the Capitol was the predictable conclusion of a presidency marked by four years of emotion trumping reason, and of a national narrative built on propaganda and fed into the participatory disinformation loop of Trump, his supporters and his boosters. It's a cautionary tale for us and for those who would seek to emulate his rise to power based on a whipped frenzy of falsehoods and fake realities.

Its echo may long ring throughout all democracies, the United States first and foremost, as that most fundamental reality—the power to govern—has shown itself to be eminently disputable. The power to govern is a powerful fiction that holds our societies together, but it is a fiction nonetheless, as the Trump ecosystem has exposed. In the astute words of the County Clerk for Houghton, Michigan, Jennifer Kelly, as she faced relentless pressure from the MAGAphone to open an investigation into her county's voting results: 'I don't know if the November 2020 election will ever be gone.'

Part Four
The Psychology

19 / Why Do We Fall for Fake News?

And now while round the shearing floor the list'ning
shearers gape,
    He tells the story o'er and o'er, and brags of his
escape.
    'Them barber chaps what keeps a tote, By
George, I've had enough,
    'One tried to cut my bloomin' throat, but thank
the Lord it's tough.'
    And whether he's believed or no, there's one
thing to remark,
    That flowing beards are all the go way up in
Ironbark.

—From 'The Man from Ironbark', A.B. Paterson

Though she professes to never holding this opinion nor remembers ever expressing it, my mother at some point in our young lives told my sisters and I something that we mistakenly took as gospel: 'Don't trust anyone with earlobes attached directly to their head.'

It's not scientific (I can reassure all readers with such earlobes). Today I know better. I categorically reject the link between genetic auricular structure and trustworthiness.

In fact, I first questioned the earlobe theory upon discovering that Mrs Wharvill, my beloved third grade teacher, was most honest and dependable—despite her prominently attached earlobes. Yet to this day I find myself inadvertently checking the structure of people's earlobes upon first meeting them. My sisters do the same.

This is a common psychological phenomenon known as the 'Continued Influence Effect'. Long after we learn a falsehood to be wrong, it still leaves an impression in our brain that survives the correction of that falsehood.

It is one of the many psychological phenomena that explains not only why we are so likely to believe and spread misinformation, but why many of the most common practices to combat it are ineffective—and often counterproductive.

We cannot begin to fight disinformation before understanding these phenomena.

As we discovered in our brief history of truth, humans have had a long and complicated relationship with truth and falsehood. It's been made all the more confusing by the Enlightenment declaration of the triumph of reason, which ignored many of the yet to be discovered psychological phenomena discussed in this section.

It has conditioned us to assume, in our Western liberal tradition, that if we 'educate', 'inform' and 'reason with' people then they will reach a logical conclusion from the presented evidence. You will notice this in how most people and platforms respond to misinformation: give them *the facts* to inform them they are wrong, or *factual arguments* to convince them to change their minds.

There was only one problem with this approach: when psychologists began looking at the brain and how it actually works, they didn't find evidence to support this conclusion. All they found was that the more educated, informed and reasonable a person was, the better they became at appearing rational and masking the fact that our brains sidestep logic in favour of a strong desire to conform to each other and our pre-existing worldviews.

In thinking we were enlightened beings, we believed our own brains' deception.

Imagine you are at your book club meeting, discussing this very book you are reading right now. You know it to be thoroughly enjoyable: a pithy and at times hilarious account of a topic of great importance to our modern society, as told by a ruggedly handsome author. You come prepared to share that perspective, and a few of your favourite highlights. But when you arrive, book club member after book club member has a different perspective: they think this book a confusing and pretentious hodgepodge of highfalutin unoriginal half-thoughts that overblows the importance of a fringe concern. Everyone else roundly and enthusiastically agrees. When it comes to your turn, that churning feeling in your stomach is rising to your throat: do you agree with your peers, or defend your contrary opinion and tell them they are wrong and crazy for not knowing they hold in their hands the next great opus of Australian intellectual thought?

All of our instincts tell us to do the former. Even if you do buck that urge and express your opinions in support of this book, you are likely to at the very least temper them, concede many of the contrary points and find common ground. You are experiencing the overriding cognitive behavioural desire to conform above all else.

Likewise, if you had already formed a strong positive opinion, but then were to read a negative review of it in the newspaper (give me their names!), your brain would be looking for ways to discount the review's criticisms: questioning the bias or motives of the reviewer, disagreeing with the conclusions they form or chiding them for selectively over-looking all the great bits.

This all sounds very obvious, but the extent to which our brains will do this is shocking—especially to our notion that we are evolved rational beings.

Just take a step back after reading this chapter and honestly ask yourself how many times you read the following psychological phenomena and caught yourself doubting them, or questioning the extent to which they are true or applicable to the situations described or to yourself.

Finding out that humans are not as rational as we assumed upends our existing worldview, and our brains will work overtime to resist or reconfigure that information.

The same is true when we encounter disinformation.

People who study our brains and those who manipulate them with propaganda would not be surprised by the rise of social media disinformation. At its heart, this disinformation works because of a time-honoured principle familiar to both: we are hardwired to respond to and share emotive content if it accords with our pre-existing beliefs.

Study after study shows people are unable to reliably distinguish between fake and real news (older demographics even more so—though young people may be a little more anti–covid vaccine) and that fake news spreads much faster and further than real news (six times as fast, by one count).

In addition, attaching a warning to fake news articles (as Facebook and Twitter do in an effort to mitigate their spread) can be counter-productive. At best they are helping address that particular article but sowing doubt over all other news, at worst they are drawing greater attention to it and helping its spread.

The crux of the problem is that psychological reality disagrees with our assumption that humans are rational and when presented with information will draw the logical conclusions. Here it is laid out most starkly by some of the leading cognitive psychologists—shout out to Australia's own Stephan Lewandowsky who has led much of the best research on disinformation in recent years (well we'll claim him like we do Phar Lap):

> When confronted with information compellingly debunking a pre-existing belief, only a minute proportion of people—2 per cent of participants in one study—explicitly acknowledged their beliefs were mistaken. The majority of people display some form of motivated reasoning by counter-arguing against the refutation.
>
> This is consistent with other research into 'motivated skepticism' which shows participants expressing active skepticism to worldview incongruent information. The most intransigent people engage in a strategy termed 'disputing rationality': insisting on one's right to an opinion without it being supported by factual reasoning.

That's psychology talk for: we fit facts to our pre-existing beliefs, not the other way around.

This part will outline a number of key psychological theories that will help us understand the forces at play behind disinformation and efforts to combat it.

20 / Imprints

'It ain't what you don't know that gets you into
trouble. It's what you know for sure that just ain't so.'
—attributed to Mark Twain

How do you know the Earth is round? The belief that it is, which you no doubt formed at a young age, is hardwired into your brain as reality. You've never been into space to see it first-hand (I assume. Apologies to any astronauts, cosmonauts or taikonauts reading this—you are excepted.) So how do you know for sure that it is round? What level of evidence would you need to see before you believed otherwise? *The Earth is round* is a belief that carves a deep permanent groove in your cognition. Rewiring that groove would be an uphill battle.

As we discovered with our fine earlobed friends, the continued influence effect of misinformation ensures that because of these deep grooves our beliefs carve, people who have been exposed to misinformation often continue to believe in it even after it has been thoroughly debunked.

More maddening, even when corrections seem to reduce people's beliefs in false information, the misinformation lingers under the surface, continuing to influence their thinking. Hence the name of this effect.

Imagine if I told you I had food poisoning from eating at a certain restaurant last night. I won't name it for fear of being sued. And also because it's not true—I just made it up. Even if I subsequently told you (and proved to you) that I had made the whole food poisoning episode up, you would still be likely to avoid eating at that restaurant. It's like disinformation *Inception*, without the theatrics of Leonardo DiCaprio or mind-bending special effects.

Your brain maintains a healthy scepticism against the correction, as it is biased towards the original information. Just like the attached earlobes theory, which made it to my brain first and now lives there rent-free.

This poses a big problem for the default approach of 'fact-checking' a piece of disinformation adopted by many news organisations and social media platforms.

Fact-checking and corrections work on the surface. In general people will report no longer believing the original misinformation and repeat back the correct information. They themselves will believe they have been accurately corrected.

Job done, right? No. When it emerges later or in other scenarios, the zombie misinformation will reappear in that person. It's like those novelty birthday cake candles you can't blow out.

Perhaps this is because we are simply not good at remembering context. One study showed participants a handout from the US Centers for Disease Control and Prevention that had 'myths' and 'facts' about the flu vaccine. When quizzed immediately after, people could correctly identify the information as either a myth or a fact. They embraced the context—of thinking about vaccines and the information they had just received about them. But a mere 30 minutes later, out of the immediate context of the experiment, it had all become muddled. People who were shown the handout incorrectly remembered more myths as 'facts' than people who never received a handout to begin with.

Worse still, in that experiment people were less likely to want to receive the flu vaccine after reading the handout designed to calm their fears about the flu vaccine. But still we see the most common reaction to disinformation being 'myth-busting' resources and information just like that handout.

What hope did we ever have against the armies of covid vaccine disinformation?

Just think of the imprint that was carved in so many people's brains, that covid is a disease that affects old people. Once the Delta strain emerged and began hospitalising young people at a much greater rate, this imprint was hardwired and extremely difficult to dislodge. Even for those who rationally embraced the new information, their brains were wired to revert to the 'covid is an old person's disease' perception once they stopped actively thinking about it. And what of other mutations that are yet to occur, that you may already be grappling with by the time you are reading this? Our brains have accepted a covid reality that is frozen in time—the disease we first came to know and love in early 2020. What amount of evidence would be needed before we started readjusting our behaviours and perceptions to a version of covid that bypassed the vaccine or masks, was primarily transmitted through touch, or was most severe in babies? This is a large part of the problem of compliance with rapidly changing public health advice. Daily briefings with new instructions—like Premier Gladys Berejiklian's gripping 11 am reality TV fixture I was glued to during lockdowns—are a drastic mismatch for how our brains want to receive and retain information.

Luckily there have been some proven antidotes to the continued influence effect that can be deployed to overcome the brain's preference for the original misinformation, as we will discover later.

21 / Shortcuts

> 'A wealth of information creates a poverty of attention.'
> —Herbert A. Simon

I hate to be the one to break it to you, but your brain is essentially lazy.

You can't blame it—it is tasked with taking in millions of pieces of information at the same time, sorting and filing them, and then prompting the rest of your body to act on them. This means it will always be looking for ways to take shortcuts.

I lived for a decade in New York City. As anyone who lives there will tell you, you avoid Times Square like the plague. They will tell you it's the tourists, the creepy guy in the Elmo suit and the overpriced restaurants, but in reality our brains don't like places like Times Square because there is simply too much information for our senses to process. The hordes of people, the flashing neon signs, the cacophony of horns and whistles, the three-day-old trash mixed with the unmistakable stench that can only be human urine: this is information overload for our brains.

It's obvious to us when in crowded settings like Times Square, but this information overload is actually happening all the time. In order to save brain power, stay sane and reduce blood pressure, our brains are trained to shut out all but the very important information our senses are receiving at any given moment.

That feeling when everything goes into slow motion when you drop a vase or see the oncoming car about to hit you? That's your brain changing gear to allow you to process more of the information it usually filters out as inconsequential background noise. It knows that in that moment the information may not be inconsequential, but lifesaving. It processes it.

Think of your brain as a sophisticated filing system. If your office looks anything like mine, your actual filing cabinet is overstuffed with largely inconsequential and forgettable paperwork (I'm sure I'll need that five-year-old utility bill at some point!). Your brain hates that, and is programmed to retain order and efficiency.

The 'perfect storm' of our new information ecosystem has been an unmitigated disaster, largely because it has played into these cognitive shortcuts. Unable to process the volume of information we are now exposed to, we instead defer to our cognitive biases. Our mental shortcuts decide what we should pay attention to and how we respond to it.

Your brain doesn't think that article you just saw on Facebook is of life-or-death importance, so rather than using a lot of brain power to assess and file it, it takes a shortcut. 'Seems legit? Sounds about right? Let's file it under "true".'

Our brain takes these kinds of shortcuts all the time. Psychologists call them 'heuristics', from the Greek for 'I find'. It helps ease the burden on our brains—for example having a 'rule of thumb' or 'educated guess' instead of using the brainpower to actually work something out.

One of the key cognitive reasons we take these shortcuts when looking at a headline on Facebook is called the 'illusory truth effect' which says that the brain favours familiar information.

We have trouble distinguishing between familiarity and truth. So if that article reinforces something you already know (it is 'familiar') then it will be filed under 'true'—regardless of whether you also know it to be blatantly false or from a dodgy source.

If the information is repeated then it becomes easier for our brain to process, and so we subconsciously favour it over new information that would take a bit of our brain power to correct and rewrite. After all, our brains are supercomputers, but they are wired for efficiency.

Our ancestors would rather burn a scientist at the stake than rewire their brains to see the Earth as round and not at the centre of the universe.

It took centuries of facts to overcome the ferocity of the familiar and turn those brains around.

In fact our brains are so lazy that it's not just repetition that has this effect. One group of researchers even demonstrated how the brain will see statements written in easier to read fonts as 'truer' than statements in difficult to read fonts. Another found that statements by someone with an easily pronounced name were viewed as more truthful than statements from those with harder to pronounce names. Disinformation featuring images is also more effective, as are corrections, because we can't be bothered making sense of words. Squinting, it appears, is a little bit too much for our poor brains to put up with.

The more times a person encounters a piece of misinformation the 'stickier' it becomes in our neural pathways and the harder it is to rewrite. Repetition of a falsehood makes it truer and truer as far as our lazy brains are concerned. Think of how many times Trump would repeat the same lies, over and over and over again. His supporters didn't stand a chance.

One study kept telling people that 'The Atlantic Ocean is the largest ocean on Earth' until even the people who knew the Pacific Ocean was larger started to accept it as true—because it became so familiar to them they stopped conducting the taxing mental process of checking it against their actual knowledge. Even warning people that they are about to be shown false statements doesn't stop this from happening.

Consider how far the brains of poor covid victims in rural America had to stretch to accept the reality they were dying of a disease they did not believe was real. Many of them couldn't. A South Dakota nurse told CNN her patients' 'last dying words are, "This can't be happening. It's not real."' That is some impressive hardwiring.

New Day ✓
@NewDay

A South Dakota ER nurse @JodiDoering says her Covid-19 patients often "don't want to believe that Covid is real."

"Their last dying words are, 'This can't be happening. It's not real.' And when they should be... Facetiming their families, they're filled with anger and hatred."

Another key factor is that, in terms of neuroscience, there is a race to the brain: whichever information gets there first will likely win.

That makes it even more incongruous that we default to a 'fact check' and 'correct the record' approach to fighting fake news. By the time facts are checked, they have already lost. It's like the winning golfer holing that last putt at the 18th hole of the US Open, only to turn up at the clubhouse to see the guy who finished earlier already wearing the green jacket. 'Sorry, mate, finders keepers. I got here first.'

This effect underlines the importance of *pre*-bunking—getting out early with the facts to inoculate an audience against disinformation *before* it takes hold (don't worry, we'll cover this in detail later). An ounce of prevention is better than a pound of cure, and quite often the only opportunity to counter disinformation, as these next phenomena show.

22 / Social (Media) Dynamics

> 'All that once was directly lived has become mere
> representation. All real activity has been channelled
> into the global construction of the spectacle.'
> —Guy Debord, 1967

First, let's take a quick pause for me to ask you to answer a simple question.

A bat and a ball costs $1.10 total.

The bat costs $1 more than the ball, so how much is the ball?

Did your brain immediately blurt out *10 cents*? That's wrong, of course—think about it some more.

Correct—if the ball is 10 cents, then the bat is $1.10 and the total is $1.20. Actually, the ball costs 5 cents ($0.05 + $1.05 = $1.10).

The two things your mental process did above are the two types of reasoning our brain does. The first is intuitive. It doesn't matter how smart you are—one study gave high-achieving MIT, Harvard and Princeton students the same question, who also answered '10 cents', the first answer that popped into their heads. The answer that 'seemed' right through instinct.

The second type of reasoning is when you actually think about it. You deliberate until you arrive at the correct answer. No doubt you were able to do this after your initial gut-based intuitive response. As this bat and ball experiment shows, we can override our instincts with analytical thinking.

The problem with social media–driven disinformation is that when posting online we don't think or deliberate too much about what we do first. People, as we have already established, will avoid having to think too hard. We are much happier to trust whichever judgment springs to mind and seems plausible with what we already know. We opt for instinct.

Psychologists will tell you how our brains approach the $1.10 problem in a neutral vacuum, and that's really helpful. But what happens when we layer on top of that a topic that triggers other less rational and more political parts of the brain and then puts it in the environment of social media, which layers social and performative considerations on top of the existing layers?

Let's put it this way: in a vacuum, you ask, 'A bat costs $1 more than a ball, how much does the ball cost?' and you get '10 cents'. But ask on social media, 'A vial of covid vaccine costs $1 more than the syringe, how much does the syringe cost?' and you get the answer, 'Death to Bill Gates!'

Social media is not a vacuum. In many ways it replicates some of our social dynamics, but in others it gives us a free pass from having to follow them.

Have you ever said something to somebody online that you never would have said to them face to face? This is one of the key problems behind the terrifying rise of bullying and trolling on social media.

Ask any female journalist or commentator what happens any time they commit the heinous crime of having an opinion on the internet. Violent threats of murder and sexual violence are the shocking but predictable result. Were we always this horrendous, and the anonymity of the internet allowed us to surface our real selves? Or is there something about the forum that brings out a darker beast detached from our real-world alter egos?

Yale psychologist Molly Crockett was able to show how the usual things that stop us from being vile in person—physical proximity, time to cool off, a social cost to being a dickhead (my words, not hers)—aren't present on social media. Instead it fuels moral outrage 'by inflating its triggering stimuli, reducing some of its costs and amplifying many of its personal benefits'. In other words, it tips the scales heavily towards your inner dickhead.

In the petri dish of social media, researchers have often fallen for a mistaken assumption: that just because people are sharing something on social media they therefore believe it to be true. There is no evidence to support this assumption. In fact, there is plenty of evidence to show that knowing the 'truth' of an article has little impact on a person's decision to share it.

There are many reasons why we share things on social media. Often we do it without thinking about the veracity of the content if it accords with what we already think. Sometimes we are just virtue signalling. Sometimes we simply have a barrow to push and want to advance our own ideas even if we know they are probably bullshit. Sometimes we just want to mess with people, like that urge to knock over the Jenga tower mid-game.

As the $1.10 exercise demonstrates, the most common reason is simply a failure to put our brain in gear before using it. The attention economy of social media distracts us and encourages intuitive reasoning. One study we will cover later demonstrated this by 'nudging' people to think about accuracy before posting (i.e. engaging the deliberative '5 cent' part of our brain over the intuitive '10 cent' one). This massively reduced the number of fake articles shared (by about half), suggesting a lot of the sharing of disinformation is unintentional.

It certainly brings out our gullible selves. Social media is able to quantify something that has always been essential to guiding our behaviour: how many of our peers agree.

Researchers in the US were able to recreate this to show that the more 'likes' a post has, the more likely we are to believe it, even if false: 'Social engagement metrics can strongly influence interaction with low-credibility information. The higher the engagement, the more prone people are to sharing questionable content and less to fact-checking it.'

Likewise, the more we see a piece of disinformation shared the less unethical the decision to spread it seems. One study found that even seeing an article *one time* reduced how unethical participants thought it was to share it when they saw it again—even when it was clearly labelled as false and the person sharing it disbelieved it themselves. This is amazing. It clearly shows that social media provides an environment that disrupts the usual norms of our social behaviour.

The messenger is also important. Trump supporters are more likely to believe disinformation that comes out of Trump's mouth. Researchers were able to show this empirically in a study that also showed political figures can become a 'heuristic' (a shortcut) our brains use to assess whether something is true or not. Even when shown it was false, it didn't change their opinion of that candidate.

This also speaks to Trump's role as an authority figure, and the effect that has on our ability to objectively respond to him. The famous Milgram experiments in the 1960s showed that, under the instruction to obey an authority figure who asked them to go against their conscience, an incredible 65 per cent of participants would deliver electric shocks to strangers strong enough to kill them. One hundred per cent delivered at least a 300-volt shock, enough to inflict serious pain (thankfully no strangers were actually harmed). Social factors can easily cloud our moral judgments.

It goes without saying, but I will note it anyway: fear does the same. Take a trip down your toilet paper aisle in the supermarket during a lockdown to answer the question of whether fear triggers our rational or irrational thinking.

The social dynamic is even more pronounced when the disinformation being shared is emotive. We have already looked at how social media algorithms give a leg-up to the right-wing echo chamber. Unfortunately it is also given a leg-up by our brains. A study in 2020 saw this borne out: they found that when we read fake news there is a correlation between heightened 'emotionality' and believing it. They couldn't replicate this for real news, only fake news.

Psychologists had already long known that anger triggers those shortcuts our brains like to take. (It would surprise no one to find out we are less likely to deliberate rationally and analytically when fired up. See: rage, road.) But this had never been tested in regard to fake news.

Where more reason was present, people could reliably judge the accuracy of headlines; where more emotion was present then they couldn't. To compound this, prior studies had already shown that fake news articles are likely to provoke emotion through shock, anger and moral outrage. Fake news triggers our emotions, which then clouds our judgment.

And lest we just blame the bots, this last point is particularly human. Robots, it is well established by science fiction, cannot make sense of the salty discharge we call tears. In fact, when MIT researchers pitted them against each other to measure the spread of fake news, they found the preference for falseness was unique to humans: '. . . robots accelerated the spread of true and false news at the same rate, implying that false news spreads more than the truth because humans, not robots, are more likely to spread it.'

The same study found that fake stories inspired 'fear, disgust, and surprise' and spread 'farther, faster, deeper, and more broadly than the truth in all categories'. Emotion is a great trigger for our shortcuts to fake news.

None of these psychological effects are unique to social media, but social media uniquely provide the environment for them all to thrive at once. It brings out our emotional, intuitive, anti-social selves and enlists those characteristics to spread disinformation.

23 / Motivations

> 'It is a habit of mankind to entrust to careless hope
> what they long for, and to use sovereign reason to
> thrust aside what they do not desire.'
> —Thucydides

Now see if you believe this next phenomenon. If you don't, you may be experiencing it.

Backfires

'Confirmation bias' is the term for our tendency to reject information which contradicts our beliefs or to misinterpret it so that it still confirms those beliefs.

The most fierce subset of confirmation bias is a possible 'backfire effect', a hotly debated concept among cognitive researchers, where people double-down on their beliefs when these beliefs are shown to be factually incorrect. You may have experienced it in any argument with a friend or family member on opposite sides of a political debate (or anywhere on social media).

Let's just repeat that for effect: if you take someone who already believes a piece of disinformation ('vaccines cause autism') and show someone *proof* of the contrary ('here are 100 peer-reviewed studies showing it doesn't and the recant of the one academic who said it did'), the backfire effect means they may in fact be *more likely* to believe vaccines cause autism, not less likely.

Misinformed people shown evidence that Iraq did not have weapons of mass destruction were *more likely* to believe they did. Misinformed people shown evidence Obama's healthcare act did not have 'death panels' were *more likely* to believe they did. Telling people he was a Christian made people *more likely* to believe he was a Muslim.

That initial doubt your gut may have had on reading that, that this actually happens? That's the backfire effect at work.

The vaccine example above isn't hypothetical—several studies have found showing information about the safety and efficacy of vaccines to parents who refuse to vaccinate their children made some either more likely to believe vaccines cause autism, or less likely to get their kid vaccinated. How did we encourage people to take up the covid vaccine? Show them information about its safety and efficacy.

---

cat
@cafernblue

i still think my favourite thing that's ever happened to me on the internet is the time a guy said "people change their minds when you show them facts" and I said "actually studies show that's not true" and linked TWO sources and he said "yeah well I still think it works"

7:07 AM · Dec 11, 2019 · Twitter for Android

32.2K Retweets   **738** Quote Tweets   **174.4K** Likes

Experts suspect this effect occurs because we feel threatened when we come across information that contradicts our beliefs—especially when that information is challenging something central to our self-identity, like a strongly held political belief.

Being threatened is a powerful motivator in our evolutionary biology. It causes negative emotions, which cloud our ability to properly process the new information and instead causes us to retreat into familiar territory. Basically, our brain runs home to mummy when it gets uncomfortable. It can also trigger what psychologists call 'naïve realism', where we believe our perception of reality is the only accurate view, and that those who disagree are simply uninformed or irrational. (Sound like any covid denialists you may know?)

A correction can also remind us of the original source of the misinformation, and cause our own internal repetition of it; and hence trigger the illusory truth effect as it makes it more familiar.

Yet 'best practice' still tells us to 'correct the record'. Does this do more damage?

It likely depends on the context. There is some pushback against just how pronounced the backfire effect can be. Some more-recent studies have questioned the original ones because they can show the backfire effect is more or less pronounced, or indeed absent, depending on the circumstances—sometimes debunking can actually work.

Many experts are currently recommending frequent repetition of the debunking, in line with our brain laziness: let's just make the truth more familiar. Studies show this works to reduce any backfire effect but there is also a very big caveat: unless someone is also repeating the disinformation. As the leading researchers found in their pursuit to identify any backfire effect:

> Strengthening of the initial misinformation seems to have a stronger
> negative effect than strengthening of the retraction has a positive
> effect. This unfortunate asymmetry results in an unlevel playing
> field, with a seemingly natural advantage ceded to initially encoded
> misinformation.

That's bad news for us. We are never handed such an advantage when trying to debunk deliberate disinformation campaigns. In politics, family disagreements and pretty much everywhere on the internet you won't get far counting on the other side to go quiet. If they continue to push their disinformation, it will win out over the debunking.

The backfire effect has even spawned a couple of its own spin-offs. The 'overkill backfire effect' suggests the brain will prefer simple explanations over complicated ones (hello, climate change debate), and the 'familiarity backfire effect' which biases the brain to revert back to misinformation once its correction has been forgotten (as we will see later when we bust open myth-busting).

A lot of the controversy around the backfire effect stems from the fact that often when we think we are seeing it (a brain acting counter to what they see) we are actually seeing something else (the brain wilfully ignoring what they see). We can easily mistake sticking to an incorrect belief for a polarised doubling down on it.

That, we call 'politically motivated reasoning'.

Gymnastics

Being social animals means we need to get along to survive. Our basic behavioural motivations simply don't align with 'finding the truth'. It is just not part of our biological make-up. We have bigger fish to fry: fitting in, forming connections, winning arguments, having moral values.

That means our brains will go to great lengths to take a piece of information and contort it to fit and reinforce what we already believe. This sometimes involves great feats of cognitive gymnastics—like the mental contortion the brains of Donald Trump's supporters had to do in 2020 once election results trickled in. As the vote counts put Trump ahead in some states but behind in others, they applied their logic that the count should stop in the states he was ahead but continue in the states he was behind. They failed to see any contradiction in these beliefs.

At literally the exact same time, his supporters were chanting 'STOP THE COUNT!' in Arizona while others were chanting 'COUNT THE VOTE!' in Pennsylvania. Sometimes the mental gymnastics all got a bit too much for the Trump supporters' brains—in Phoenix they had to be reined in for chanting 'STOP THE COUNT' when Trump was behind.

Politically motivated reasoning is another subset of confirmation bias. It is critical to understanding how disinformation works.

Effectively, people will use their minds to protect the groups to which they belong from grappling with uncomfortable truths.

In one classic experiment (the 'Asch experiment') a room full of people were shown three columns and were asked to choose the tallest one. One column is obviously the tallest, but everyone in the room except for one poor unsuspecting sod is in on the experiment. They all

Nancy Leong ✓
@nancyleong

As I understand the state of the race, Trump is seeking various forms of relief in his lawsuits:
- recount WI
- stop counting in NC
- count faster in NV
- count backwards in PA
- count only the ballots he likes in GA
- don't count Detroit

9:53 AM · Nov 5, 2020 · Twitter Web App

7,074 Retweets   **1,011** Quote Tweets   **26.1K** Likes

pick column B, despite it being very obviously shorter than column C. Which column does the poor test subject choose? Column B, to go along with the crowd.

Let me put it here in lights, because this is really important:

The motivation to conform is stronger than the motivation to be right.

This helps explain the rise of the partisan echo chamber and the difficulty in penetrating it to counter disinformation.

Adding fuel to this partisan fire is when politically motivated reasoning pulls in opposite directions at once. This is called 'belief polarisation': people on opposite sides of the divide see the exact same information and update their beliefs in opposite directions. It poses a huge challenge for persuading or dissuading voters who have already formed negative opinions towards an issue or a political party.

There's a lot of debate in the psychology community about the extent to which we do this because we are consciously partisan, or simply because we are mentally lazy. In any case, it means the information (and disinformation) we see affects us all differently, depending on our motivations.

In 1951, two Ivy League schools in America—Dartmouth and Princeton—squared off in the final gridiron game of the season. It was a particularly brutal encounter which saw tempers flare and punches fly. The star Princeton player, who had just appeared on the cover of *Time* as the Ivy League player of the decade, exited with a broken nose. A Dartmouth player was carted off with a broken leg.

In the aftermath, both campus newspapers told starkly different versions of the same events, variously with Princeton and Dartmouth cast as the villains. 'The blame must be laid primarily on Dartmouth's doorstep,' thundered the *Daily Princetonian*. Meanwhile *The Dartmouth* saw it differently: 'When an idol is hurt there is only one recourse—the tag of dirty football. So what did the Tiger coach Charley Caldwell do? He announced to the world that the Big Green had been out to extinguish the Princeton star.'

This was remarkable to a pair of psychologists—one from each school. In a heart-warming display of our abilities to overcome this effect, they teamed up when they realised the reality they were seeing in each school was entirely different. The results of their landmark experiment upended traditional beliefs about how we process information.

They showed students from Dartmouth and Princeton the same footage of the game and then gave them a questionnaire about the fouls they saw committed in the footage:

> When Princeton students looked at the movie of the game, they saw the Dartmouth team make over twice as many infractions as their own team made. And they saw the Dartmouth team make over twice as many infractions as were seen by Dartmouth students. When Princeton students judged these infractions as 'flagrant' or 'mild,' the ratio was about two 'flagrant' to one 'mild' on the Dartmouth team, and about one 'flagrant' to three 'mild' on the Princeton team.

Despite the controlled setting, and viewing exactly the same evidence, the students only strengthened their existing beliefs as to which team had started the fight.

Another study in the 1980s found the same effect: after militia in Beirut massacred thousands of mostly Palestinian refugees in plain sight of the Israeli Defence Force in 1982, researchers from Stanford University showed the same TV news footage of the events to pro-Israeli and pro-Palestinian students. Both sides rated the exact same media coverage as biased against their own side. They also reported significantly different recollections and perceptions of the same footage, each group seeing more negative references to their side.

More recently, when Robert Mueller handed down his report into Russian interference into the 2016 US election, a similar national experiment was borne out. Everyone in the country read exactly the same report, but half of the country saw collusion and crimes and the other half saw vindication and innocence.

Same information, increased polarisation of tribal beliefs.

24 / Tribes

'One can be deceived in believing what is untrue,
but on the other hand, one is also deceived in not
believing what is true.'

—Søren Kierkegaard

We prefer 'in-group' information from people we trust.

When researchers at Columbia University allowed people to see what songs other participants were downloading, they ended up downloading similar songs. What's more, when they divided people into social groups who could only see the song choices of those in their own group, those groups rapidly became their own 'bubbles' which diverged radically from the other bubbles. The impulse to conform trumped individual preferences, and these closed song groups exhibited groupthink hostile to outside reality.

These effects also help explain why people have a hard time understanding how *other* people can accept disinformation.

We may see a piece of information ('hospitals are at capacity because of the pandemic') that accords with our worldview ('covid is real'), and accept it as true. We can't comprehend how someone else could see *the same information* and reach a different conclusion ('the media is hyping this, hospitals are fine'), because we can't conceive of the alternative worldview ('covid is just a bad flu').

In fact, there is a body of research showing that belief in conspiracy theories, such as the ones we are seeing proliferating around covid, is motivated by exactly this type of tribal reasoning that aligns with and protects our group's worldview.

We have always formed ourselves into 'tribes' and evolution would then compel us to think the same as each other in order to become a stronger, more cohesive group. It helped us survive. We still do this, but how it now manifests in our age of social media tribes is hostile not just to other groups who do not think the same, but to reality itself.

Tribal Bonds

If you want to understand why nearly everyone in the media and who was opposed to Trump failed to see his victory coming in the 2016 presidential election, this tribal groupthink is a big part of the reason. They lived in a world where if you showed people photos of Trump's inauguration crowd and Obama's inauguration crowd, the answer to which was bigger was objective.

That's not the world we live in. Despite no objective comparison of the two crowd sizes possibly seeing more Trump supporters than Obama supporters, 15 per cent of Trump fans in one survey were willing to look at both photos and declare the Trump crowd bigger.

Can you spot the difference? Trump's crowd (left) vs Obama's crowd (right). These are the same images used to survey Trump supporters 'Which photo has more people?'

Even if they knew themselves the answer to be false, it shows they were willing to place loyalty to their political belonging over their loyalty to the truth. By extension, they can often then fool themselves as much as they fooled those asking the question. When they see information that aligns with their political beliefs, their brain will sidestep the work of evaluating it for trueness or falseness and skip straight to the part where it is accepted as reality.

This may outwardly seem highly irrational. We can all see the size differences between the crowds as plain as the white flooring exposed by Trump's sad numbers. But to look at it another way, motivated reasoning is actually highly rational—it just pays no heed to truth.

If we, as humans and human societies, derive most evolutionary benefit from working together then it makes perfect sense for us to process information in a way that reinforces the bonds of our groups. If our interests are served by motivated reasoning then it shouldn't surprise us that our brains are geared towards favouring group bonds over accuracy.

Yale psychologist/law professor Dan Kahan calls this 'tribe before truth'. We don't stand to gain much by going against our crowd. But we stand to lose a great deal by alienating those we depend on for support and companionship:

> For members of the public, being right or wrong about climate change science will have no impact . . . Yet the impact of taking a position that conflicts with their cultural group could be disastrous.
>
> Take a barber in a rural town in South Carolina. Is it a good idea for him to implore his customers to sign a petition urging Congress to take action on climate change? No. If he does, he will find himself out of a job, just as his former congressman, Bob Inglis, did when he himself proposed such action.

This helps explain why we do this even when we can reason well. Which takes us back to our $1.10 bat and ball experiment. Remember? One way of thinking is to say the first thing that pops into our head, the other way is actually using brain power to work it out. One of Kahan's studies showed that the higher our ability to do the latter the *more* likely we were to fit facts to our worldview, not the other way around. It's just us being highly rational.

Do Trump's fans seem so stupid now, for ignoring visual reality? It was in fact a display of deliberative thinking triumphing over instinctive thinking. Further demonstrating this, the survey found that those Trump supporters with a university degree were much more likely to give the wrong answer about the crowd size.

It's also a big lesson that in countering disinformation we may have to step outside our own worldview and into those of others.

And there is hope, Australia—pat yourself on the back. One encouraging finding is that these effects are more pronounced the more polarised a society already is—for example in the US. Even in studies where Trump supporters could be convinced something their candidate said was not true, it wouldn't damage their intention to vote for him. An Australian study on the other hand found Australians are *less* polarised and *more* capable of changing our minds, at least when presented with information about a politician's 'untruthfulness'.

This may have been what blunted mining magnate Clive Palmer's false claims in the 2020 Queensland state election. Despite spending millions of dollars promoting the same disinformation campaign he used successfully during the 2019 federal election (Labor having a 'death tax'), it was largely ineffective this time around. In the intervening period between the two elections there had been a lot of negative publicity about Clive Palmer's untruthfulness and untrustworthiness, which may have shifted the dynamic of voters being prone to believe his disinformation.

Alarm bells should still ring, however: the more polarised we become, the more of an effect politically motivated reasoning will have on our society.

And this polarisation is not just happening along traditional ideological lines.

Tribal Lines

Did you ever think a hippie Byron Bay influencer mum on Instagram would have much in common with a far-right White nationalist neo-Nazi? They may represent a new political constituency that transcends geography, religion, demographics and political persuasion, if their beliefs align on covid vaccinations and anti-lockdown protests.

This is an age of new tribes formed by the digital echo chamber, and they are not forming along the traditional lines of political ideology or parties. The bonds these new tribes feel are stronger than their previous political identities, and are formed along the same fault lines disinformation exposes (covid lockdowns, vaccines, etc).

This need for tribal belonging accords with the politically motivated reasoning discussed above: the need to belong trumping the need to be correct.

When studying Brexit tribal lines in the UK, researchers found:

> The need to belong to a tribe can influence people's psychological biases, such as the willingness to believe information that supports the tribe's viewpoint while being overly critical about information that challenges it. Tribe members use disinformation to broadcast their identity as part of the tribe, and seek approval from other members. Approval comes in the form of likes, comments, and shares. This has implications for the spread of online disinformation, as the search for tribal approval may encourage people to broadcast content that reflects the views of the tribe, veracity notwithstanding.

In the lead-up to and following the Brexit vote in the UK, the traditional political fault lines (Labour, Conservative, Liberal Democrats) shifted, with many finding their new homes in the 'Brexiteer' or 'Remainer' camps that ignored previous party affiliation. Tribal behaviour on social media widened the gulf between Remain and Leave voters, and the tribalism made people more vulnerable to disinformation. As a result, the traditional political constituencies in subsequent British elections have changed.

In May 2021, the UK Labour Party convincingly lost one of their safest seats in a by-election deep in Labour heartland. The seat, Hartlepool, had never been in any hands other than Labour in its entire history.

But it was staunchly pro-Brexit. A new political map was redrawn along new Brexit tribe lines.

When the nonpartisan organisation More in Common released their research project looking at the 'Hidden Tribes of America' they found something similar. New tribes had formed:

> Our research concludes that we have become a set of tribes, with different codes, values, and even facts. In our public debates, it seems that we no longer just disagree. We reject each other's premises and doubt each other's motives. We question each other's character. We block our ears to diverse perspectives.

Psychologists even have a term for something that falls in between a white lie (generous lies) and a black lie (selfish ones): a 'blue lie'. Blue lies are falsehoods told on behalf of a group to strengthen the bonds of that group. Trump excelled at telling these sorts of lies to forge the bonds of his tribe, and it explains why lying became so central to his presidency. As others scratched their heads at how people could support a politician who lied so brazenly, Trump supporters viewed these blue lies as symbolic protests on their behalf. His inauthenticity made him more authentic in the eyes of his tribe.

Another group of researchers thought all of this disinformation and digital echo chamber malarkey sounded pretty familiar to their own field of study: the psychology of cults. Their prior study of cults is now informing our understanding of disinformation. The behaviours are strikingly similar.

Most people are drawn into cults by an open question—now so much easier to do online than in real human conversation. The complex process that would have then pulled people into real-world cults is much more easily automated in our digital ecosystem.

Dylann Roof, for example, the racist mass murderer who killed nine Black churchgoers in South Carolina, began his journey to radicalisation with a simple Google search: 'Who is Trayvon Martin?' (the Florida teenager killed by a White neighbour for looking suspicious). The next suggestion Google offered to search was 'Black on White crime'. He told investigators 'For some reason it made me type in the words Black on White crime. And that was it.' So began his descent into a racist rabbit hole that eventually culminated in a tragic White on Black hate crime in a Charleston church.

In a cult, a group will pull you in and then isolate you from all other realities. We already discussed some of these group dynamics when examining echo chambers and the closed online communities that populate them.

A quainter term for a closed online community would be 'cult'.

Those within cults distrust those on the outside. We see this with disinformation echo chambers, where members are unlikely to have real-world connections but are bound by shared beliefs. Like a cult, inside these closed online communities outside voices are discredited and are treated with great hostility. That hostility now plays out online: the new form of harassment for dissent is usually doxing (publishing private information about someone like their address) and cancelling (removing the ability of those who disagree with you from having a public platform).

Tribal Realities

This cult-like behaviour usually coalesces around one big, scary elephant in the room: the psychology of conspiracy theories.

As cult expert Rachel Bernstein told *Wired* magazine, 'Secret information . . . makes them feel protected and empowered. They're a step ahead of those in society who remain wilfully blind. This creates feeling similar to a drug—it's its own high.'

You have no doubt already had a relative or friend succumb to the covid-lockdown side effect of the posting of ridiculous conspiracy theories.

The covid pandemic has sparked another pandemic of conspiracy-fuelled disinformation, this time infecting your Facebook feed. As we already saw, of the 71 per cent of Americans who have heard of the conspiracy theory that powerful people intentionally planned the covid outbreak, more than one in every three people say it is either definitely or probably true.

While we've already looked at conspiracy and QAnon in previous chapters, the similarity to cults makes it useful to look at some of the psychology behind why movements like QAnon and other conspiracy theories have found such salience in the pandemic era.

One underlying factor is the increasing complexity and confusion of the world around us as fundamental things changed rapidly. They often happen after a sudden change that brings collective uncertainty and needs to be interpreted, like 9/11 and covid. The covid pandemic may have been a 'black swan' event—a rare event that is beyond the realm of normal expectations, and so confounds us (before the European arrival in Australia, the Old World believed every swan in the world was white).

To make sense of that confusion, many people turn to conspiracy theories, which behave very similarly to cults (in history, cults often formed in times of great social and political upheaval too).

'There are people who would choose to believe in complicated nonsense rather than accept that their own circumstances are incomprehensible, the result of issues beyond their intellectual capacity to understand, or even their own fault,' as Tom Nichols put it in *The Death of Expertise*.

Our brains really want the world to be predictable and organised. We don't do a good job of coping with the fact it is neither.

We don't like unanswered moral questions. We want to know who did it and why. ('Could a virus just randomly jump like that from the animal to the human world for no reason? Not a good enough explanation!') Conspiracy theories (like cults) make us feel special, as we have a secret knowledge nobody else is smart enough to see, and connected, in that we find other people with that same special knowledge.

They are also a symptom of information overload, and our innate desire and ability to find patterns, even where there may be none (another result of how our brains are hardwired). This is another motivation that is key to understanding disinformation.

Conspiracy theorists, like those in cults, take random bits of unrelated information and see connections—and in these connections they infer meaning. One problem with the internet these days is it supplies a hell of a lot of information. It's not difficult to find overlap in an infinite supply of proof points when looking for a pattern. This is exactly why everyone who consults Dr Google will ultimately lead themselves to the self-diagnosis they have terminal cancer. Given enough information you can find a link to anything.

Once these beliefs take hold, they are very difficult to uproot. Every counterpoint is explained away somehow. Take for instance the bizarre theory many people believe, that Australia does not actually exist (yes, this is real—those who believe the Earth is flat also think the First Fleet sailed off the edge of it, and to cover that up the British government has been involved in a centuries-long ruse to make up a fictional country the missing sailors colonised). How would you 'prove' Australia to them? Maps? Made up. Satellites? Faked. Australians? Actors. It is easier to explain away these counterpoints than to admit the core belief—the Earth being flat—is wrong.

Making matters more complicated, Italian researchers found that in the rare cases where conspiracy theorists popped their heads out of their bubble to encounter science-based dissenting information, those conspiracy theorists were then more likely to interact with conspiracy content in the future (not less likely). Conspiracy theorists who had never encountered such material, on the other hand, were twice as likely to one day move out of the conspiracy filter bubbles. Hence why it is very difficult to remove people from a cult.

Thankfully, another group of researchers put their hands up and said, 'This looks pretty familiar to our field of study!'—those who had been tracking the radicalisation of people into extremist groups and the best methods to deradicalise them.

How do you remove someone from a cult or an extremist group? The experts say it has to come from people who are within these trusted communities already, and it is best done by reaching out to an individual one on one, and over the long term.

These community-based approaches over a long period have been the most effective way deradicalisation experts have been able to extract people from their bubbles, but that is very difficult to scale online. If prevention is also not possible, how can we replicate the methods to deradicalise people from disinformation, and overcome all these cognitive phenomena that makes it so hard to do?

In later chapters we will explore the ways in which we can do that from our very own homes.

25 / Opinions

> 'The human understanding when it has once
> adopted an opinion . . . though there be a greater
> number and weight of instances to be found on
> the other side, yet these it either neglects and
> despises, or else by some distinction sets aside and
> rejects, in order that by this great and pernicious
> predetermination the authority of its former
> conclusions may remain inviolate.'
> —Francis Bacon, 1620

I've got to tell you something the political parties don't want you to know: they have absolutely no idea why you vote the way you vote.

Elections are contested these days, in Australia and elsewhere, along a simple rationale: people have opinions on issues, parties make policies to appeal to these opinions, and voters then choose the parties whose policies align with their opinions.

It is, of course, all bullshit.

It presumes we are rational creatures, and if this book has served to convince you of nothing else it should have been to demonstrate that we are absolutely not.

It's a myth that is so pervasive it has even spurred an entire industry around it: 'public opinion'.

Public Opinion

Walter Lippmann was well ahead of his time. He coined such concepts as the 'Cold War' and the 'stereotype', but by far his biggest contribution to political science was the idea of 'public opinion' as we know it. Lippmann wrote a hundred years before our current filter bubbles, yet still described how voters 'live in the same world, but they think and feel in different ones'.

Without first-hand knowledge or experience of complex questions or public affairs, he said, people instead form political opinions on a whim—largely by outsourcing that thinking to others.

Now we have the tools to measure and track in great detail the 'public opinion' Lippmann described, we do so obsessively. Discussion of the results dominates our political discourse. More than one recent prime minister has had their job sacrificed on the altar of public opinion, as if it can be measured like the height of a dam.

We report weekly shifts in 'opinion' as a snapshot of voters' genuinely held desires, and then when elections are held we are stunned (again!) when the methods have proved to get it wrong. We do the required fortnight of naval gazing about the methods we used and how we relied on measurements that in hindsight were inaccurate, and then get back to the business of doing it all over again. We conveniently ignore the fact a celebrity octopus in a tank has as good a chance of predicting the outcome as our measurements of public opinion do.

It's because the entire industry is built on a myth which social psychologists have long exposed: that voters are rational.

People, of course, are emotional. And we don't set aside our true forms when it comes to voting choices, or opinions on issues of public importance.

As Lippmann argued, we live in a personal fiction we mistake for reality:

> For the real environment is altogether too big, too complex, and
> too fleeting for direct acquaintance. We are not equipped to deal
> with so much subtlety, so much variety, so many permutations and
> combinations. And although we have to act in that environment, we
> have to reconstruct it on a simpler model before we can manage it.

Lippmann's hunches were borne out when psychologist Drew Westen started scanning the brains of Democrats and Republicans in the US nearly a century later. He saw in stark neuroscientific relief what we discovered earlier in other cognitive experiments: his scans showed the brain activating its 'emotion' parts when presented with negative information about their candidate. It uses emotion to contort the information into something instead biased towards them. Then it rewards that bias with a good hit of dopamine. The 'reason' parts of their brain? They remained dormant in the scans.

Another way to put this, if we again think of the $1.10 experiment, is that whereas the politics of public opinion assumes when a voter walks into a ballot box they will make their choice with the *deliberative* way of thinking, these brain scans showed that in reality they use the *instinctive* thinking shortcut which in the bat and ball experiment yields the wrong result. Starting to understand Trump's election yet?

Contrary to most assumptions and the logic of nearly every political campaign ever, we don't vote in self-interest. One of Trump's first decisions as president was to remove the crucial economic support for poverty-stricken coal miners in Appalachia who had voted for him nearly unanimously. Did it change their opinions of him? Of course not. They voted for him again four years later.

And yet a political party will continue to appeal to the reason parts of their brain: 'Maybe if I give them a tax break, or retraining, or keep their mine open they will vote for me!'

We know this, because neuroscientists have studied people who have had damage to the emotional decision-making parts of their brains. They spend an inordinate amount of time deliberating the pros and cons of a very simple decision, weighing up with reason what emotion could have decided for them in a fraction of a second.

How do we form our opinions in reality? We never let the truth get in the way of a good opinion. We connect with each other and form our opinions through feelings. How do we 'feel' about the candidate, the party, the issue? It's governed by our subconscious, not our conscious, mind.

Moral Opinion

This all accords with social psychologist Jonathan Haidt's work on morality. According to his 'social intuitionism' theory, our positions on moral issues are determined by—you guessed it—that instinctive 'intuition' way of thinking that we then rationalise after the fact.

Let's pause for a minute here to recall the grand history of intellectual thought we discussed in Part One: the centuries-old search for and debate over truth. For most of that time the great philosophers who argued that we are rational and that truth was knowable through reason won that debate handily. We were rational before we were emotional.

But just look at any kid to see the reality of how we make decisions. As our brain develops, we take our morality from our parents. We don't know why we need to hold hands to cross the road, but we do know the importance of the connection we have to our parents who are telling us to do it.

I can't get my toddler to stop poking that dog in the eye through understanding the intrinsic value of all mammalian wellbeing or even because she grasps the consequences of being bitten. But I can get her to understand my anger, through her feelings and social connection.

Whereas the old 'rationalist' school of thought (like Piaget, for any of you teachers out there) said that as she grew older she would learn to make moral decisions using her rational brain, in reality as an adult her moral reasoning will be just as intuitive. But she will have become much better at rationalising her choices after the fact.

How do you feel about euthanasia? Did your brain just rattle off a list of very comprehensible reasons why it is a good or bad idea? Like: people have a right to die with dignity; people will do it anyway; people should have autonomy over their own bodies; etc. Those reasons are not why you are in favour of or against euthanasia, they are your *justifications* for holding the opinion you hold.

We'll demonstrate this in a subsequent section when we hypothesise your reaction to receiving information that disproves your justifications, and if that would then change your opinion? Hint: no, it would not.

And so it is for disinformation. If you were to see an article about euthanasia you will not form your opinion as to whether that article is true or false through a deliberative rationalisation of the information it presents and the context it is presented in—you will form your opinion intuitively and then fit the information to your predetermined conclusion.

As Haidt perfectly put it, 'The reasoning process is more like a lawyer defending a client than a judge or scientist seeking truth.'

Our moral reasoning is not just intuitive, it's also biased. Our brains try to do two things to make sense of our world: it fits our opinions to agree with our friends, and it fits our beliefs to fit our central identity. We saw this earlier, where people were presented with the same information but interpreted it differently to conform with their peers (the Dartmouth/Princeton game) or our central identity (the Mueller report).

Haidt's other great contribution to our understanding has been to extend this concept into an explanation why people are conservative, progressive or libertarian—based on the evolution of our moral foundations.

We are all calibrated differently on a range of values: care/harm; fairness/cheating; loyalty/betrayal; authority/subversion; sanctity/degradation; and liberty/oppression. Progressives, for example, calibrate 'care/harm' (e.g. 'Should we look after refugees?') significantly higher than conservatives, who calibrate 'sanctity/degradation' (e.g. 'Should we have sex before marriage?') much higher than progressives.

As a result, conservatives often have an advantage over progressives (see Chapter 14 on the MAGAphone) because they are simply better at framing their opinions in terms of their moral foundations, and so triggering the emotion parts of our brains, while progressives love tickling our intellectual parts.

Even when framed emotively, progressives won't resonate with conservatives for this reason. Greta Thunberg's famous 'How dare you' speech to the UN was incredibly polarising. It brought tears of joy to progressives' faces and tears of rage to the faces of conservatives. Haidt's moral foundations theory shows why: using his framework, researchers analysed the speech to find 'care' words were three times as frequent as 'authority' and 'sanctity' words.

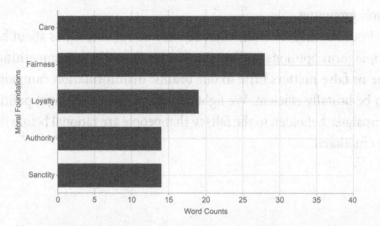

Detected Moral Words Per Moral Foundation

'How dare you' had great appeal to progressives but alienated conservatives.

Haidt's moral foundations theory helps explain our gut-based opinion-forming and why we retreat into like-minded filter bubbles online when offered the chance. It gives us a culturally supplied foundation to make our intuitive opinions and then dress them up in reason. On social media we have the tools to connect with others who share our moral foundations, and then broadcast our opinions to others.

Haidt outlined the negative consequences of this:

> We often think of communication as a two-way street. What
> happens, though, when grandstands are erected along both sides
> of that street and then filled with friends, acquaintances, rivals,
> and strangers, all passing judgment and offering commentary? . . .
> Citizens are now more connected to one another, in ways that
> increase public performance and foster moral grandstanding, on
> platforms that have been designed to make outrage contagious.

Our preference is to forge strong social bonds with those who agree with us—or perhaps more accurately, we agree with people *in order* to form strong social bonds. Social media has meant this process no longer reaches some kind of stable equilibrium in the middle ground of tradition and collective memory, but fractures into infinite parallel moral groupings.

Pour the arsenic of disinformation into these realities about how people form opinions and we see that because whether something is true or false matters little to our brains, disinformation campaigns can be brutally efficient. We fight disinformation as we fight political campaigns: beholden to the fallacy that people are rational before they are emotional.

Cheat Sheet: The Brain and Disinformation

Effect	Description	Example
Continued Influence Effect	People continue to believe an earlier piece of disinformation, even after it has been disproved by newer information.	Growing up with an old wives' tale like 'going outside with wet hair causes a cold' makes you dry your hair even though you know it to be scientifically false.
Illusory Truth Effect	What is familiar is accepted as true, even when contrary to sense (e.g. it comes from an untrustworthy source).	Hearing an advertising jingle so many times you start thinking that maybe you *should* nip into Natrad.
Confirmation Bias	General term for the tendency to reject information which contradicts beliefs or misinterpret it to confirm those beliefs.	Someone makes a spectacular recovery from a serious illness. A religious person may see it as a 'miracle' due to prayer, as opposed to a triumph of medicine.
Backfire Effect	Clear facts that disprove a strongly held belief only reinforce that belief. The reaction can be strong or violent.	Showing a voter negative information about their candidate (e.g. 'he paid off a porn star') increases their support for the candidate.
Politically Motivated Reasoning	Our brains are wired to prefer fitting in than finding facts. New information is contorted to fit with the current worldview of oneself and the group they belong to.	Confronted with evidence of consistent global temperature rises, climate sceptic Andrew Bolt declares that global warming is 'overall, a good thing' for the planet (actual quote).
Belief Polarisation	People see the same information, which reinforces their opposing beliefs in opposite directions.	I might see David Hasselhoff's German pop success as an indication of his versatility and resilience, while my friend sees it as proof that he was always a hack. It really depends on your underlying view of The Hoff going in.

Part Five
Defeating
Disinformation

26 / What Not to Do

Part Five
Defeating
Disinformation

> SOCRATES: And if they can get hold of this person
> who takes it in hand to free them from their chains
> [of ignorance] and to lead them up [to the truth], and
> if they could kill him, will they not actually kill him?
> GLAUCON: They certainly will.
> —Plato, *The Allegory of the Cave*

Every time linguistics professor George Lakoff started his Cognitive Science 101 course at the University of California, Berkeley, he asked his students not to think of an elephant.

In the 44 years he taught there before retiring in 2016, not a single student was able to accomplish that task.

This has been, in essence, the world's approach to tackling disinformation: bring attention to the disinformation they are trying to defeat.

When the Labor Party was faced with the 'death tax' disinformation campaign in 2019, they bent over backwards to make sure everyone in the country had heard of it—prosecuting a media campaign to loudly complain to everyone who had not yet seen it that Facebook was refusing to take the offending material down.

Anyone tasked with the job of tackling disinformation would be well served to have read this far, to gain an understanding of why it occurs. But as you will see, the standard practice for how we deal with disinformation flies in the face of everything we have learned about our information ecosystem, our human brain and our motivations for embracing and sharing disinformation. What our instincts tell us to do when confronted with false information often has the opposite effect.

As the world has been gripped by our recent disinfodemic, collective efforts to find a cure have yielded some promising antidotes, but they are very much the exception to the rule. First, we need to acknowledge the flaws in our responses thus far.

No Negating (irony intended)

This next piece of information will not surprise any parent: our brains don't process negations.

Tell any child 'Don't touch that sparking electrical wire!' and all they will hear is 'Touch that sparking electrical wire!' The brain does a terrible job of hearing the 'no', 'don't', 'stop' part of instructions, and does a much better job of processing the action part of the sentence.

If you want your kid to listen (I can't guarantee this works 100 per cent of the time) child psychologists tell us instead of saying what *not* to do ('Quit hitting your sister!', 'Don't run!', 'Stop screaming!') you should instead tell your kids positively what you *want* them to do ('Keep your hands to yourself!', 'Walk!', 'Be quiet!').

Don't look for any political leadership to model your parenting on: 'don't negate' is one of the best-known and least-followed precepts in political communications. The instinct to refute or deny a falsehood about oneself is simply hard to resist. Hence Labor's protestations of 'We do not have a death tax!'

Maybe Richard Nixon could have hung on as president if only he'd told the American people 'I am a law-abiding citizen' instead of 'I'm not a crook'.

Think how the Biden campaign successfully modelled this in the context of disinformation. As previously outlined, they tried to ignore the actual disinformation itself to give the positive alternative. They didn't say 'Joe Biden does not have a mushy brain' they showed clips of him talking coherently, clearly possessed of a working brain.

I don't want to let the Biden campaign completely off the hook, as their campaign was also rife with blatant negating of Trump's attacks which achieved nothing more than the opposite of what they were setting out to do.

When Facebook posts started circulating with disinformation that Biden would increase taxes for people earning under $400,000 the campaign responded with a Facebook post of their own: 'Joe Biden won't raise your taxes if you make under $400,000'. It followed on the heels of other classics like 'Joe Biden won't ban fracking' and 'Joe Biden will never defund the police'.

They may as well have run with 'Joe Biden won't make you think of an elephant'.

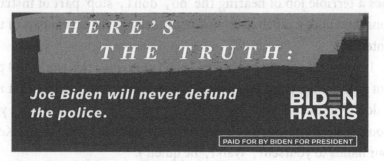

HERE'S
THE TRUTH:

Joe Biden will never defund the police.

BIDEN HARRIS

PAID FOR BY BIDEN FOR PRESIDENT

I wasn't worried about Joe Biden defunding the police . . . until I saw this ad.

Bust Myth-Busting

Even correctly framed without a negation, there is another big problem with this approach.

Fact-checking, myth-busting and correcting the record—society's default response to disinformation—usually doesn't work.

It shouldn't come as any surprise given the preceding chapters. Presenting facts simply does not erase falsehoods within the cognitive maze of our minds in the social media ecosystem.

It again assumes the age-old trap that we are open-minded rational beings; that we are governed by a dispassionate deliberative process of thinking. We are anything but.

Consider the best-case scenario: that when presented with countering facts we will willingly accept we have been wrong and change our minds on a previously held falsehood. In a neutral setting, cognitive psychologists have shown this can work: repeating the myth was more effective than not mentioning it, when issuing a retraction. Another, similarly neutral and devoid of polarising content, showed it can be safe to repeat misinformation when correcting it. In this scenario, the increased familiarity with the myth could be overcome by the correction.

But usually the case scenario is far from best.

A factual correction is not typically found in a willing retraction, it is usually up against a hostile mind—hostile not only to the particular information being promoted and the messenger promoting it, but also hostile to the whole idea that their identity merits correction in the first place.

Our knee-jerk reaction when fact-checked is cognitive dissonance: we are motivated to reject the factual correction in order to maintain our pre-existing worldview.

If I had tasked you or any group, before you had read this, with the objective of coming up with a plan to tackle covid disinformation, chances are you would have recommended compiling a list of all the common covid myths and presenting factual information to debunk them.

Don't feel bad—that's what everyone else came up with too. Intuitively it should work.

It's what you see all around you too.

A number of studies have been able to show the more familiar a piece of disinformation, the more likely you are to think it is true—even if you originally thought it was false, or it didn't align with your beliefs. Myth-busting familiarises people with the myth being debunked, which they are more likely to have seen than any factual correction (and that you are showing them once again in order to debunk it). This is the 'illusory truth effect' we talked about.

We have a preference for the familiar. We're much better at remembering a claim we have heard than we are at remembering the circumstances of where we heard it (like in a myth-busting article) or the true/false 'rating' we attached to it or saw attached to it.

This is even more pronounced in older people. One study showed that the more times they were told something was false, the better they could identify it as false in the short term, but the more likely they were to think it was true when asked about it a few days later.

It also has the effect of making us think, the more times we hear it, that its acceptance is more widespread. We are notoriously bad at estimating how many other people share our beliefs, and even more so if we are exposed to biased social media feeds. Psychologists call this 'false consensus'.

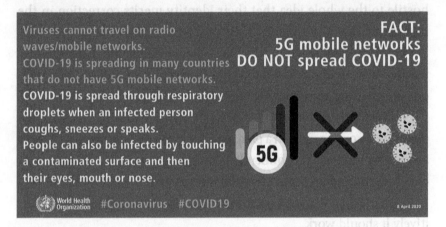

Viruses cannot travel on radio waves/mobile networks.
COVID-19 is spreading in many countries that do not have 5G mobile networks.
COVID-19 is spread through respiratory droplets when an infected person coughs, sneezes or speaks.
People can also be infected by touching a contaminated surface and then their eyes, mouth or nose.

FACT:
5G mobile networks
DO NOT spread COVID-19

5G

World Health Organization   #Coronavirus   #COVID19

8 April 2020

An example of the World Health Organization's amplification of the 5G conspiracy.

None of this is to say you can't myth-bust your way to a correction, when done properly (as studies have been able to demonstrate). It's just that the typical *way* we myth-bust nearly always favours the myth over the correction. It's just not a battle you are going to win. Myths are usually way more entertaining than facts.

Julius Caesar, for example, was born by natural birth. The myth that he was from his mother's womb untimely ripped (hence us calling it a 'caesarean') is much stickier in our minds and in history because it is novel and interesting, even if it was a medical impossibility at the time (his mother survived).

Similarly, Napoleon Bonaparte was well above average height. In fact, he was taller than many modern leaders, despite average heights being significantly taller now—Dmitry Medvedev, Nicholas Sarkozy and Silvio Berlusconi are all shorter than Napoleon. But that he was short was a great *story*. It was one of the original disinformation campaigns made up by his enemies to undermine him, and it was so successful that no doubt hundreds of years later you still bought it.

Likewise, the fact that the covid vaccine was created by Bill Gates as a secret plot to sterilise people and solve overpopulation is a *great* yarn! Well, at least a significantly more interesting story than 'a number of research projects incrementally added to the body of scientific knowledge that ultimately culminated in mRNA immunology trials'—nobody is optioning the Hollywood rights for that story.

We are social creatures who tell stories because *that's how our brains work*. The best story will win. In fact, our brains will invent stories even when there are none in order to make sense of random or complicated information.

In one famous experiment in the 1940s, a group was shown an animation of geometric shapes moving around each other. They were then asked to describe what they saw. People saw shapes but invented stories. Every single participant described things like:

> A man has planned to meet a girl and the girl comes along with
> another man. The first man tells the second to go; the second tells the
> first, and he shakes his head. Then the two men have a fight, and the
> girl starts to go into the room to get out of the way and hesitates and
> finally goes in. She apparently does not want to be with the first man . . .

This was literally an animation of no more than a triangle and a circle both moving around a square. The myth will always be a better story than the correction.

Add to this the other effects we have already outlined, like any possible backfire effect and the brain's preference for repeated and familiar information, and we see that myth-busting is worse than ineffective—it is a myth's best friend.

Yet what do we see on our biggest social media platforms? Facebook, in an attempt to address 'false information about COVID-19' proactively asks all of its users to send their friends and family to a WHO page listing every common myth about the virus.

Help Friends and Family Avoid
False Information About
COVID-19

Share a link to the World Health Organization's (WHO) website where they've put together a list of common rumors about the virus.

Share Link   Go to who.int

Don't Put a Label on Me

This is just one of the (mis)steps the social media platforms take.

You will have no doubt noticed the preferred method they deploy to deal with disinformation: attaching labels or warnings to the offending posts.

This doesn't work, and in fact can again be counterproductive.

A group of researchers in Poland divided people into two groups, and misled one of them. They were played a recording and then read a description of it. After being given a warning the description might be inconsistent with the recording, the group whose description didn't have any discrepancies began to find many where there were none.

In other words, the 'label' attached to the information they were given made them see misinformation even where there was none. Researchers are concerned the net effect of all labelling is a greater distrust in legitimate media.

That might be one thing to weigh against the benefits labelling provides against actual disinformation—if it had any.

A typical label on social media might read 'This has been rated by fact checkers as false' or 'partly false' or 'This information is disputed' or make a user have to click a warning in order to see the post in the first place.

Part of the problem is the platforms' lack of an appetite to censor any speech, regardless of whether they know it to be false. As Mark Zuckerberg said when announcing a new labelling policy: 'We'll allow people to share this content to condemn it, just like we do with other problematic content, because this is an important part of how we discuss what's acceptable in our society.'

A number of studies have been tracking the effect of this, and it's not good news I'm afraid. One early study found that while putting a label on one post made people less likely to believe that post, it also made people more likely to believe another false post *without* a label.

Donald J. Trump ✔ @realDonaldTrump · 1h   ○○○

> Some or all of the content shared in this Tweet is disputed and might be misleading about an election or other civic process. Learn more   **View**

One of the Italian researchers we mentioned, Walter Quattrociocchi, who studies conspiracy bubbles (and found exposure to dissenting viewpoints had the opposite effect), called the idea that fact-checking can prevent disinformation on social media a 'hoax' and 'bullshit'.

There is much to suggest that labelling, especially among the disinformation set, only serves to pique people's interest in it—in other words, 'flagging' content works, but for all the wrong reasons. In the same way, the well-intentioned 'trigger warning'—a label many use to alert trauma survivors to potentially disturbing content—has been shown by Harvard psychologists to simply reinforce survivors' trauma instead of heading it off. A label on social media may similarly have the opposite effect of what it sets out to achieve.

Some of it may again be our brain laziness. Just the mere presence of a disputed tag, like a red flag, catches our eye and draws us to that content which all of a sudden is elevated among the overload of otherwise unflagged content. In Facebook's early trials of their labelling system, its own developers admitted that many of the users who read the warning label actually became more inclined to share the disputed news. As a result they shrank the warnings.

Labelling has also become a 'badge of honour' for many in the right-wing ecosystem who fit it within their worldview that social media platforms are out to censor their 'truth'. In one famous example, Hollywood actor-cum-conspiracist James Woods called his labelling 'the best endorsement a story could have'.

James Woods ✔ @RealJamesWoods · Mar 18, 2017 · · ·
The fact that @facebook and @snopes "dispute" a story is the best endorsement a story could have...

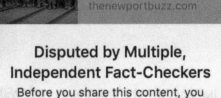

The Slaves That Time...
by G John Sit We've all be...
thenewportbuzz.com

Disputed by Multiple, Independent Fact-Checkers
Before you share this content, you might want to know that the fact-checking sites, Associated Press and

♡ 275　　↻ 1.8K　　♡ 3.2K　　⌄　　⬆

There are also many practical limitations to labelling. Fact-checking is a laborious process—an algorithm can't be relied on to label correctly; it needs a human's touch—while fake news is free.

By one count, it takes Facebook an average of 28 days to label false content (and even longer for non-English content). By the time any content is labelled it may have been viewed millions of times. If anyone thinks a four-week lag on labelling can still make it effective they haven't spent much time on social media, where immediacy is king and content stales quickly.

By the time Twitter labelled a manipulated video of Joe Biden in the 2020 election, it had already been viewed five million times and retweeted more than 21,000 times.

Even if it was particularly effective and speedy, it doesn't address another issue with labelling: cloning.

As debunked and labelled posts get removed, dozens of 'clones' appear in their place, sometimes with very minor changes to avoid detection. Some of this may not be intentional—if there is a delay of several weeks before disinformation is labelled, it will have been cloned or copied by those who think it is true (or have never thought to question it) before it has a label attached.

The disinformers freely take advantage of this to outsmart the censors. As we saw when discussing anti-vaxxers, the covid film *Plandemic* executed a deliberate disinformation campaign based on this exact strategy 'to bypass the gatekeepers of free speech'. Efforts to label and ban disinformation are always playing catch-up. One cloned version on YouTube had racked up over 7 million views before it was taken down.

Pay More Attention to Giving Less Attention

Barbra Streisand's house in Malibu, California, has a wonderful pool terrace. French doors from her house open onto a deck littered with parasols and a manicured lawn, overlooked by a sun-drenched balcony with lounges taking in a breathtaking view of the coastal cliffs it is perched on.

I know all this because Streisand tried to keep it a secret.

In 2003, an obscure blog documented coastal erosion up and down the California shoreline by posting more than 12,000 aerial photos of the slow advance of Mother Nature into the backyards of those lucky enough to live by the ocean.

Streisand was one of those people. One of the 12,000 photos showed the cliff encroaching towards her manicured lawn, and so she sued to have the website take it down as it violated her privacy. She didn't want anyone to see her backyard.

Before her lawsuit, and the national publicity it generated, 'Image 3850' had only been downloaded six times from the website, and several of those times were by Streisand's lawyers. In the month alone after the news broke, more than 420,000 people visited the website to see it. Now there are more than 7 million results on a Google image search for 'Barbra Streisand house'.

People who work in PR even have a term for doing something that brings more attention to the thing you are trying to suppress: the 'Streisand Effect'.

One of the most common 'worst practice' responses to disinformation is giving oxygen to something to make it bigger than it otherwise would have been, and make it seen by more people than otherwise would have seen it.

When Twitter banned the *NY Post* for refusing to delete a tweet linking to a fake news story about Hunter Biden, its stated intention was to prevent people from spreading harmful false material. But thanks to the cycle of disinformation—and the conservative outcry that social media platforms were deliberately censoring them—Twitter managed to do the opposite. The *MIT Technology Review* mapped how the Twitter ban doubled the number of shares of the article it was purporting to ban.

The challenge of all traditional crisis communications has always been to not unintentionally amplify something you are trying to dispel. Whenever a scandal is exposed, the company or celebrity must weigh up the need to give a response with the need to make sure people don't hear about the scandal through that response.

When addressing disinformation, often an offending tweet or Facebook post is shared as an example that people should ignore—like sharing a post you see in order to warn people about it—all the while highlighting the offending material.

The media have to ask themselves all the time when reporting on disinformation, or crackpot conspiracy theories, or the latest vile thing to come out of a racist politician's mouth: 'Are we just bringing more attention to this by reporting on it?'

When Joe Biden quietly launched his presidential campaign website in 2019 it didn't generate much traffic.

When a Trump consultant bought a similar web address and launched a spoof website focusing on all the stories of Biden's inappropriate behaviour, nobody took much notice either:

> Creepy Uncle Joe Biden is back and ready to take a hands-on approach to America's problems! Joe Biden has a good feel for the American people.

It featured bad wordplay and sold T-shirts with slogans like 'Hidin' from Biden'.

But then, a few months later, the media started reporting on the spoof website. All of a sudden the traffic to it began to dwarf the number of visitors to the real Biden campaign website. When a *New York Times* article identified who was behind the site in June 2019, traffic spiked— getting more than four times the amount of traffic the real Biden site was receiving. As a result of the news coverage, when you Googled 'Joe Biden' it gave you the spoof site over the real one.

Consider this: how did you first hear the idea that 5G towers spread covid? Or that QAnon exists? Or the name of any Australian far-right extremist group? Or that an anti-lockdown protest was gathering? No doubt you heard it first in a news article rather than coming across it organically in your own networks.

The news media were slow to realise their role in the disinformation fabric and how they were unintentionally fuelling its spread, giving outsize importance to fringe actors and legitimacy to their narratives.

Extremist groups, fully cognisant of this, were quick to capitalise.

The leaked manual of an Australian neo-Nazi group instructed members to: 'stage media provocations to make the organisation itself better known and recruit suitably committed people'.

They laid out a model to do so, where members would create fake 'non-White' accounts and then use them to report fake stories to media outlets, in an incredibly self-aware practice they called 'media baiting':

> Media baiting is a huge portion of our recruitment drive. There are currently hundreds of minor nationalist groups in Australia, but none of them ever amount to anything without media attention. Even if the articles are mostly negative, the readers of the article are not the target audience.
>
> When an article is released, jump into the comment section and start praising the group and defaming the media for distorting our group. Pretending to be offended by the organisation in the post is a good way to promote the organisation in hostile groups. This way your post won't be deleted.

As the mainstream media began to wake up to these realities, including first and foremost their complicity in Trump's rise to prominence, they began to reform the way editorial decisions are made when stories covered may contain disinformation.

For many well-trained journalists this was a recalibration of everything they were taught. They were forced to collectively confront the traditional 'journalistic imperative' which says that all information needs to be spread and published. It was this, and other norms—like giving an equal hearing to two sides of a story—that had to be dramatically revisited in the wake of disinformation.

By the time the 2020 US election rolled around, and its bloody aftermath, they had finally begun to more carefully consider that they were *part* of the ecosystem, and not merely reporting on it, and so tempered their coverage accordingly.

For the most part, however, it was too late. Disinformation stories of voter fraud were mapped by researchers at Harvard, and in many cases they began with Trump and spread out through conventional media reports. Social media spread was often secondary.

Their reporting of the increasingly extreme things coming out of elected officials' mouths without consequence had moved the 'Overton window'—the things that are politically possible to say and do—to where more outlandish ideas (like disputing an entire election result) were now politically acceptable. One hundred and forty-seven Congresspeople voted to overturn the Constitution they had just sworn to uphold and an election result they themselves had just been victorious in, without consequence.

Whitney Phillips is a disinformation expert who compiled the 'Oxygenation of Amplification' handbook for journalists in the light of their new-found complicity.

> Just by showing up for work and doing their jobs as assigned, journalists covering the far-right fringe—which subsumed everything from professional conspiracy theorists to pro-Trump social media shitposters to actual Nazis—played directly into these groups' public relations interests.

In the handbook, she outlines how journalists should approach reporting disinformation and extremism in a way that doesn't merely amplify the thing journalists are describing. The media need to ask themselves three big questions first: has the story already reached people outside of the community being discussed; will the story have a positive social benefit; and will the story produce harm or allow others to cause harm?

Timing is everything. Reporting something too early gives it new audiences; too late and the window is closed to frame it as false before it takes hold.

First Draft, the organisation established to help journalists confront disinformation, was able to track this successful timing in a French and a Brazilian election. On both occasions the timing and framing of the reporting was able to slow down the spread of key conspiracies.

For all the journalists reading this, I encourage you to read Whitney Phillips' full report and Claire Wardle's work with First Draft. For everyone else, don't think this advice is not relevant to you: you play the role of journalist in microcosm every time you publish something to social media. And in fact, you even play the role of publisher each time you comment or like another person's or page's post.

We'll talk in more detail about the practical steps each of us can take as individuals to address disinformation, but you should be aware of the dynamic you feed into on social media when you comment on a post that you disagree with or share a story in order to debunk or disagree with it.

This is your own form of harmful amplification.

Every time you comment—even if it is to comment on a post saying covid isn't real (i.e. 'hey this isn't true, here is a link to the WHO facts')— your action will mean more people see the original disinformation.

First, your comment may all of a sudden make the original post visible to all your friends, depending on your privacy settings. Second, your friends and followers may receive a notification that you have commented on it which draws their attention to it. Third, it may elevate it in people's newsfeeds because your recent comment has made an older post more timely. And fourth, it may elevate it in the original post's network because the algorithm will see more comments as an indicator this is an important post that everyone else should see.

You've generated your own mini backfire effect event, though your intentions were noble.

Craig Kelly ✓
January 8, 2020 · 🌐

THANK YOU LEFTY TROLLS ! !

A special thanks to all my new found lefty troll friends.

Firstly, thanks for demonstrating how brainwashed you are, and your inability to articulate a single logical alternate argument shows that you are losing the debate.

And secondly, and more importantly, thanks for helping spread the facts and the data which undermines your simplistic groupthink and cultish beliefs.

For every time you post a 'comment' this helps with the Facebook algorithms and results in the facts in my posts appearing on more and more people's newsfeeds.

So please keep up the good work.

👍😆❤️ 4.4K   2.6K Comments 493 Shares

Craig Kelly gets it: 2600 people baited into spreading his post by commenting.

Remember, the social media platforms love engagement but are terrible at distinguishing between positive and negative sentiment. It all counts the same, and so your condemnation of or correcting of a post you disagree with helps elevate that post's prominence.

What should you do instead? We'll cover that in the next chapters.

27 / How to Defeat Disinformation

> 'Let us remember that the lie did not creep into
> politics by some accident of human sinfulness.
> Moral outrage, for this reason alone, is not likely
> to make it disappear.'
> —Hannah Arendt

Thinking that there is a silver bullet to defeat disinformation means you probably only skim-read the first half of this book, or perhaps looked at the index and skipped straight to this section to find out the answer. GO BACK AND READ IT FROM THE START, DO NOT PASS GO, DO NOT COLLECT $200.

To think that we can merely turn off the tap of bullshit by stuffing the faucet with facts is to misdiagnose disinformation. It is not a set of unrelated falsehoods appearing in a vacuum, moles that can be conveniently whacked as they pop up. We are in this disinfodemic because we have turned the corner on an entire epoch of human society and development.

There is no turning back. We must move forward.

Instead, we have to develop coherent ways of navigating these new waters where the old lighthouses of a shared baseline of facts and central media narratives, and the old harbourmasters of our politicians and our institutions, no longer provide us safe passage.

We have had our linear progression towards enlightenment, truth and reason violently disrupted, and now lie shaking in disbelief as those who would exploit our disinformation age do so with near blanket impunity and ruthless efficacy. We cede them this battle through our own disbelief, ignorance and assumption. As the military maxim goes: Generals always fight the last war, not the current one.

We fight in the Disinformation Age as we fought falsehoods in the information age—and then despair at the results. The times do not suit us. Closed groups live in parallel realities wilfully embracing the contested nature of their truths; the media landscape is a business geared to feed them their opinions, not rein in their ignorance; and it all takes place within platforms designed to reward the worst parts of our nature.

Should we just give up then? Of course not! The stakes are simply too high. Disinformation is tearing the fabric of our society, and so we need to pick up the needle and thread.

To do that—and to labour our metaphor a little further—we will need a sewing pattern.

There has been an overwhelming amount of literature dedicated to understanding the forces that make disinformation so brutally effective. Cognitive behaviouralists, social psychologists, computer scientists, evolutionary biologists, political economists, you name it—much ink has been spilled in the effort to understand and describe what is happening. What you have read so far has been an attempt to synthesise much of it.

Luckily, in doing so a few promising leads have been discovered that offer us hope that we can redesign our approach to regain the upper hand.

Like in all things, prevention is better than cure.

28 / Infection Control

'Science is truth.'
—Dr Anthony Fauci

The handy parallel metaphor of a virus is the literary gift that keeps on giving: many of the approaches we take to prevent the spread of viruses apply equally to disinformation.

The first and most promising lead is that it appears we can vaccinate against it.

Inoculate

If covid lockdowns have taught us anything, it is a thorough working knowledge of exactly how vaccines work. If you're anything like me, you've spent hour upon hour meticulously poring over every article that paved the road to duly authorised covid vaccines.

Here is the crux of it: you administer a weakened or deactivated dose of a virus to someone, and this triggers the body's immune response to produce protective antibodies.

Well, it works exactly the same with disinformation.

In 1961, some psychologists thought they would see if they could stimulate some kind of immunity to persuasion by presenting weakened counter-arguments first.

They gathered a group of people with terrible teeth and asked them if they agreed with the statement 'Everyone should brush his teeth after every meal' (clearly women were exempt from oral hygiene back then). What the psychologists found was that the people given weakened doses against that statement in advance were much more likely to stick to their belief about teeth brushing when it came time to face stronger arguments about it later.

It's all a bit convoluted, but what they discovered is essentially that you can vaccinate someone against being persuaded by something by first stress-testing it with arguments they'll later face. It gives them mental protection.

Decades later, taking this so-called 'inoculation theory' a group of researchers in Cambridge thought they would see if it worked the same against exposure to disinformation. And so they made an online game called *Bad News*.

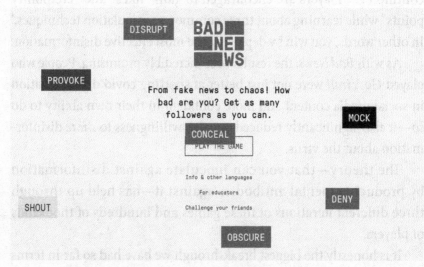

In it, you play the role of a 'disinformation and fake news tycoon'. The goal is to recruit the greatest number of followers by spreading disinformation, using a range of common disinformation techniques (like starting a fake news site, impersonating famous people, and making emotive bot tweets—you would recognise all these from earlier chapters).

In reality, it's not actually a game—it's a vaccine. The researchers tested the first 15,000 people who played it to see if it had created 'mental antibodies' about fake news.

It had.

Across *all demographics*, including age, political ideology and education levels—and even across both those who think a bat costs $1 and those who think it costs $1.05 (our good old intuitive and deliberative thinkers)—people much more reliably downgraded fake news articles after playing the game.

Not to be outdone by their excellent contribution to our body of knowledge against disinformation, once covid struck then the same researchers made another game called *Go Viral!*.

In this game, players are 'slowly lured into an echo chamber where misinformation and outrage-evoking content about COVID-19 are common . . . Players are encouraged to gain "likes" and "credibility points" while learning about three common manipulation techniques.' In other words, you win by deploying the most effective disinformation.

As with *Bad News*, the results were incredibly promising. People who played *Go Viral!* were not just better at spotting covid disinformation in social media content and more confident in their own ability to do so—it also significantly reduced people's willingness to *share* disinformation about the virus.

The theory—that you can inoculate against disinformation by producing mental antibodies against it—has held up through three different iterations of these games and hundreds of thousands of players.

It is honestly the biggest breakthrough we have had so far in terms of concrete things we can do to combat disinformation: exposing people to the topic of disinformation and its techniques *in advance of their exposure to actual disinformation* generates mental antibodies to protect against it.

So if we could only get everyone in the world to play that game then we'd be alright? Not quite. Yes, it would defend us pretty well against the unintentional spread of disinformation, but as we have discovered, that is not always the case. Often disinformation is spread consciously and willingly.

It does teach us some valuable lessons, however.

A screenshot from the *GoViral!* game.

This type of inoculation has been found in other studies too, not just limited to having everyone on Earth sit down and play a video game.

In 2017, another experiment—again a shout out to Australia's Lewandowsky and friends—explained to a group of participants the tobacco industry strategy from the 1960s, where fake experts and fake debates were used to confuse the public about scientific consensus on smoking causing cancer:

> Groups wishing to cast doubt on science often use fake experts to convince the public that the science isn't settled . . . The tobacco industry pioneered this approach through ad campaigns featuring long lists of doctors endorsing smoking. These ads conveyed the impression that the scientific case linking smoking to lung cancer was not settled. However, the cited 'experts' actually consisted of tens of thousands of non-experts.

The participants who heard about the tobacco disinformation campaign became more resistant to subsequent persuasion attempts using the same misleading strategy against climate change science. They recognised it.

In other words, the researchers had successfully inoculated them against disinformation.

It's closely related to another most promising breakthrough: while it is incredibly hard to *de*bunk disinformation once the genie is out of the bottle, if we get to a person first we can much more effectively *pre*bunk.

Prebunk

Shortly before announcing an election to be held later that year, in 2020 New Zealand Prime Minister Jacinda Ardern fronted the cameras to tell the nation she was pledging to conduct a 'positive, factual and robust campaign':

> New Zealanders deserve a factual campaign, one that is free from misinformation ... It is incredibly important for us as the Labour party that New Zealand does not fall prey to what we've seen happen in other jurisdictions.

While to the untrained eye it seemed like any other political announcement, what Ardern was actually doing was practising one of the most effective techniques to combat disinformation: warning people that it is coming, and what to look out for.

Prevention, as with so many other things in life, is indefatigably better than cure.

As we saw with the tobacco experiment, the audience were able to have climate change disinformation *pre*bunked before it needed to be debunked.

If you recall our discussion on psychology, there is a very straightforward reason why: the brain prefers the information that reaches it first. It is a race to be imprinted, so when laziness kicks in the easiest thing for your brain is to believe the truth which has already taken up residence.

There are two main ways we can achieve this: get the factual information about something specific out there first, and also warn people about disinformation in general.

The psychology of disinformation is clear: it is incredibly difficult to rewire a brain that has already accepted disinformation as reality. To defeat disinformation, the absolute most important thing we can do is to get out ahead of it.

Have you ever convinced a sibling that the type of music you listen to is better than the type of music they listen to? Or a friend that your favourite sporting team is better than their team? Good luck with that. It is very difficult to change a mind once it is made up—though there are some tips on how to do so in the next section.

Instead imagine that if *before* your sibling formed their musical tastes, or your friend decided any sporting affiliation, you had gotten in there first: 'Hey, listen to this Midnight Oil album!' or 'Hey, check out this clip of Chicka Ferguson scoring a try on the buzzer with one shoe on in the Canberra Raiders' famous 1989 Winfield Cup grand final victory!'

You might just have a convert for life. The same is true if you can get information in there before disinformation.

Part of this solution is long term. If we embrace an education curriculum that teaches about disinformation techniques and builds media literacy skills, we will be building brains that are much more resistant to subsequent disinformation they encounter in adulthood.

But our needs are much more immediate. We can educate adult minds simply by talking about the general problem of disinformation.

In the short term, prebunking has three main elements:

1. Bringing public attention to efforts to spread disinformation in general (without repeating any actual disinformation).
2. Eroding trust in the individual messengers carrying the disinformation.
3. Getting ahead of the specific disinformation by spreading the truth first.

If at the start of an election campaign a leader speaks openly about the dangers of what to look out for in election disinformation, voters will be less predisposed to buy it when it arrives—exactly as Ardern did in 2020. This is the inoculation theory in effect.

But the most important thing anyone can do is to make sure that the reliable, factual information reaches the audience first. If for example a political party was able to effectively communicate their tax cuts policy first, then outside efforts to convince people they were planning on raising taxes would be less effective. But if instead people had already embraced a narrative that the party was high taxing, or had not yet formed an opinion, brains would be primed to readily believe the tax hike disinformation as reality.

It is much better to have your narrative on the front foot, to win that race for hearts and minds. The fact that prebunking could work successfully on a topic as politically polarised as climate change, as it did in the tobacco experiment, is extremely encouraging.

Similarly, in another study some people were shown a petition of 31,000 scientists saying that there was no evidence of global warming. If participants were first forewarned (e.g. that the signatories were not verified; that they were not climate scientists; that 'the Spice Girls' and 'Charles Darwin' were among them; that 97 per cent of actual climate scientists disagree . . .) they showed strong resistance to the misinformation.

Another study showed that you could even prevent Russian Facebook bots from convincing unsuspecting Germans that Russia didn't poison the Skripals by warning the Germans about the arguments they were about to be exposed to. Another study still repeated the effect against anti-vaxxer conspiracies by showing anti-conspiratorial material first.

Sometimes it won't be possible, and instead disinformation will need to be responded to after the fact. Here, the principle remains the same: rather than repeat the disinformation to negate it, positively tell the opposite factual truth.

This was crucial during the 2020 US election in response to claims that mail-in voting was susceptible to fraud or may lead to arrest or deportation. The best practice response was not to say 'There is no mail-in fraud, this is fake news' or 'ICE agents will not be waiting in the wings to arrest you,' but instead offer the positive frame: 'The mail-in ballot system *is safe.*'

FEATURED

Colorado's mail-in ballot system is safe, Montrose clerk and recorder tells voters

Katharhynn Heidelberg | katharhynnh@montrosepress.com   May 22, 2020 Updated May 22, 2020   💬 0

Hopefully the message sinks in before the alternative—which we saw in great volume after the election results—takes hold. If we carve deep neural imprints in people's minds through frequent repetition that 'climate change is real' then those imprints are very hard to dislodge.

Our political leaders have the greatest responsibility here to be reminding people at every possible opportunity that disinformation is expected, to disclose the techniques the disinformers will use, and what in particular to look out for. This is confounded, obviously, when it is our political leaders who are doing the disinforming.

The more such politicians and their disinformation is normalised the greater this problem becomes. We saw this realised in the US where Trump and his echo chamber were able to move the window of potential political reality to where even violent insurrection was tolerated in many corners, even by those Congresspeople directly in harm's way.

The onus, therefore, is on not normalising the people we know will be spreading disinformation. This is its own form of prebunking.

When I put the Australian context to one leading US expert on alt-right disinformation, and asked her what we could be doing over here to combat disinformation, her response was unequivocal: you know exactly which politicians will embrace extreme disinformation in Australia—so start monitoring them and working with the media to ensure their views aren't normalised or accepted.

Not long after, Craig Kelly—famous adherent of conspiracies, ranging from climate change denial, to covid quack therapies, to the Capitol storming being a 'false flag' Marxist hoax—resigned from the Liberal

Party in the face of probably being disendorsed, and took up residence with that other great disinformer Clive Palmer. George Christensen, fellow crackpot who spent time in Facebook jail for his disinformation activities, announced he wouldn't seek re-election. More important than the loss of their seats will be the loss of their megaphones, which is no foregone conclusion.

These ideologues followed the Trump playbook to the letter, and as a result their engagement on social media dwarfs most of their colleagues.

Remember, an added importance in shutting down these political culprits early is the information out of the US that tracked the source of voting disinformation. It found the major election disinformation began with an 'obvious elite-driven triggering event'. In other words, disinformation comes from the top: someone high-profile like Trump makes the statement first, not a common user.

Just as Fox News viewers were more likely to believe Iraq had weapons of mass destruction at the turn of the century, in our current disinformation age the lies are fed from on high before they ricochet around the internet. Exposing the people who do so in Australia, and removing them from the perch they sing from, can help collectively prebunk us.

Nudge

As I was scrolling through my own Facebook feed today, I saw a post that grabbed my eye:

In 1999 this house was $105k

Today it's $405k

In 1999 a teacher's salary was $65k

Today it's $69k

It struck a chord (it should go without saying it was an American post; basically no house in an Australian city costs so little). I care about rising house prices and low teacher pay, and the economic unfairness in the root causes of both. It said something I wanted to say and thought was important. As I considered sharing it, my brain turned over the pros and cons of doing so: *Would I offend anyone I know? Did it say something about me as a person I wanted other people to see? Would I look smart, or dumb? Would I get 'likes'?*

But never once did I think to myself: *Is this true?*

There is an underlying debate you may have sensed in our discussion about the psychology of disinformation: do we primarily share disinformation because we are politically motivated, or because we are simply lazy?

The answer is a combination of both: our laziness makes us likely to lean in to our subconscious political biases. Had the above post said the opposite—that house prices are down and teachers' pay is up—I would have dismissed it immediately.

But whereas our political conditioning is pretty hard to overcome, the laziness of our brains is a lot easier to bypass: just prompt us to think first.

Close your eyes and picture the last time you shared something on social media—not something original, like a photo of your kids or a boozy selfie with your girlfriends doing duck lips, but something you saw someone else post and felt compelled to share it to your own networks.

I'll go first: the most recent thing like that I shared on social media (I decided against sharing the house price post) was an article I saw someone else post about a twelve-year-old boy in the Arctic tundra who'd died from anthrax poisoning when an ancient reindeer carcass was exposed by the melting permafrost.

It was an emotional decision. Looking at it with ruthless self-analysis, I was prompted by my pre-existing belief that climate change is real and we should be aware of the dire consequences: like long-dormant bacteria and viruses, trapped in the permafrost for centuries, reviving to kill us all thanks to unprecedented melting. I posted it in the middle of a pandemic that I worried could become the norm due to climate change. And I wanted my friends to care.

Things I didn't notice before posting it: how old the article was (more than four years old!); who had shared it originally and why (can't tell you, I have no idea); which website it was on (phew, I am relieved to see it was the BBC, but honestly it could just as well have been 'bobsrandomsciencerumours.com' and I wouldn't have noticed); or any subsequent fact-checking, corrections, or labels applied to it.

I posted it without thinking critically. Did you do the same with your most recent shared post?

We simply don't pay too much attention to potential disinformation when we see things that affirm our worldview, tug our heartstrings or simply say something we want to say but better.

Social media sharing is a reflexive art of self-identity and performative signalling, yet we never feel like that as we post; our brain is rarely in gear. We are experiencing many of the subconscious shortcuts and heuristic tools our brains apply to everything before we act.

In 2020, more of our helpful psychology researchers—where would we be without them!—looked at this in detail in a study about why people were sharing covid disinformation. They gave them fifteen false and fifteen true headlines about covid and presented them in the format of Facebook posts. They then asked if they would share them.

The researchers found evidence 'that people share false claims about COVID-19 partly because they simply fail to think sufficiently about whether or not content is accurate when deciding what to share'.

Then the researchers went one step further: what if they could overcome this?

This time, participants were asked to rate the accuracy of a single headline.

The researchers found that giving this 'simple accuracy reminder' at the beginning of the study more than doubled the level of 'truth discernment' in deciding whether to share the covid disinformation: 'Our results, which mirror those found previously for political fake news, suggest that nudging people to think about accuracy is a simple way to improve choices about what to share on social media.'

This is most relevant for the social media platforms themselves, and is one of the most promising empirical findings to date about preventing the spread of digital disinformation. Facebook and Twitter could replicate this breakthrough with a simple prompt before people submit a post to think about what they are posting. Something like, *'Hi, it looks like you are sharing an article about covid. Have you double-checked the sources to make sure it's true?'*

With this simple nudge, we could reasonably expect the amount of misinformation shared on their platforms to halve.

Of course, the promising powerful tools of inoculation, prebunking and nudging have one enormous shortcoming: they assume the sharing is unintentional.

What do we do when those posting do so with relentless intention to disinform?

Deplatform

Sorry losers and haters, but my I.Q. is one of the highest—and you
all know it! Please don't feel so stupid or insecure, it's not your fault

—@realDonaldTrump

Donald Trump loved Twitter. It allowed him to circumvent the traditional filter the mainstream media would apply to his narratives, with their pesky predilection for fact-checking, even largely foregoing the press briefings every other modern president had duly given.

It was the spigot with which he tapped his cask of disinformation, the intoxicating elixir of liquid bullshit spewing forth all over his thirsty fans.

In the wake of the Capitol riot, Twitter shut the spigot off. The @realDonaldTrump account fell silent on 8 January, and other social media and online platforms including Facebook, Twitch, Snapchat, Spotify and Shopify soon followed suit.

In the week after the platforms turned off Trump's microphone, misinformation about election fraud declined an *unbelievable* 73 per cent across all platforms, dropping from 2.5 million mentions to just 688,000 mentions.

It wasn't just Trump's solitary account. At the same time, the platforms were removing the worst offending accounts who had fomented violence before the Capitol uprising, many of them related to QAnon.

It may seem rudimentary, but it works: removing the worst offending accounts from social media platforms altogether—or 'deplatforming' them, in the lexicon of Silicon Valley (who similarly like to 'deplane' at an airport and 'detrain' at a station).

It has proven to be very effective in slowing the spread of disinformation—with a couple of caveats as we will discuss below.

There are a couple of converging factors that explain why.

First, we have already examined that while it feels like our social media feeds are littered with pervasive disinformation, in reality the vast majority of it can be traced back to a very small handful of accounts who act as 'superspreaders'.

Before the 2020 election, just twenty pro-Trump Twitter accounts—including @realDonaldTrump itself—were the original source of 20 per cent of retweets pushing voting disinformation. Half of all the vaccine disinformation on the most vaccine-hesitant Facebook groups originated from just 111 accounts.

This gives us a great opportunity to disrupt the integrated disinformation ecosystem by ripping out its heart. This may, however, only give us temporary reprieve.

The second factor is that it removes the unfair advantage their megaphone is given by the platform's algorithm. Taking away these accounts' megaphone entirely makes it increasingly difficult for their ideas to be given oxygen. No algorithm can favour content that does not have an airing on the platform to begin with.

We ran this experiment already, when seeing if anyone would read Trump's blog without the advantage of algorithmical amplification: they did not.

Facebook was very hesitant to suppress any form of political speech, including QAnon's. But as soon as the US authorities declared QAnon a domestic terror threat in October 2020, it gave them the cover they needed. The platforms were quick to suppress their content and ban their groups and adherents. The engagement in QAnon content subsequently fell off a cliff.

They needed no such declaration to deplatform an entire political party in New Zealand two days before the 2020 election. Advance NZ, who were vocally opposed to any measures to lock down in response to covid, had their entire Facebook page deleted due to repeat offences of spreading disinformation about the pandemic. Between late June and early October 2020, the Advance NZ page generated more than 5.3 million views—for a new political entrant in a nation of just 5 million people, this was far more activity than the mainstream parties generated.

Here, Facebook used this cover: 'We don't allow anyone to share misinformation on our platforms about Covid-19 that could lead to imminent physical harm.' At around the same time, Facebook also banned a politician from India's ruling Hindu nationalist BJP for hate speech: 'violating our policy prohibiting those that promote or engage in violence and hate'.

Deplatforming subsequently gave rise to another consequence: the insufferable whining of conservatives—who are happy to censor anyone who disagrees with them—that 'free speech' was under assault.

You could hear the whining across the oceans, from Fox News' studios in New York to Canberra's Parliament House. Australian Government ministers lined up to vocally criticise Twitter and Facebook for banning Trump while somehow being unable to find the words to criticise Trump for the seditious acts he got banned for in the first place. Even renowned Trump bestie Boris Johnson still managed to do that.

The furore gave rise to an interesting exposé of some of the concepts we've explored already: the networked infrastructure of how disinformation spreads online and the omnipresence of social media in our lives. Taking away the president's toys was decried in terms of violating his fundamental rights—as if an account on a private company's app is a divinely granted birthright.

What they were really saying is that even though these are private companies, the role of social media in our society has become so pervasive that they constitute the new de facto public square. It logically follows that preventing access equates to a form of exile.

One of the caveats to the success of deplatforming is if it is a piecemeal or temporary exile. There is a tension between effective deplatforming and 'banning', which we have previously shown can be counterproductive when it leads to increased oxygen on other platforms, or on the same platform once the ban expires. Deplatforming works to fire up the narrow base of the firebrand, but it can also send a strong signal to other audiences that the attitudes of those banned are not normalised.

Trump was effectively deplatformed because it happened simultaneously across all mainstream platforms. There was initially no safe harbour for his disinformation that provided the same favourable 'perfect storm' for dissemination.

Another caveat however is that the gains provided by deplatforming may prove to be short-lived if he and others can find that harbour elsewhere. Trump, his pundits and supporters quickly moved to the purpose-built Parler app, or Gab, or Frank, where they hoped they wouldn't be censored or fact-checked. In July 2021, Trump's team launched 'GETTR' to 'fight cancel culture and challenge social media monopolies', which imported users' Twitter followers. Its first trending term was '#VirusOrigin'.

They also retreated underground to encrypted messaging apps like Telegram, where their disinformation could proliferate unencumbered by the interfering invisible hand of transparency.

And Advance NZ? Like a serpent-headed Hydra, once banned they simply started a new page under a slightly different name.

29 / Change Minds

'Nothing is so painful to the human mind as a great
and sudden change.'
—Mary Shelley, *Frankenstein*

When my best friend at high school would have me round for dinner, his mum would train our young minds by picking a deliberately provocative political position and have us all argue vociferously about it.

It was a great exercise, no doubt formative in my subsequent career arguing about politics. She was, in her mind, training us to become creatures of reason—thinking men, skilled in persuasion and logic, and curious enough about the issues around us to inform ourselves and take coherent defensible positions.

But a closer inspection of the recent moral psychology of our minds shows she may have inadvertently been doing the opposite—she may have in fact been training us to become *less* flexible in our thinking and *less* equipped to convince others to agree with us. The better at reasoning and arguing you are the more inflexible your thinking becomes.

Bear with me now as I insult your brain some more—yours, in particular. Not everyone's. Yours. Because I am going to go out on a limb and make an assumption about you: that as you have been reading this miserable journey through disinformation, conspiracy and extreme fruitloopery, you were thinking to yourself, *The people who believe these things are fact-resistant, ignorant and wrong. I am neither. I am open-minded and use facts to reach my conclusions.*

In fact, you are the *worst* type of person, when it comes to changing your mind.

The more intelligent, educated, better at reasoning and better at arguing you are, the *less likely* you are to change your mind when presented with evidence that challenges your prior beliefs.

Remember from our tour of psychology that we fit our facts to our worldview—not the other way around. And you sophists out there are not any less gut-driven—you are simply better at reverse-engineering a rationalisation. You dress it up in facts and coherent arguments.

As a parent in America I would often find myself debating other parents over the safety of guns in the home (no thanks!), but never once would we debate swimming pools. Yet swimming pools kill more children than handguns in America. Would you rather have a swimming pool or a handgun in your home? You are a rational person—so surely you must think swimming pools are a greater threat. Unless of course this is a moral position, not an empirical one.

What if a study came out that found the death penalty was an effective deterrent to violent crime? Your views on the death penalty are likewise rooted in your moral reasoning—your value of a human life, for example, or the state's power to take one. It is not a product of the evidence—that comes later.

It is easy to find evidence for both the death penalty being ineffective and it being effective—your brain will subconsciously select for the former and dismiss the latter, and your ability to reason will be deployed to justify your subconscious choice. If you are better at arguing and reasoning than a person who holds the opposite belief then your beliefs will appear more fact-based and rational.

Your skills make it easier for you to find flaws in any contrary evidence you see, and better at finding reasons to justify your position.

In fact, being interested enough in our society to reach this chapter means that you are the type of person who is much more likely to hold ideological positions, to believe in causes and to support a political party. That in turn makes it more difficult to sway you with facts.

Unfortunately for you, it also makes you more likely to discriminate against people who don't share your positions in any of those causes.

This is particularly relevant, because you are our frontline warrior against disinformation, and the person most likely to want to intervene to address it when you see it—hence you are reading this book.

But it also means you are not the most ideally suited person to be doing it.

The way your instincts tell you to approach a debate—moralising, presenting facts and statistics, appealing to universal standards—are not at all effective in changing another person's mind. In fact they have been shown to only polarise them further.

Would an advertiser sell you a soft drink using the same tactics? 'Only stupid people drink your preferred brand. You must be stupid. Here is a list of the ingredients in ours and the steps in the manufacturing process. Every other soft drink brand also quenches thirst like ours does.'

No. That's a terrible ad. It's right up there with Kendall Jenner preventing police brutality by giving a cop a Pepsi. Instead, good advertisers provide an emotional hook that meets the consumer where they already are and makes them feel good about themselves.

There are, in fact, ways to disagree with someone that are much more effective when it comes to moral reasoning (that's the type of arguments you need to address disinformation, where people have formed strong moral beliefs around things such as vaccinations or the climate).

Let's explore them together. Sorry about all the insults to your brain. I know you'll rationalise your way around them.

How to Disagree with Someone

If you've ever been to South Florida, you won't hold high hopes for rational progress. As voters, they looked at four years of Trump as president and thought to themselves, *I'm convinced, let's have four more!* It swung further towards Trump in 2020 than anywhere else in the country. (I'm being unkind, the panhandle part of Florida is still a deeper hue of red—but come on, Miami, are you serious?!)

You shouldn't expect them to care too much about climate change either, despite suffering the increased batterings of hurricanes and coastal erosion like no one else in the country. They are a wonderful case study in cognitive dissonance, as they wade up to their ankles in climate change effects but still maintain an allegiance to the fact it's not really happening.

Not to be deterred, some researchers thought they'd test a sure-fire way to crack that nut. Sure, they hypothesised, sceptical South Floridians might not be moved by a climate scientist or charts showing unprecedented heating in historical data, but they are sure to care about one thing: their property prices, which would be wiped out by coastal erosion and rising seas.

I know what you're thinking—that this is the bit I now say, 'It worked! Putting your issue in your opponent's frame is the key to breaking through!' Sorry to disappoint. It was a dismal failure.

The people who saw the information about their property values, the ones who saw on a *map* how their *actual house* would be underwater in fifteen years? They cared *less* about climate change after seeing it, were *less* likely to think climate change is happening and were *less* likely to think it would impact their property value.

Another study might reveal the clues why, and it has particular relevance to the crucible of disinformation—which is designed to stoke passionately held markers of our identity.

The backfire effect is triggered when we are asked to compromise a 'sacred value'.

Both Israeli settlers and Palestinian refugees were able to be incentivised to reach a hypothetical peace deal through simple mechanisms like paying them or showing how their people would be better off. The Israelis would cede land; the Palestinians would cede the right of return. But these same incentives had the opposite effect when they were asked to compromise something they viewed as a 'sacred value'. The stronger the incentives, the more opposed they would become. Another study replicated this with Indonesian madrassah students over Sharia law.

As soon as the issue was 'sacred', the brains stopped applying a cost-benefit analysis and started applying moral rules and instincts. And the conclusions were the opposite.

To Republicans in South Florida, their brains consider climate change a 'sacred value', because it is so closely related to their political identities. It triggers not a cost-benefit analysis of their property values, but inflames their moral instincts.

I'll give you $100 (seriously, send me your address) if you can tell me who said this:

> The danger of global warming is as yet unseen, but real enough for us
> to make changes and sacrifices, so that we do not live at the expense
> of future generations ... It may be cheaper or more cost-effective
> to take action now than to wait and find we have to pay much more
> later.

Conservatives weren't always so climate denialist. That was Margaret Thatcher, praising the creation of the Intergovernmental Panel on Climate Change (IPCC) in 1990 (the same IPCC that has become the favourite punching bag of her acolytes). Richard Nixon created many of the environmental laws that Trump subsequently tore up. John Howard introduced the same emissions trading scheme his party then crucified Kevin Rudd and Julia Gillard over. What happened in between? Conservatives adopted climate change denialism as a 'sacred value', integral to their political identity. Now it engages the moral part of their brains, not the rational.

That is the cerebral crucible that disinformation also engages. In fact, it is specifically *aimed* to target sacred issues. The vast majority of fake Russian ads in 2016 mentioned race for this very reason—in the US it was an easy trigger for the moral brain.

But I am not here to make you despondent that the task is too hard. We just need to be aware of the dynamics that sit behind our efforts to change a mind.

Those same Republican-voting minds in America were very effectively convinced, for example, by another experiment. It showed videos to Republicans in Georgia and Missouri, but with unexpected messengers.

One had a retired Air Force General explain climate change poses a national security threat. Another had an evangelical Christian explain the consistency between her faith and caring about climate change. Another still had a former Republican Congressman from South Carolina explain how his conservative values compel action.

Each video increased Republicans' belief in, understanding of, and care about climate change. By several percentage points.

The videos exhibited the first point of today's lesson: putting your message in their *values* frame.

The Values and Identity Frame

Another study told free-market conservatives that it was free enterprise (i.e. companies) that were driving the response to climate change; they *loved* it.

It aligned with their worldview all of a sudden. Although it is incredibly hard to get someone to think something different, it is incredibly easy for them to agree if you present it as fitting something they already think.

I'm also not going to get very far starting a sentence to an American by saying, 'As an Australian . . .' because I am emphasising the differences in our identities. As soon as identity is triggered within us, our brains get a signal for What should this identity think? (remember that urge we have above all else to conform). If on the other hand you said, 'Hey, we're both mums who care about our children . . .' or 'We're both Buddhists . . .' then you will start to get somewhere.

Even better, put yourself in their identity shoes.

Imagine you have been given the task of persuading a QAnon anti-vax conspiracy theorist to get vaccinated. Which of these two approaches below would be more effective?

'I'm a scientist and I know the science. It is clear that vaccines work and are safe.'

or

'As a Q patriot, aren't you concerned Russian spies are trying to weaken our great nation by tricking us into not taking a vaccine that will save our economy?'

Sure, that latter reasoning may be a stretch, but the principle remains the same. If you are talking to a religious person about climate change, the same arguments will not be effective talking to an atheist, and vice versa.

If you are talking to someone about the election fraud disinformation they just shared, it's much better to say to them, 'As a Republican you must be concerned about government overreach into our election process . . .' than to say 'As a Democrat I am concerned about the right of every voter to be heard . . .'

There's a wonderful scene in James Jones' novel *The Thin Red Line* which demonstrates the power of our own framing on others' perceptions. Caught stealing a pistol shortly before landing on Guadalcanal in World War II, our protagonist instead flips the script with his framing by putting the issue in a frame familiar to those he is addressing, thereby triggering their mental 'shortcuts' to make sense of it:

'That's my pistol you're wearin, soldier,' the private said. His voice held injured accusation.

Doll said nothing.

'He saw you take it off the bunk,' the sergeant said. 'So don't try to lie out of it, soldier.'. . .

Doll still did not answer, and forced a slow, cynical grin to spread across his face, while he stared at them, unblinking now. Slowly he undid the belt and passed it over. 'How long you been in the army, mack?' he grinned. 'You oughta know fucking better than to leave your gear layin around like that. You might lose it someday.' He continued to stare, unflinching.

Both men stared back at him, their eyes widening slightly as the new idea, new attitude, replaced their own of righteous indignation. Indifference and cheerful lack of guilt made them appear foolish; and both men suddenly grinned sheepishly, penetrated as they had been by that fiction beloved in all armies of the tough, scrounging, cynical soldier who collects whatever he can get his hands on.

'Well, you better not have such sticky fingers, soldier,' the sergeant said, but it no longer carried much punch. He was trying to stifle his grin.

'Anything layin around out in the open that loose, is fair game to me,' Doll said cheerfully . . . The private himself had a hangdog look, as if he were the one at fault. The sergeant turned to him.

'Hear that, Drake?' he grinned. 'You better take better care of your fucking gear.'

Doll's frame—the 'guilty thieving party'—is so quickly and easily supplanted by a frame his opponents are familiar with—the 'resourceful scrounging soldier'—because it fits their worldview and so their brains are quick to make sense of it.

There's an easy exercise to do before engaging someone who disagrees with you. Try to think of all the arguments that can be made against your position, and then see if you can find any common ground in any of them and your position. That would be a great place to start.

Arguing with a religious person about same-sex marriage? Your opponent might argue about the sanctity of marriage. That would be a great place to start: isn't it better for all children to grow up in the stability of a marriage? Or if you are arguing with a small-government conservative, you could start with an agreement that the government has no right to interfere with private relationships.

Arguing with a fiscal conservative about government-funded healthcare? Your opponent might argue about the costs. That would be a great place for you to start: countries with fully government-funded healthcare systems pay a lot less for their medical care than those with private systems like the US. Wouldn't a fiscal conservative support the option that most drove down costs? No free-market capitalist could support paying $600 for an EpiPen like they do in the US when others pay $38 like we do in Australia.

It's important to remember this is about 'values' and not 'ideology'. In all my years in politics the most frustrating mistake I see people commit every day is to assume there is a political spectrum between left and right that naturally gravitates towards the middle. People see it as a bell curve.

It's why many couldn't understand how an American could vote for Obama in 2012, Bernie Sanders in the 2016 Democratic primary and then Trump in the 2016 election.

In terms of ideology, instead of a bell curve in America only 7 per cent of people are 'middle of the road'. Even fewer are 'somewhat liberal' (progressive) or 'somewhat conservative'. The biggest grouping by far? 63 per cent of Americans don't have a political ideology at all.

The implications of this are profound. Political candidates almost always appeal to ideology to win support, but for two-thirds of the population that doesn't speak to them at all.

Remember from our tour of psychology that most fundamental discovery: identity pre-empts ideology. Instead we need to speak to each other in something we all understand: values.

A 'value' is like the moral foundations we discussed. Should we cheat? Is it okay to hurt the individual to protect the group? Should you obey orders no matter what they are? We all fall somewhere different on the values spectrum, and a range of factors influence them.

But if we want to defeat disinformation then we have to start speaking to people inside the filter bubbles of falsehoods in terms of their own value sets.

Don't Make Stupidity the Price of Admission

We also have to stop talking to them like idiots.

One of the biggest flaws with current approaches to disinformation is that we frame our arguments in a way where for someone to agree we are right then they must first admit they are stupid.

Picture how we correct most disinformation: often it is mocked. We point out just how wrong it is in order to strengthen the scope of our own factual correction. We rush to judge those who buy it as lacking in judgment and reasoning, and often worse—that they are crazy or brainwashed.

We tend to treat disinformation as a zero-sum game—that there is only room for us to be 100 per cent right and the people we are correcting to be 0 per cent right. That's an unhealthy approach to any good faith discussion. We want to make them aware of their own biases while remaining blind to our own.

When we see someone sharing a piece of disinformation, say 'hydroxychloroquine can cure covid', we are quick to dismiss their intentions as disruptive and their understanding as ignorant. We respond accordingly.

But we could equally focus on other elements of what they are saying without ceding any claim to our own factual correctness. The poster no doubt is expressing some fidelity to medical knowledge and practice, as misplaced as the details are. They are also exhibiting care and empathy, in that they seek to share a solution to ease people's suffering. They also might be displaying a healthy scepticism of pharmaceutical company motives—that is by no means irrational.

Likewise if a friend posts questionable material about the covid vaccine. Do we tar them with the same 'anti-vaxxer' brush we paint Pete Evans or Jenny McCarthy with, or anyone who sees a link between the MMR vaccine and autism? Their hesitancy may well be just as rational as your acceptance of the vaccine as safe. We have never approved a vaccine so quickly with no long-term data on its safety, that part is true. Their apprehension is not irrational, either. They may just reach a different rational conclusion to you on the cost-benefit analysis of getting a jab.

Our focus, however, is usually predicating our ability to be 'right' on their being 'wrong'. It therefore makes the stakes too high for them to agree with us, as it necessarily involves such an admission on their part—that they were wrong.

It is much easier to admit we are wrong about some things than others. If I tell you the next bus to arrive at a bus stop will go to the city and it turns out to be heading to the beach, I can easily laugh it off.

But if I was the Transport Commissioner then the whole thing would be a great blow to my ego—as this knowledge is central to my identity.

If my argument is that people who don't recycle are selfish, nobody is going to then put their hand up and say, 'You're right, that's me, I'll change!' I have made the argument for recycling about identity, what it says about a person, and so I have raised the stakes.

Likewise, if I disagree with a friend about police killings of minorities, it is unlikely I will convince them of my opinions if to do so they first have to admit theirs are racist.

We saw this as the Black Lives Matter movement swept a wave of racial reckoning across our societies in the wake of George Floyd's murder by police in Minnesota. For many it was (quite rightly) a welcome overdue recognition of everyday biases and microaggressions that could now be publicly called out. For others, however, they retreated into private disapproval of that trend because they felt the stakes were too high to admit their behaviour had been wrong all these years, lest they be branded a racist. They found refuge with others who felt the same and reinforced their biases instead of taking advantage of a learning opportunity to evolve.

By making the disagreement central to the identity of the person we are disagreeing with, we remove it from the realm of persuasion and into the realm of the personal.

We already touched on this phenomenon when we discussed 'tribe before truth'. The stakes of a barber in South Carolina dissenting from his or her peers on climate change were much higher than the stakes of them going along with the prevailing crowd.

We've also explored at length the degree to which people will fit facts and arguments to their existing worldview. Often when we argue with people we are really asking those we disagree with to abandon their entire worldview. That is simply a bridge too far. Better to try to have someone concede their government did a good job managing covid than to have them admit they were wrong about the whole concept of small government in the first place.

You can have your Liberal-voting mate admit their Labor state premier had the right border policy without them also switching their vote or entire political allegiance.

Sweat the small stuff—get agreement on that. Find consensus where you can instead of leaping straight to the conflict. Be prepared to be as wrong as you want them to be right.

Remember that even the best experts can be wrong, and that it is impossible to have completely value-neutral political positions. If you model the intellectual humility you want the person you disagree with to possess, they are more likely to reflect it back to you.

As we saw in the scene from *The Thin Red Line*, we are wired to reflect the behaviour we are seeing. You can model the mental flexibility needed to draw someone out of their disinformation bubble if you want them to come around to your way of thinking.

This can be as simple as listening—a long-forgotten art in our social media age. Researchers in the US had activists knock on strangers' doors to promote transgender rights. But instead of trying to convince people by 'bitch-slapping them with statistics' (a doorknocker's words, not mine), they just listened for ten minutes. These conversations substantially reduced transphobia, even three months later. They also increased support for a non-discrimination law, even after many had begun the conversations vehemently opposed. Just by *listening* to the other person's perspective, we can inoculate them against prejudice and change their mind on strongly held moral positions.

The more we can approach such a conversation with good faith, the less likely we will be to fall back on the emotive and conforming parts of our brains which come out when we are challenged or threatened.

Don't get me wrong: it's incredibly difficult when addressing dis-information to model open-mindedness to the other person's point of view—especially if that view is that the world is flat or run by one Jewish banking family. But it is important to step behind the disinfor-mation and ask what *value* they are representing, and be open to their point of view. Remember that their view, no matter how batshit-crazy, is genuinely held.

1–1

There's also another key factor in allowing them to change their mind: it will not happen in public.

Traditionally, the pressure to conform to a particular way of thinking came from the elites: a king's decree, a priest's sermon. Immanuel Kant's plea for the Enlightenment in 1784 was: 'Have the courage to use your own understanding.' He also introduced me to the wonderful term 'nonage', which is the period of one's youth or immaturity (from which my wife sometimes wonders if I am still yet to fully emerge):

> Enlightenment is man's emergence from his self-imposed nonage. Nonage is the inability to use one's own understanding without another's guidance . . . *Dare to know!* (*Sapere aude.*) 'Have the courage to use your own understanding' is therefore the motto of the enlightenment.

Now the pressure to conform comes from social media, which makes us more likely to invert this process and reject elite ideas. We take our instruction from the mob (with the glaring exception of where the elites have cottoned on to this and feed the mob, as in Trump's case).

Lest we end the same way as the lemmings, we need to find a circuit breaker for this type of social pressure, to enable people to have the courage to use their own understanding.

The best circuit breaker for the pressure to do something in public is to take it private.

It is obvious why: when correcting disinformation, you are essentially asking people to admit they are wrong, as discussed earlier. Even if we follow the advice of this chapter, it is still far more embarrassing to admit you are wrong in public to your entire peer network than it is in private to a single person.

A group of researchers who were interested in deliberative democracy took small intimate 'enclaves' and found that they were much more likely than large groups with power imbalances to consider a diversity of viewpoints, and were much less polarised at the end of it. Instead of adopting 'groupthink', the more intimate setting allowed them to hash out a much more genuine form of consensus.

Consider the 'virtue signalling' element of social media—the modern form of 'grandstanding'. Often on these platforms we are not saying something to state its intrinsic merits, but instead to signal to others that we have certain values and want to declare them publicly. We want our peers to know we are good people. Our statements become currency for our social status.

What if our peers believe the covid vaccine is harmful? To signal our virtue to these groups, we would then have to define ourselves by posting the latest 'proof' that vaccinated people can shed the virus and cause unsuspecting pregnant women around them to miscarry.

Asking these people to admit publicly that this view is not based in science is asking them to admit to their group they don't share the same virtues: they are not a 'good' person. That is a high barrier to expect them to leap over in the name of your contrary views.

If instead we can take our conversations somewhere away from public view then we decrease the amount of pressure they are under to conform. We blunt the effect of mob rule and groupthink.

What is the online version of having a private conversation? Moving it from a comment thread to a private message just between the two of you, or—heaven forbid—picking up the phone and having an actual conversation.

Once a debate is less visible, it becomes less about self-promotion and more about self-understanding. The imperative at a podium is to be loud and right; the imperative in a conversation is to hear the other person out and see if you can reach common ground.

Think again of the vile way people conduct themselves online, as we discussed in describing the perfect storm of disinformation. They say things they would never say to a person's face.

If you have ever had the thankless job of answering emails to a generic email inbox (like an 'info@' address or 'contact us' page) or moderating a comment thread on a forum, then you will have experienced this phenomenon: if you respond to someone being nasty, nine times out of ten you will get a profuse apology once they realise an actual human being was on the receiving end of their message. 'Sorry, I was having a bad day, I actually agree with you' is the common refrain.

Taking the conversation private also means that it won't be hijacked by others. A comment thread—the terrible new 'marketplace of ideas'—is performative: we get to not only signal our virtue but also increase our standing by knocking down those who disagree with us. It is a hyper-competitive environment not conducive to compromise. 'You know what, that's a great point I hadn't considered before' said no Facebook comment ever.

As one study found, 'Adversaries attribute their ingroup's actions to ingroup love more than outgroup hate and attribute their outgroup's actions to outgroup hate more than ingroup love.' In layman's terms, this means that we all think we are the good guys. We stick up for each other against those out to get us. Israelis in that study said they were driven by love and the Palestinians by hate, and vice versa. American Republicans and Democrats did the same.

The net result of this effect is that conflicts become intractable when you think the other side won't negotiate or compromise. It is an effect that is recreated in the threads of social media. Nobody will change their mind in that contested 'group' environment.

To convince someone who has shared disinformation to change their mind about it, you will not be able to do it in the same place they shared it.

The Fact Sandwich

Okay. I've tried and I've tried to get you to resist the temptation to repeat disinformation when you see it, but I know the temptation will be hard to resist. You will probably do it anyway.

So if you do go down that path, I am going to arm you with the *correct* way to debunk if you absolutely, positively, categorically, definitively, unconditionally and unquestionably *have to* repeat the disinformation you see.

Let's just repeat the threshold you should reach before responding, just so I feel better about this: that the person or people you are talking to have already heard about the misinformation, that it is doing harm, and a debunking would cure that harm. Seeing a post about drinking bleach to cure covid and sharing it on your Facebook page does not meet this threshold: you will be showing the disinformation to people who have not seen it before, and as far as you are aware they are not currently drinking bleach to cure their covid. Correcting this disinformation will have no public health benefit, only amplify the bleach cure.

But let us assume for a moment they *are* drinking bleach. If they survive, there is a correct way to explain the science that concludes bleach is more suited for our bathroom tiles than our stomach lining: you put it in a 'fact sandwich'.

Our friend George Lakoff, in between warning his students not to think of an elephant, is a big proponent of this. Likewise, many of the elements in it have been reinforced by various social psychology experiments over the years.

A number of prominent disinformation and debunking experts then came together—I'm not going to list them all; there were 22 of them from various institutions—to codify the fact sandwich in a bit more detail in an excellent resource, *The Debunking Handbook*. Of course they called it something a bit more dignified than a 'fact sandwich', but seeing as their first instruction was to make it sticky, I am going to go with 'fact sandwich'. You may remember nothing else.

First, state the *fact*.

Then warn them they are hearing a *myth*. Mention it if you have to—only once.

Explain how and why it misleads.

Lastly repeat the *fact* again. Ideally a bunch of times.

In other words, you want to follow a few key principles: if you ever have to repeat a myth you want it surrounded as closely and as often as possible with the facts. Never leave it hanging. You also don't want to leave it hanging without context. Explaining why it is false (maybe by giving the motives of those saying it, e.g. 'these people who spread anti-vaccine lies do so to generate a lot of traffic to their website, where they sell quack remedies and make a ton of money from their disinformation'), and give a factual alternative.

Let's give it a whirl:

FACT: 'The covid vaccines have been through many rounds of rigorous testing.'
WARN: 'You may hear some people suggest all sorts of crazy rumours about the safety of these vaccines.'
EXPLAIN: 'They do this because they sell alternative remedies and want you to buy those instead, so undermine confidence in the vaccines by distorting the data.'
FACT: 'The fact is covid vaccines are safe, thanks to layers of rigorous safety trials.'

You'll note I hardly even needed to repeat the actual disinformation in order to debunk it.

You might recreate this in a conversation with a friend who is sharing disinformation about climate change being a hoax:

FACT: 'We are experiencing unprecedented heating because of human-made climate change.'
WARN: 'A lot of people have a hard time accepting this, so repeat misleading claims like the one you may hear about the Earth always going through warming cycles.'
EXPLAIN: 'They are cherrypicking statistics to make you think this is normal, because they are funded by fossil-fuel companies. It's like saying winter doesn't exist if we get one warmer than average day.'
FACT: 'But the science is clear: this is way beyond normal cycles, this level of heating is unprecedented.'

30 / Win the Story

> 'The best lack all conviction, while the worst
> Are full of passionate intensity.'
> —W.B. Yeats, *The Second Coming*

There's another very simple way to beat disinformation: be less shit at ideas.

The disinformation ideas? Wonderful! Tell me what is not to like about a gripping yarn of heroic internet detectives banding together and collecting breadcrumb-like clues to save vulnerable children they have never met from the grips of Satanic organised crime—other than the fact it is not actually true?

If we want the truth to reign supreme, we need to tell better stories about it.

Our brains love a good story—it's why we tell them and remember them. They are an evolutionary tool we developed in the caves once we realised we'd have more chance of bringing down the woolly mammoth if we worked together. Stories help us make sense of the world.

As we have already seen with the experiment in the 1960s where participants were shown a bunch of random shapes and asked to describe what they saw, the brain will take in information and create elaborate narratives to give it meaning.

The best story wins. That's why viral advertiser Jonah Sachs called his book about this *Winning the Story Wars*. He saw social media as a return to the days of oral tradition—a time when if something needed to stick, then its story had to be pretty darn good to rise above the rest of the noise.

Disinformation does not win *because* it is false. It wins where it tells a more compelling story—regardless of how true or false that story is. That's much easier to do when you can make it up from whole cloth, but it doesn't mean the truth can't be just as entertaining. It's just that we're in the habit of making it boring.

This is another by-product of our fallacy that facts will speak for themselves, and therefore that the most rational explanation will win. It won't on that basis alone. You also have to give facts their own story.

Facts in a Vacuum

Sometimes we lose sight of what is happening with disinformation because we focus on the fact that it is *false*. Its tenuous relationship to reality gives it a leg-up over the truth, but it is by no means material to whether our brains respond to it or not.

Disinformation is about a competition to establish the dominant narrative.

Is covid real? The dominant narrative says yes: it spread from animals in a Chinese wet market to humans, and from there to our increasingly mobile and connected world. The competing narratives (that it was created in a lab; that it is a hoax; that it is a tool of population control; that it exists but is harmless) have become dominant in certain subgroups but not in the mainstream. Our battle with disinformation is to ensure it stays that way.

We have cause for concern that we are losing the battle over the vaccines narrative (not just covid vaccines, where narrative defeat stands in the way of us exiting the crisis, but all vaccines). While the current pro-vaccine narrative is dominant, the anti-vaccine narrative is exploding.

A team of prominent physicists and computational social scientists in the US modelled this in 2020. The results were alarming: by 2030, the anti-vaccination narrative will become the dominant one.

> Although smaller in overall size, anti-vaccination clusters manage to become highly entangled with undecided clusters in the main online network, whereas pro-vaccination clusters are more peripheral.

Our theoretical framework reproduces the recent explosive growth in anti-vaccination views, and predicts that these views will dominate in a decade.

Their analysis found that undecided people were more prone to become dominated by anti-vaccination opinions because of how online networks operate.

Unless pro-vaccination narratives can figure out a way to speak to these people more compellingly, this nightmare vision will be realised. Millions may die.

We need to learn how to place our truth within a bigger picture.

The big lesson Labor took from the 2019 Australian election, which they had been expected to win but didn't, was that they had a suite of policies but no coherent story to pull them all together. Their election review laid it bare: *'Labor did not craft a simple narrative that unified its many policies.'*

It created not just a losing environment, but one that was prone to disinformation.

When the Liberal Party began circulating a disinformation campaign that Labor would introduce a 'death tax' it had all the hallmarks of the type of creature we described in the fake account chapter. Clusters of suspicious accounts took their direction from the political elites to create a new reality for many voters, that Labor would tax their inheritors.

But this policy accusation, false or fair, did not exist in a vacuum.

We have already established that voters are peculiar animals who don't make up their minds rationally, so it logically follows that no one voter actually decided their vote on the sole proof point of Labor's fictional death tax. What the disinformation did, however, was to feed another compelling narrative which was much more likely to actually determine voting behaviour: that Labor would *tax you to death*.

It was a narrative the Liberal Party pursued relentlessly: 'the Bill you can't afford' who had a raft of new taxes to fund his big-spending ways. A real policy (regarding franking credits) became a 'retiree tax' within this story. A 'death tax' seemed plausible in this context.

To effectively rebut it, Labor didn't need a comprehensive description of their inheritance tax policy to negate the accusations—it needed a better narrative than the 'we are high taxing and high spending' one their opponents were successfully prosecuting. That is a narrative that the 'death tax' disinformation feeds.

If a voter had already, on the other hand, formed the opinion that Labor stood up for low-income earners by reducing their taxes and taxing the rich instead, that mind is much more impervious to 'worldview incongruent information' (i.e. things they hear that don't fit the view they've already formed). It's inoculated against specific disinformation that aims to dislodge existing opinions implanted in their brain. We know how difficult that is to do.

So where was Labor's 'better story'?

The political party fell into a similar trap in the same election by being silent on climate change for the first few weeks of the campaign. In a vacuum, this allowed the Liberal Party to get to voters' brains first and define the frame on their terms—the cost of Labor's plan to reduce emissions—rather than on Labor's terms of the moral imperative to act. Once the narrative was lost it proved impossible for Labor to regain. A defensive scramble to explain away a scary price tag only reinforced the opponent's winning narrative (cost) instead of supplanting it with a stronger one (opportunity). The cost story won.

A focus on facts when disinformation occurred in that election clouded the real problem: the underlying story the disinformation was created to validate. Facts don't occur in a vacuum, though we often treat them as if they do.

We fight vaccine disinformation in the same way. The factual contention is obvious: does the MMR vaccine cause autism or not, for example. We answer it with peer-reviewed scientific studies that are thick with data. But that is not the *story* the anti-vaxxers are telling. Their story is much grander: that we cannot trust the vested interests of pharmaceutical companies and their similarly vested government regulators who care only about propping up the medico-industrial complex they profit from.

And they're not wrong—the core of that story is true (though their logical extension that therefore vaccines harm us is not). But we don't fight vaccine disinformation on that playing field; we don't mount a defence of our medical research and regulation by telling a compelling story to outflank the alternative, like how there is no great profit in a drug you only administer once. We don't create a dominant narrative about miraculous scientific breakthrough and altruistic motives. We treat factual points along the way of that story as if they exist in a vacuum. We treat the hit but leave the wound gaping.

The best story wins.

Fastest Finger First

You can also give your story a massive boost if it gets to people's brains first. The brain favours the familiar and the repeated.

We discovered the 'continued influence effect' already, and all got a little depressed to find out that even when a piece of misinformation is corrected it still leaves an impression in our brains (like avoiding that restaurant at which you know I didn't actually get food poisoning).

There are some antidotes, thankfully. For example, researchers found they were able to mitigate this effect by providing an 'alternative account' at the same time. That's when you can basically shove an explanation in the gap left behind when you remove a falsehood (another reason why it is key to have a better story). In our vaccine example above, having an alternate explanation ready that pharmaceutical companies often make no profit from vaccines helps fill the imprint left behind if you successfully convinced someone they were wrong about profit motives.

But as we know, convincing someone they are wrong is a massive uphill battle.

By far the easiest way to supplant a false reality is to make sure you beat it to the brain, before that false reality is firmly implanted. We often only have a brief window to act. We get this opportunity when a new issue arises, like the covid pandemic.

By acting promptly, preferably before there is any disinformation circulating around an issue, we can reach people first—remember that once out of the gate, disinformation travels six times faster than truth, so you have to have your information skates on. By acting compellingly we can then help that information get to as many brains as possible (that's where the strength of your story will help).

It didn't take long for covid disinformation to rear its ugly head (remember the nature of these events made them perfectly ripe for alternate realities to spring up quickly). Any delay in spreading the truth-based narratives cedes the advantage to those with another story to tell.

In 2020 one political experiment in the US confirmed this assertion that disinformation is best beaten by acting fast with a better story, while brains are still forming their opinions.

A Democrat-aligned group named Acronym turned their digital war room's attention to hitting Trump on his pandemic response as early as February (remember those earliest days of the pandemic? 'It's one person coming in from China. It's going to be just fine,' in Trump's words). They faced a strong backlash from the establishment Democrats who wanted to see how it played out with voters first, which is typical of mainstream political campaigns whose instincts tell them to be led by voters' opinions rather than trying to influence them.

In hindsight that narrative of Trump's failed response seems self-evident, but it certainly wasn't in February 2020.

By Acronym's measurement, that early pivot moved swing voters 3.4 percentage points away from Trump by creating that narrative without waiting for Trump to create his own and then the Democrats to push back against it, or for voters to form their own opinions. This was the crucial 'persuasion window'.

Acronym founder Tara McGowan told *Marie Claire* magazine at the time:

> We got a ton of heat from Democrats who thought it was insensitive,
> but it turned out to be the most strategic, effective pivot we've made.
> We moved persuasion voters away from Trump in those critical
> weeks we call the 'persuasion window,' before the narrative was

baked about his response to the pandemic. Within weeks, every Democratic super PAC and campaign started to hit the president, after criticizing our strategy to do so.

Getting to those voters' minds *first* was crucial for what was to come subsequently: a flood of election disinformation targeting the very same individual voters (everyone in US politics has a detailed voter file identifying persuadable voters, and they target them relentlessly). Knowing what we now know about the psychology of disinformation, 'waiting to see' what people think about something can be a fatal mistake. It merely opens the door for disinformation to get their first, from which it will be incredibly difficult to dislodge. There's a race to the brain between the facts and the disinformation, and usually it's a case of winner takes all. Once one gets there, it shuts the door behind.

In fact, once disinformation has reached the brain then you can't retract it even if you yourself created it. That's how fast and hard it takes hold as reality. Once the toothpaste is out of the tube, good luck trying to squeeze it all back in.

In 2007, when UK artist Dan Baines thought he'd have a lark on April Fools' Day, he posted prank photos of a mummified fairy corpse that he'd made. Once he came clean, he then couldn't convince the people who saw it that it was a hoax. To them, his denials and admissions were part of the cover-up rather than an explanation of how they had been duped by his fabrication. 'I've had all sorts of comments including people who say they've seen exactly the same things and one person told me to return the remains to the grave site as soon as possible or face the consequences,' he told the BBC.

Once disinformation takes root it is incredibly difficult to dislodge—even if it is clearly an elaborate fairy tale.

How Curious

It is incredibly important *how* we tell our stories.

One of the key features of the evolving news model we studied earlier was 'clickbait' headlines. The need to drive traffic to news sites led to an annoying way of packaging articles with headlines designed to achieve one thing: pique your curiosity.

Subeditors were only following the lead of our brains' characteristics. We engage a different part of our mental map when we are motivated to find the answer to a question, rather than when we are simply given it.

But when we fight disinformation we ignore this concept completely in order to 'tell' the truth rather than inspire a mind to seek it themselves. That is a big mistake.

When we present our stories in the usual adversarial format from one point of view, as partisan content, people will perform mental gymnastics in order to protect their own group and form even stronger opinions contrary to the evidence provided. When we allow people to explore and get to the answers themselves, on the other hand, like the transphobic people whose doors were knocked on for a chat in the example we discussed earlier, their journey takes them to a different destination altogether.

We know that is the big challenge in defeating disinformation, yet we still do the former all the time.

If only there was a way to present our factual information in a way that prevented people from retreating into their pre-existing beliefs and bubbles when we do it. Good news: there is.

When you engage a person's scientific *curiosity*, their politically motivated reasoning is negated.

Dan Kahan, the Yale psychologist we already met when discussing the motivations to conform to our groups, managed to replicate this effect in a study.

He found that regardless of political outlooks, those who displayed higher curiosity were able to offset their politically motivated reasoning:

> Curiosity promotes open-minded engagement with information that is contrary to individuals' political predispositions.

In his experiments he hypothesised that people find some intrinsic pleasure in awe and surprise, and some of us more so than others. 'For that reason, subjects higher in science curiosity might be expected to show a preference for the *surprising* story—the one conveying unexpected evidence—*regardless of its relationship to their predispositions.*' (His emphasis.)

We can hope that all our subjects we need to convince about disinformation are particularly scientifically curious. But we can also use this insight to frame our facts in a way that stimulates whatever curiosity they do have, regardless of their propensity to watch the Discovery Channel or follow Dr Karl.

This can be a backdoor to disarming the 'worldview backfire effect' by presenting the same information in a different way to prevent the brain retreating into its old familiar habits.

When a brain sees these two headlines, its response is radically different in each instance:

> 'Report: 200 years of scientific data on vaccinations shows widespread efficacy.'
> 'Researchers asked what happens when you mess with our immune systems for 200 years. You won't believe what they discovered.'

In the first headline, where a statement is given, we employ our mental shortcuts to file this away where we think it is most appropriate. If we already believe in vaccinations, we see it as affirming our worldview and we reinforce our confidence in vaccines by filing it under 'true'. If we don't then we dismiss it (as biased, inaccurate or misreported) and file it under 'false propaganda'.

When we see the second headline, however, we don't automatically come to any conclusion. We want to know the answer, and we welcome being surprised by it.

When we read the information it links to then we have bypassed to some degree our mental defences that want to take the shortest path to what we already know: we are prepared to devote some mental energy to engaging with it, and are open to the possibility of being convinced of something new. We lower the drawbridge to let facts in.

If the answer is framed correctly, we may even find something we embrace because we want to appear smart to our peers by possessing new or contrary knowledge.

Most likely related to this same process, another study showed how we could bypass the backfire effect on people who were opposed to welfare spending by engaging their brains in another non-confrontational way.

When asked first to *guess* the level of welfare, and then what level they think it should be, people responded positively to being corrected and finding out they were wrong (and that welfare was much lower than they themselves had said it should be—some thought it was 90 per cent of the US budget at the time; it was 1 per cent). They did their own work of realising welfare should be higher rather than having someone else convince them, because their minds had been opened to the fact they were about to learn something.

They had received the correction and internalised the overcoming of their own ignorance. Instead of telling someone a fact, if you ask the right questions to lead them to their own conclusions then you bypass the parts of the brain that defend their own worldview.

Echo the Echo Chamber

Just as the two headlines above triggered different mental responses, it is also key *who* the story is coming from.

Our politically motivated defences are triggered when we see a partisan voice telling us something, as we are predisposed to either reject or accept the information depending on who the messenger is.

This is a hard reality for political parties and candidates; it's why they find proxies to advocate on their behalf. Political figures are great messengers for their supporters (people use it as a mental shortcut to automatically believe the information), but predictably terrible for convincing anyone who doesn't already agree.

Commercial advertisers have long known this, and so often recruit someone you look up to, usually a sports or movie star, to tell you to buy their product. The same works for our opinions on social media, which often come from someone we care about or whose opinion we care about. That's a big reason our entire information ecosystem has been upended: social media has enabled peer-to-peer marketing of ideas but forgot to include the bit where they go through a fact-checking filter first.

On top of that, studies consistently show that social media posts from peers have more influence over people than expert opinion or organisations.

The right-wing echo chamber in the US uses this to devastating effect to spread disinformation. As we have described it contains three arms: high-profile individuals with large megaphones, fake news websites, and large groups (public and private) of connected supporters who can easily share content between them.

Going up against this disinformation network without a similar constellation is fighting a losing battle. I am not advocating we defeat disinformation by adopting it—but sometimes you need to fight fire with fire.

There are elements of the success of disinformation wildfires that we need to replicate if we are ever to hope to match them. The doomsday scenario mentioned earlier, for example, where anti-vaccination becomes the dominant narrative by 2030, is realised because of how the echo chamber ecosystem will persuade undecided audiences. It is a competition for their attention, and to cede the echo chamber to the disinformation is to fight with one hand tied behind our backs. Might as well call it quits already.

Our fact-based narratives need to be seeded and spread like wildfire too, and to do that we can learn from our disinforming opponents.

We won't have the high-profile individuals with large megaphones anytime soon, as the media landscape is too far tilted towards the disinformation-spreading shock jocks who win the ratings war both on- and offline.

We already have the media properties to house fact-based stories (that's our mainstream media, for as long as it exists in its current form), so that isn't the problem.

Where we lack is the large group of connected supporters of the truth to be superspreaders of the real story, in the same way there are 'clusters' of groups who do the same vociferously for fake news and the narratives it sells. They have built a dominant digital disinformation infrastructure (say that ten times quickly).

The same study that found anti-vaxxers will overtake us in a decade mapped the pro-vaccination infrastructure and found it both weakly networked and on the periphery to the main online conversations.

The answer lies in creating the organic ecosystem to enable factual narratives to thrive. It can be done through organic grassroots groups that can align and share content.

It reminds me of something I painfully discovered while working on gun control in the US (the most thoroughly depressing exercise of my professional life). It's called the 'intensity gap'.

If the slaughter of five-year-olds is not going to prompt you to do something about gun control then nothing will—and in America it didn't. In 2013, in the aftermath of the mass murder of kindergartners and their teachers at Sandy Hook Elementary, the US Congress failed to pass a bill closing a loophole allowing people to buy guns without a background check.

The overwhelming majority of Americans—over 90 per cent in most polls (hell, even 83 per cent of gun owners and 85 per cent of Trump voters too)—support background checks for gun sales. But the 10 per cent who don't support this *care way more about it* than the 90 per cent who do. This is the 'intensity gap' which prevents any action.

In the same way, even though the vast majority of people on the internet aren't wild conspiracy theorists, anti-vaxxers or political meddlers, the relative few who are generally are *way more motivated* to spread their lies than you are to spread your truth. So they win.

They know what they are doing. 'Let's get this trending,' they say on Twitter, while on Facebook they form innocuously named groups to avoid detection, and once they are kicked off that platform they create Telegram groups to give their ideas a secret express lane to the world.

Anti-vaxxers are on a crusade to spread their disinformation while you are happy to sit quietly knowing that science is on your side. QAnon followers are busy building secret networks with the express purpose of spreading lies while you shake your head in disbelief but take no such pains to spread the truth. It's not a level playing field when disinformation fights like hell and reality is quietly taken for granted.

We need to conspire to share truth with the same organised fervour. You need to see yourself as a combatant in a battle over reality, not a neutral observer, if we are to defeat disinformation.

In the next chapter, we will look at how to do that.

Cheat Sheet: Defeating Disinformation

WHAT NOT TO DO

Effect	Description	Example
Don't negate disinformation	Our brains skip the 'no' or 'don't' or 'I am not' and only hear the rest of the sentence which you are trying to refute.	I wasn't worried about the covid vaccine making me grow horns until you just told me 'the covid vaccine will not make you grow horns'.
Don't myth-bust disinformation	Factual corrections are at best ineffective but likely do more harm than good. Repeating the myth makes it stickier and more familiar.	I see a myth-busting article about the covid vaccine not causing horn-growing, and a week later my brain can only recall the link between 'covid vaccine' and 'horn-growing'.
Don't label disinformation	Putting a label on a social media post is a big flag that raises its prominence, provides a badge of honour, and makes people worse at judging other posts.	You are scrolling through your Facebook feed and something catches your eye: the post that has a big label on it. Minutes later you're drinking bleach to cure covid.
Don't amplify disinformation	The 'Streisand Effect': trying to suppress something can bring more attention to it. Sharing, commenting on or condemning disinformation gives it more prominence and a leg-up in the social media algorithm.	The government bans Milo Yiannopoulos from entering Australia, and the media coverage about what ideas were barred from entry spreads them much further than the university forum he was going to speak at.

WHAT TO DO

Effect	Description	Example
Inoculate	By being exposed to weakened doses of disinformation techniques first, people develop resistant antibodies.	Playing a game about disinformation then makes you less likely to share disinformation when you see it in the real world.
Prebunk	Warning people about the dangers of disinformation, what to look out for, and who will do it, blunts the impact of subsequent disinformation. Getting the truth to them first is the best defence against any lie.	If I outbid Clive Palmer and put an ad on the front page saying '*Clive Palmer spreads misinformation*', then his ad which I had relegated to page 2 would be much less effective with those who saw mine first.
Nudge	Most disinformation is shared because we are lazy, not evil. Prompting someone to think about accuracy before they post can halve the number of shares of disinformation.	I watch another great episode of *Bachelor In Paradise* and want to rave about it on Twitter. My wife reminds me I'm supposed to be a highbrow author and should probably think what that says about me first.
Deplatform	Removing the worst or most high-profile accounts from the social media platforms significantly suppresses the spread of disinformation. It may however just move it deeper underground.	Pete Evans being banned from Facebook and Instagram proves the only thing more insufferable than hearing from Pete Evans is hearing from people who can no longer hear from Pete Evans.
Argue in their value frame	As soon as an argument triggers our identity or values, the brain behaves differently. We can only convince people if we frame our arguments in ways that appeal to their values, not ours.	I will get much further telling those Pete Evans fans 'We're both *My Kitchen Rules* fans, and it will be cancelled for another season unless we get vaccinated' than I would sending them a WHO factsheet.

Effect	Description	Example
Lower the stakes	We often address disinformation by making the other person have to admit they are stupid in order to admit they are wrong. It's better to find common ground and model open-mindedness.	I ask someone to tell me more about their reasons for not getting vaccinated and see if I agree with part of any of them. Emphasise those ('*I guess you're right, I* should *do my research.*')
Take the chat private	The social pressure to conform means we have to take the conversation private if we want someone to admit they are wrong.	When my crazy uncle posts a hilarious meme that global warming is a hoax because it's cold today, I send him a private message to chat weather patterns, rather than comment on his post.
The Fact Sandwich	If you absolutely have to ever state a myth to debunk it (but please don't), you need to surround it by facts and an explanation of why it is wrong. State the facts as many times as you can.	I can no longer ignore your ignorance: 'Cast iron is the best non-stick cooking surface. You may hear other crazy ideas, like Teflon being better. But that is PR spin, after a month you need a new pan. Cast iron is non-stick forever. It is the best cooking surface.'
Tell a better story	Disinformation doesn't win *because* it is false, but because it's usually a better yarn. Facts don't speak for themselves, they need to be packaged in a more compelling story than the myths they are trying to dislodge.	Winning over voters in coal mining regions by telling a great story about how clean energy will improve their lives and their children will thrive, as opposed to giving them a set of facts about emissions.
Get to the brain first	Unlike Scott Morrison's vaccine rollout, this *is* a race. If you can get to a person's brain before a falsehood, the truth takes up residency and is hard to dislodge.	Concerned about Clive Palmer's forthcoming vampire accusations, the head of ASIC runs front-page ads saying '*I sleep at night and love garlic*' before anyone sees disinformation to the contrary.

Effect	Description	Example
Pique curiosity	By engaging people's curiosity, you bypass many of the brain's defences to fact-resistance. They will be more open to changing their opinion.	I ask my flat-Earth friend: *'I bet you'll never guess what the first astronauts said about the Earth when they saw it from space'* instead of flat out telling him the Earth is round.
Echo chamber	Those spreading disinformation are way more motivated and organised than those who believe in facts. Match the intensity gap by sharing reality with the same organised fervour.	Instead of waiting to respond to your vaccine-hesitant friends, you conspire with a group of peers to all share the same article about vaccine safety, and to boost each other's posts like our lives depend on it. Because they do.

31 / What to Do When You See Fake News?

> 'What do I do when my friend shares an anti-vaccination conspiracy on Facebook?'
> —My mum, and no doubt thousands more mums around the country

Do you cough or sneeze into your elbow?

Good, then we have already overcome the first hurdle: you are aware that you yourself can be a viral vector. You are a good infectious citizen.

In the same way you are conscious of being a potential viral vector for covid, so too are you a vector for disinformation. These false narratives spread via the piggybacking of social proof and social capital—things you possess in your social networks, real or online.

And so in the same way you are conscious that you are a vector for viruses and so will wash your hands, wear a mask or cough into your elbow, so too must you practise good social media hygiene to help avoid becoming a vector for this disinfodemic.

It's not all up to you—our final chapter will explore broader solutions beyond the role of the individual. By teaching good disinformation hygiene, each of us has a big role to play.

You are on the front lines. What takes place in your social media feed could be the germ of a damaging false narrative that may end up taking the lives of your neighbours, family and friends. Knowing how to respond when you see it could help prevent that from happening.

At the very least, it might make Christmas lunch with your relos more tolerable.

There is such a great appetite to do something. When they asked their readers in 2020 what the news site *Mother Jones* could do for them, the top answer, from a third of all respondents, was to 'debunk misinformation that threatens people or instils fear'.

But the answer to this key question remains open: how to do this without inadvertently causing more harm? Responding to disinformation is incredibly fraught, and so should be approached with great caution.

If responding had a cheat sheet then the below would be it. But it is issued with the large caveat that each and every encounter with disinformation is different, and so you must use your best judgment how you apply all the wonderful precepts you've learned along the way. Just remember that 'your best judgment' is often clouded by harmful mental shortcuts. Be conscious of not applying 'your laziest judgment' inadvertently.

STEP 1: GET YOUR FRIENDS TO BUY THIS BOOK

Okay, the real Step 1 is to inform yourself to understand our disinfodemic, but congrats—you've made it this far, so we can check that off! Now make sure everyone else you know reads it too.

Let's start again:

Step 1: Identify

It goes without saying that the first step is to identify something as false. This is sometimes easier said than done, especially as the disinformation methods become more sophisticated. A good rule of thumb is that if a story grabs your attention then you need to take a closer look and engage the rational part of your brain to trump the emotional part being triggered.

There will be all sorts of clues, like whether you have heard of the website it links to and whether the date on the content is recent. Often disinformation uses content that is absolutely true, but the context makes it disinform. Much of the worst racist disinformation in the US election for example used real stories but from years earlier.

It also may be manufactured context too, even though you are just reading other people's opinions—this is what we see with inauthentic accounts trying to make it appear the whole country feels strongly about something. Pay attention to who is posting and where an opinion began its life.

This also applies to yourself—are you the one doing the posting? Nudge yourself first to think about the accuracy of what you are posting, even if you excitedly agree with it.

Step 2: Decide

As we already outlined in 'what not to do' there is an overwhelming consideration for you to take into account when you see disinformation in your own thread:

Will I bring more attention to this by responding to it?

We are collectively confounded by the paradox at the heart of responding to disinformation: usually the correct response to disinformation is to do nothing.

Even something as innocuous as a comment to 'correct' disinformation when you see it can have the opposite effect, as we discussed earlier:

First, your comment may make the original post visible to all your friends all of a sudden, depending on your privacy settings.

Second, your friends and followers may receive a notification you have commented on it which draws their attention to it.

Third, it may elevate it in people's newsfeeds because your recent comment has made an older post more timely.

Fourth, it may elevate it in the original post's network because the algorithm will see more comments as an indicator this is a great post everyone should see.

So the first thing you need to do when you see disinformation is ask yourself if you will do more harm than good if you do anything at all.

Remember how the journalists decide on whether to report on disinformation: do people already know about it; is it doing harm; will your talking about it cause more harm?

Step 3: Report

Before you do anything else once deciding something is fake news, report it to the platform you saw it on.

This won't elevate its importance in the algorithm at all, won't bring any new oxygenation or amplification to the post and hopefully will have the opposite effect: suppress its spread.

There is real debate as to how efficiently the platforms respond to this type of feedback, but it is an easy step for you to take. At least one study has found that reporting disinformation has some positive effect: 'We find [it] may indeed have an effect on reducing false news sharing intentions by diminishing the credibility of misleading information.' It's difficult to tell: Facebook doesn't provide the data themselves.

It's also easy to manipulate: in Syria there's a pro-Assad 'Electronic Army' unit who report every Syrian opposition group's posts until Facebook flags them as false.

Every social media platform has a mechanism for reporting disinformation. On Facebook at time of writing, for example, you click on the three dots on the top right of a post, click 'Find support or report post' and then click 'False Information' to leave it in the lap of the Facebook algorithm gods.

Step 4: Respond

Okay, so you've met your threshold for responding directly (once again, are you *sure* you really want to?). Now it is a question of how.

This is where you will use your good old friend the Fact Sandwich. As a reminder, it is:

FACT: state the truth first.
WARN: people they are about to hear something false. Say it once and briefly.

EXPLAIN: how what they just heard misleads and why.

FACT: state the truth again. Over and over again.

Remember all the conversation resources from Chapter 29 about the tenor of this conversation. There are effective ways to talk to someone when you disagree with them, and then there are ways that will only reinforce the disagreement. Put it in their values frame.

You also don't want to be doing this in the comment thread on the original post. A good idea if you see a certain friend who has posted disinformation is to share a new post with a factual article and tag them in it, rather than share a correcting article in their comment thread. This will achieve the goal of bringing it to their attention without amplifying their original disinformation.

If you know the person, then move straight to Step 5.

Step 5: Engage privately

You saw something on social media, should you respond in kind? No.

As we outlined in the last chapter, it is a hell of a lot easier to admit you were wrong in private than it is to the entire world. You need to decrease the visibility of your response.

There are many ways you can do this, and it will depend on the situation and the relationship you have with the person posting disinformation. I know the temptation when seeing disinformation is often to hit delete and hit defriend, but then they are lost to us forever. If every truth-teller heads for the exits, then all that will be left behind are the disinformers and the disinformed: all now in furious crackpot agreement. If you can stomach it, and if you know them personally, it is much better to write to them than to write them off.

If they are a friend or family member, ideally you could pick up the phone or failing that email them directly (a face-to-face conversation is always more amenable to common ground than any other form of communication).

If not, it should still be possible to engage them privately through the platform you saw the disinformation on. On Facebook, for example, you can send them a private message. On Twitter, a direct message. If in a group text or WhatsApp or Telegram group, send them an individual message.

You are the best-placed person to respond to your friends—we know this from the research. As one academic paper found, people are much more likely to accept a correction if it's between people who follow each other: 'Social connections between fact-checkers and rumor spreaders encourage the latter to prefer sharing accurate information, making them more likely to accept corrections.'

This is really the most important step in this entire process. It's the only way radicalisation experts have been able to consistently deradicalise people in the real world: through one-on-one conversations with their peers. Keep in mind that it usually won't happen quickly.

In fact, if you take nothing else away from this entire tome, let it be this: *Don't engage with disinformation publicly—take the person aside and have a private chat.*

Step 6: Tell the truth

Now this one may seem obvious enough, but it's a fundamental step in this process.

We need to tell our true stories in order to supplant the false ones.

Remember the 'continued influence effect'? That's where the falsehood remains even after a person who believed it thinks it has been corrected. If you can provide a factual alternative at the same time as the debunking (i.e. telling the truth when also pointing out the lie) then the brain is more likely to accept it as it supplants the lie, and also more likely to recall it down the track.

More so, researchers even found that warning about the continued influence effect itself reduces its effect and instead increases the likelihood it can be replaced by the factual alternative.

If you are a peer of the person you are correcting, you yourself will be a trusted source. If not, it will be most effective to tell the truth using a source they trust (e.g. the Pope's statements about disinformation have been found to be effective in changing Catholics' perceptions. Side note: in a great messaging frame, he called Eve's snake temptation in the Garden of Eden 'the first fake news'.)

Before you even see any disinformation, there's something crucial you can do to defeat it: put reality out there first, and in a compelling way. If your facts reach a person before any fake news does, we've won half the battle.

Share copious amounts of truth, always: spruik the wondrous benefits and scientific marvel of vaccines; warn of the climate change–related disasters we see around us; tell stories that build faith in our institutions that have taken such a battering in our new disinformation ecosystem. And remember: make sure none of these stories contain the myths you are trying to pre-empt.

If you have a better story, one that also happens to be grounded in truth, you'll build a fortress against any disinformation that subsequently tries to attack.

You should also support those whose job it is to tell the truth. Pay for a subscription of a dying newspaper and share their content. Support journalists who go out on their own. Donate to organisations who stand up for journalists and public media. And don't support those outlets whose business model is built on spreading emotive disinformation.

Step 7: Talk about disinformation

Don't just tell your truth loudly from the battlements of our new information fortress: sing a song of disinformation itself.

This is an incredibly important feature of 'prebunking'. We know from the research that the more we can warn about the dangers of disinformation (without repeating the specific disinformation itself), and explain how it works, the more immune people are to its effects.

The more you can encourage a person to engage with the *idea* that disinformation is out there, and to have them think about how they may encounter it, the more resistant they will be when they see it. This will wake your peers up to what is often unintentional—simply by them thinking about what they are posting and sharing, we can expect misinformation to as much as halve.

So really, I wasn't joking: tell them to buy this book.

If you go to the book's website www.FactsAndOtherLies.com you will find a list of great articles and resources to share about disinformation itself.

Now, if all of the above is a bit too much to remember on the fly, then you should just remember to:

ERR on the side of caution.

There, we couldn't discuss this much psychology in one book without then giving our brains a trick to remember what to do: a mnemonic!

When you are on the go, relying on all those lazy brain patterns we all like to deploy (especially when on social media, which we generally do in 'downtime' for a break from arduous thinking), just remember the three key features: *ERR on the side of caution.*

EVALUATE: Am I seeing/posting disinformation?
REPORT: Flag the disinformation for the platform.
RESPOND: If you have to, in private.

I know you feel compelled to respond when you see something harmful in your feed—it's a very natural reaction. And a noble one! By following the above tenets you can scratch that itch without inadvertently doing more harm than good. Remember, you are influential to your peers and the first line of defence against disinformation. You have the truth on your side.

Part Six
A Shared Reality

32 / Towards a Healthy Ecosystem

> 'What is the cost of lies? It's not that we will mistake them for the truth. The real danger is that, if we hear enough lies, then we no longer recognize the truth at all.'
>
> —Professor Valery Legasov in *Chernobyl*

I want to finish by highlighting some of the ways we can begin to re-establish a common grounding in a healthy information ecosystem, more broadly than addressing specific disinformation. This is not a case of rediscovering our old habits that were fit for the information age—this is a case of learning how to better navigate a new era currently dominated by an information disorder.

We need to first accept we are living in a new epoch and then learn to thrive in it.

We've outlined the best practice ways to defeat disinformation itself, but there are also things we can do to rework our disinformation age into a healthier ecosystem. Here, our role is not just in focusing on our own behaviours but to urge others—chiefly our institutions—to pick up the mantle of reclaiming our collective reality.

None of these things alone will cure our disinfodemic in its entirety, but all are necessary elements of its remedy.

Individuals

First, the navigators.

Focusing on the actions—or rather, lack of understanding—of the individual can sometimes veer into the disinformation equivalent of victim-blaming. Given the nature of our brains' wiring that's been forged over tens of thousands of years of evolutionary reward, there is no amount of coaching of the individual that can cure the neural realities of our thinking processes.

Likewise, any susceptibility to disinformation is hardwired, and some of us will be naturally more resistant than others. In fact, psychologists can even map a trait in the brain they call 'bullshit receptivity'. But to focus on this again obscures the fact that disinformation campaigns are deliberate efforts to take advantage of our human nature. Thinking we can therefore tweak or suppress our human nature to defeat disinformation is a fool's errand.

Still, there is a place for building resilience in our brains in the same way we can train any muscle to peak performance.

Teaching digital media literacy skills is one such intervention.

Digital media literacy skills are what allow us to navigate this new information ecosystem. They enable us to function in a new environment, which for the first time has an asymmetry between age and experience. Knowledge is no longer passed down linearly.

At both ends of the age spectrum there's a dire need to build these competencies. Older citizens are foreigners in a new land; Albert Camus's absurd stranger. Young citizens are thrust into this landscape without a roadmap; digital natives but rudderless without context.

They are emotional skills as much as they are motor skills; as much social as they are computational. When I was at high school, 'media literacy' would have meant the ability to distinguish between a TV and a newspaper. Now it demands a complex sociological understanding of networked engagement and civic relationships.

Nonetheless, they are core skills we must add to our curriculum, like sin, cos and tan (actually, I would argue even significantly more core—I use the internet every day, but I can safely say I haven't had to measure the angles in a triangle since Year 10 trigonometry).

Recent studies have reinforced that the teaching of these skills builds resistance to disinformation. But more than simply training a test subject to better identify fake headlines, a generational shift in understanding will lay a different foundation for our digital engagement in the future.

In the medium and long term, an embrace of civics-focused digital media literacy programs at an early age will create resilient digital communities who are trained in the art of common purpose and progress through the harnessing of this new information ecosystem, rather than being victims at the whim of its worst realisations.

This is much deeper than a version of 'media literacy' that teaches to discern fake from real—that approach assumes the blame lies with an individual for being uninformed enough to be misled. A civics-focused media literacy is about making sure we understand the ecosystem we inhabit, and that we grasp our digital rights and responsibilities and how they can be manipulated by emotional triggers.

The first comprehensive survey of Australian adults' media literacy wasn't completed until 2021. It painted a bleak picture, especially for older Australians: 75 per cent of those over 75 years old had 'low media abilities', and almost 60 per cent of those aged 56–74 were the same.

It also revealed a media literacy divide between regional Australia, low-income and low-education levels. More promisingly, there was overwhelming support to do something about it: 81 per cent of people thought children should receive media literacy education in school.

Media literacy skills will give the next generation a framework to deal with the ongoing crisis of disinformation in a way current generations have not been able to. We have had to deal with a 21st-century problem with a 20th-century understanding. The next generation should not have to do the same.

Platforms

Like the individual, the temptation is great to blame the social media platforms themselves.

They are a welcome punching bag for governments and regulators who need a transgressor to rail against. And tech megalomaniacs make for great uber-villains—but they can be a red herring.

No amount of tweaking the algorithm of what information we digest will reinvent the golden age of journalism, or restore trust in our honest politicians, or elevate reason to a place in our brains that trumps emotion. It will not restore our prior information ecosystem.

Like Trump, these platforms are more a product of our times than the cause.

They are the realisation of our collective willingness to cede authority to unaccountable corporations whose legal obligation is to return a profit that, by necessity, must deploy an environment where disinformation thrives. Their shareholder returns rely on our worst human behaviours, and those behaviours are lucrative: in 2021 Facebook became the fastest company in history to hit US$1 trillion worth of shares.

So instead we posit that disinformation can be addressed by asking them to play 'whack-a-mole' for each instance of a falsehood poking its nose above ground. But we don't want them to turn off our access to their valuable advertising audiences in fields of rich data.

That gold mine is accumulated thanks to the encouragement of engagement. We mine the same human behaviours that generate our disinfodemic to the tune of billions of dollars.

We don't really want them to stop disinformation in any meaningful way if it means we lose access to our audiences. We realised too late that peak capitalism would put the public square behind a gated community.

Now we cry foul if locked out, as if 'free speech' is a public commodity that private companies have an obligation to uphold. We ceded that speech already—you can't ask for it back.

Still, we shouldn't also let the platforms off the hook just because they are creatures of our own shared making. We must not continue to allow them to function unimpeded by the consequences of their actions, even if we are all complicit in how we got here.

There are very real things the platforms can change to help arrest the descent towards disinformed norms.

The key one is transparency.

When we signed over the control of information from mass media to social media, we forgot to demand the same transparency we required of mass media in exchange for the control it had over our lives.

All of the fantastic research studies this book has quoted in order to help understand and explain our current predicament were based on *what they could tell* happens on social media *from the outside*. We see the tip, but the platforms themselves know the whole iceberg. Only they have the full picture of what happens below the waterline, and that information is critical to our ability to understand how and why disinformation works—and the effect of anything we do to mitigate it.

There is a very good reason why they hide it from our view: this information is commercially sensitive and therefore kept confidential. We may as well ask Colonel Sanders to share his secret eleven herbs and spices or Ronald his Big Mac sauce recipe.

Yet we would ask them for these recipes if their chicken and burgers were killing us (more acutely than they already do). It would be a public health crisis.

So too must we recognise that in ceding too much of our public domain to private tech companies, we also ceded to them a responsibility that extends beyond the usual limits of corporate regulation. They are hybrid public–private utilities, and must be treated as such.

A good start would be to bring researchers within the tent of the data troves so they can explore what the data says about disinformation. We already have well-established norms of discovery in the legal process where companies are regularly trusted to hand over relevant material to investigators. So too should the platforms cooperate with regulatory bodies and academic institutions in genuine partnerships to uncover the spread of disinformation within their digital walls, and likewise help audit the platforms' response to it.

The platforms, notoriously miserly with access to their data, instead prefer to curate carefully selected research partnerships they fund through grants from the platforms themselves—what could possibly go wrong?— or selectively release their data to the public. It creates a climate prone for self-censorship, lest access be cut off like Facebook did to a team of NYU researchers who were studying disinformation only to have their Facebook accounts disabled mid-project. Even access to engagement data on publicly available posts is hoarded: academics and journalists can apply for access but they wouldn't even grant it to your humble author, despite being from a research centre studying disinformation. Then in July 2021 Facebook executives, embarrassed by what this engagement data revealed (the complete dominance of the disinformation-laden MAGAphone nutters), gutted the team responsible for making the data available and reassigned them to other teams.

I don't want to let the good old algorithms off the hook either. We cannot continue to countenance a practice where violent extremists are radicalised thanks to recommendations and amplifications within the platforms' control. It is complicity plain and simple.

Nor can these platforms hide behind the impracticalities of volume nor the inconvenience of taking political sides. Some topics are objectively harmful. Let me list some, to demonstrate how easy this task is: neo-Nazism, terrorism, hate speech, White nationalism, anti-vaccination, child exploitation, cyberbullying . . . It's not difficult: if you don't allow people to stand up in the town square and say something then you probably shouldn't allow them to say it on social media.

Most of the platforms have reluctantly come to the party. Facebook dropped the pretence that all political speech was fair game when that speech spilled into the bloody halls of Congress. They also acknowledged the rights of users to tell people to drink bleach probably didn't outweigh the rights of users to get public health advice, and so began restricting covid disinformation. They willingly turned down the disinformation in the days after the 2020 US election to improve its 'news ecosystem quality' (another way of saying 'save democracy from disinformation'), and in the days before Derek Chauvin's trial to prevent more bloodshed.

Humans are the best machines we have to detect disinformation; actual machines have proved terribly inept at automating what is in reality a very complex evaluation. But humans are expensive and hard to scale. It makes the 'remove disinformation' frame a very impractical way to address disinformation.

Platforms can instead help advance a 'prevent disinformation' frame. Prompts and nudges about accuracy to users before they post is one great example we have discussed. But remember, where *misinformation* is unintentional, *disinformation* is deliberate. Nudges will slow the spread of unintentional sharing of disinformation, but they won't prevent its creation.

People want an authentic experience on social media and they don't get this by interacting with inauthentic accounts. If the platforms raised the bar for account creation, for example, the experience of people using the platform would be closer to that which most people expect—the original promise of truly 'social' media.

They can also directly control the degree to which we are 'bubbled' by handing some of this control to the user. I would love the opportunity to reduce the amount of hotel quarantine hysteria in my feed and replace it with professional networks, for example—or at a minimum be able to see how the platform algorithm has decided for me. At the very least it would be easy for the platforms to throw a curveball to those trapped in deep bubbles (the platforms well know who they are) by adding some diversity to their feed.

But technological solutions to a society-wide complex will never fully solve our dilemma. Market-driven corrections can throttle and slow, but they ignore the inconvenient reality of the social, political and economic forces that lie behind disinformation and its spread.

Governments

If governments truly followed the maxim that 'prevention is better than cure' then I would never have to pay for a gym membership again and my green juices would be subsidised.

But they don't, and so too with disinformation their approach has typically been to push regulation that attempts to stuff the genie back into its bottle, and to berate the platforms for not doing enough or doing too much, depending on which day of the week it is.

As we've seen in Australia, governments are much more interested in controlling the information ecosystem than preventing harm to their citizens. Australia's great regulatory invention, the News Media Bargaining Code, was a clumsy, cronyist effort to prop up News Corp in an environment it was struggling to adapt to.

Despite the social media platforms driving the majority of these news sites' traffic to their articles, News Corp instead thought the platforms should pay them for the privilege. As Facebook exasperatedly said at the time, 'the proposed law fundamentally misunderstands the relationship between our platform and publishers who use it to share news content'.

Everyone was completely surprised in 2021 when Facebook one day decided to comply exactly with the Australian Government's demands: to define news broadly as anything of public significance and to stop freely hosting this content. It accordingly called their bluff and removed all news from its platform as asked, including many unintended pages caught up as collateral damage: charities, the Bureau of Meteorology, health departments and hospitals in the middle of a pandemic, and even, amusingly, Facebook's own Facebook page.

The government then had to save face when this 'stand-off' was resolved heavily in the platforms' favour. The whole exercise demonstrates the problem at the heart of government regulation of the internet: they fundamentally do not understand how it works.

Governments are typically the last to catch up. Society changes, and then eventually drags its legislators kicking and screaming along with them (see: marriage, gay; and marijuana, medical). This poses a problem when technology moves at the speed of light and snail-paced governments are expected to ensure it doesn't do so in a way that causes us harm.

This, in a nutshell, is how a few tech oligarchs have found themselves with unprecedented power over our daily lives with minimal oversight and intervention. We are now dealing with the consequences—of which disinformation is a prominent one. Let us hope we don't have to deal with another, when unregulated AI creates robots from the future to destroy humankind before Sarah Connor can save us from the Terminator (this is not the book for that—I've given you more than enough to worry about—but artificial intelligence is an actual existential threat causing many sleepless nights for those in the know).

At its heart, disinformation is about power. And so are governments. But government intervention into the disinformation ecosystem is fraught when that intervention attempts to control speech. It's okay, because any government action that tries to address disinformation through a list of proscribed topics or takedowns of specific speech would also be hopelessly ineffective, just as the platforms' approach to remove offending content and accounts has been. It hasn't stopped governments from trying, however.

Regulation is spreading across the globe to address this in various forms. Germany gives platforms 24 hours to take down offending material or face hefty fines. The EU forces 'VLOPs' (I love that name—'very large online platforms') to get audited annually to make sure they are reporting harmful content to the authorities. Singapore can throw you in jail for twelve months if you don't remove 'falsehoods' that threaten the health, safety or elections of Singaporeans.

But these are all band-aids on a gaping wound.

Worse, all the public hears from such measures is that we should be suspicious of *all* news—it further erodes the trust in information that we need to rebuild.

There is a very real role governments play within our information ecosystem, and it is not their piecemeal laws to remove a Facebook post here or there.

They control the bloody media landscape in the first place.

Let's not forget governments' complicity in creating this disinfodemic to begin with: through decades of deliberate policy, they eroded the traditional media landscape until all that was left were a few clickbaity websites, rugby league tabloids and Alan Jones.

There is a clearly established link between local news infrastructure and disinformation: where there is none of the former then there is more of the latter. Governments deliberately created a void that was then predictably filled with polarising content farms masquerading as news. It doesn't matter if that content is coming from a Russian agent, a Young Liberal troll or an anti-lockdown crusader, it is disinformation plain and simple, fit for the landscape of our government's own creation.

So too can they rebuild the thing they destroyed.

Re-levelling the media playing field by investing in local news, investigative journalism and public broadcasting would be signs that a government *actually* wanted to address disinformation rather than use it as a cover to thumb the scale for their preferred media landscape—a sycophantic arm of their own political ends, run by their mates.

It would take an acknowledgement of the public interest benefit of news. That's a shift. News, in the current mindset, is a business product with a profit motive. We all saw in the earlier description of this perfect storm of disinformation how far that approach has gotten us.

My optimistic hope is that the worsening disinfodemic, and the broader information disorder it represents, is the long-awaited wake-up call for governments to shift this thinking. That it forces their hand to reinvest in a healthy information landscape in the same way it is expected to invest in cancer research units and mRNA manufacturing capabilities.

Burrowed away in Canberra, teams of government cybersecurity agents work furiously to build the cyber-defences of our critical infrastructure at a cost of hundreds of millions to the public purse. But they ignore gaping holes in our other defences against hackers, trolls, bots and foreign agents: the resilience of our communities to their interference and the existence of a robust information landscape to blunt the efficacy of their falsehoods. Governments should treat both with equal seriousness and resources.

Conclusion / A Shared Reality

'The antidote is citizenship.'
—Barack Obama

Seismic shocks to our society tend to bring out the worst in people.

We see it easily manifested in the cesspool of our online conversations and politics, where deliberately false realities are hurled at each other across the internet as barbed weapons.

Something as earth-shaking as the reversal of our entire information ecosystem's gravitational direction has the ability to pull down the whole experiment of modern liberal democracy with it.

It can be confronting to walk through the enormity of this shift as we have done together in this book—it is a depressing and deflating exercise. And then to learn of our in-built biological barriers to do anything about it further sucks any wind left out of our foundering sails.

We built the foundations of our modern societies on institutions who relied upon our trust to draw their legitimacy, reason to draw their authority and convention to function unimpeded. Then someone came and pulled the rug out from under it all, and we were forced to realise what we long thought permanent was in fact very fragile. One crude joker brought the whole house of cards down, and we may still be only looking over the edge of the precipice, yet to tumble tragically down into the abyss. We are definitely teetering.

But we're not there yet.

We can't despair upon making these realisations while we still have a chance to arrest our spiral into bedlam. Instead we need to grasp our new realities and learn to navigate them while many of the most harmful narratives are still fringe, before they become dominant.

And we must act fast.

Much like one of the other crises we face (one at the coal-face—pun intended—of many disinformation campaigns), climate change, simply despairing at the degree of damage will do nothing to salvage our way of life. The sooner we act against disinformation then the more damage we prevent and the easier it will be to address.

There are things we can do to preserve something around which all other healthy debates, disagreements and differences should revolve: a shared reality.

A good place for us to start is to throw out the notion that our disinfodemic is a series of discrete factual errors, each of which can be corrected in turn.

That's the kind of approach that leads to our current ineffective patchwork of solutions: busting a myth here, putting a label there, deleting a bot over there.

We can only begin to re-establish a shared reality once we acknowledge that we are operating in a new epoch. This one follows different rules from the last era, and playing by those old rules will get us nowhere. The sooner we realise the game has changed the better.

In this epoch, disinformation is a mere symptom of larger forces at work, including an erosion of trust, a fracturing of understanding and a fragmentation of realities. We no longer communicate or gather in a shared town square, and as a consequence we are losing our common points of reference and our collective sites of memory.

We have no shared baseline of information, no starting point from which we can then diverge and disagree—just parallel tracks of thought that no longer intersect at any point along the way. We are rediscovering an ancient era of hostile tribes with frighteningly modern means of information warfare, all with a callous disregard for common purpose and progress.

For most practitioners, disinformation is a Rorschach inkblot test: psychologists see faulty reasoning that can be cured by modes of cognition; political scientists see campaign skulduggery that can be trumped by messaging; computer scientists see harmful clusters that can be broken by better algorithmical models; governments see outsized tech behemoths that can be reined in by regulation; average people see deranged relatives that can be muted by metered screen time.

In reality it is degrees of all of these things, and none of these things completely.

We began this book with a tour through the history of information and of our constant struggle between the parts of us that seek reason and those parts which happily discard it in the name of emotion. We tried and failed to shake off the forces of cognition that prevent us from living up to our self-image of informed rational beings.

We painted the canvas onto which disinformation is splattered: an atrophying news media corpse picked apart by ravenous scavengers who found in the entrails a more profitable product of infotainment; an attempt to codify knowledge into the language of computer programming and the subsequent loss of nuance and context; and the organisation of our modern lives into the crucible of social media networks geared to inflame and divide.

We lived the bleak prediction of media philosopher Marshall McLuhan: we shaped our tools and then our tools shaped us.

Disinformation is the symptom of all these things. Lying is not new, manipulation is not new, irrationality is not new, tribal thinking is not new. Disinformation itself is not new. But rarely has it been so ascendant.

Our linear progression towards enlightenment truth and reason is over. We've had our 'end of history' cultural moment again: what we thought permanent (the victory of facts over emotion) was anything but. Our assumptions have again been shaken to their core.

Welcome to The Disinformation Age, where emotion once again reigns supreme.

We all know what we desire: collective truth. It's what prevents widespread harm when an unexpected pandemic virus escapes its pangolin host. It's what prevents the rise of demagogues when the leader of the free world detaches himself from conventional reality. It's what eradicates smallpox and measles and polio and QAnon.

But we are largely mistaken as to how we get there.

Our instincts tell us to go *backwards*. To reclaim something we have lost by elevating a golden age of truth that never really existed. To put a lid on the fire-breathing chimera we have unleashed as if it will be snuffed out without first extinguishing the flames that created it. We live in naïve hope that sensational edge cases are a fringe concern and that we will eventually revert to the traditional sensible mean.

Instead, we need to move *forwards*. To accept that we have entered a new epoch in the long and winding human journey, with no guarantees it will have a happy ending. To learn to live truthfully in an environment that favours falseness. To embrace our new information ecosystem as enthusiastically as those who use it to spread their own absurd realities have, or else cede it completely to irrationality and intolerance.

We know the stakes—that's why you've made it to the final paragraph of this book. And so it ends with a call to action: we will win our shared reality if the strength of our ideas are more persuasive than the disinformation they seek to supplant. You can be both a viral vector for disinformation and its antibody. Speak your truth well, understand its place in our disordered context and instead of disinformation you will spread a protective immunity from our most modern of afflictions.

Acknowledgements

I was very privileged to get to write this book, synthesising and summarising the impressive intellectual labours of so many others for you, the reader, to parse into one coherent account of many varied topics of great importance. Without that impressive body of existing academic work, and the rigorous testing of all the weird and wonderful ways our brains and societies work, this book would have been mere speculation and supposition. So firstly I must acknowledge all the academics, journalists and researchers who it pains me to say I could not list exhaustively by name in the body of the text, lest I lose the reader's attention for good. But their painstaking and science-based (facts!) study of how humans work is the shoulders this book stands on.

And then of course there was a village-like team of people closer to home who made this book what it is, though only one name appears on the cover. Chief among them is my awe-inspiring wife Summer, who had already earned the honorific 'long-suffering', but really got to put that title to good use over the course of this book's creative process. She is there on every page in equal parts muse and editor; what you have read is her perspiration if not her words. And who, for as much as we struggle uphill against the weight of social and cultural expectations, still assumes the unequal share of our family labour so that her husband can reap the kudos built on the foundations of her unrecognised toil. May our daughters inherit a world of your making that values them commensurate with their worth.

To the team at Allen & Unwin: to Jane Palfreyman for taking a chance on me, and to Tom Bailey-Smith and Sam Cooney for their hard work and thoughtful insights that made this manuscript a lot better than the one they were handed. And then to my unofficial team of helpers, Anthony White, James Woods and Jason Wojciechowski, my thought partner of many years. To my colleague Mark Connelly, this book would not have happened without you, and your wonderful ideas (and sometimes words) are found throughout. I am lucky to have access to your brain. To Anthony Reed for assuming a superhuman workload so I could write this thing. To my dear friend James Clinch, I turned to you for feedback on my thinking and ended up with your far superior thinking in its stead. I am honoured some of your wonderful brain made it into my pages, and the readers are luckier for it. To the publicans and baristas of Coogee and Clovelly, thanks for putting up with me and my laptop overstaying our welcome in your establishments in between lockdowns as my ideas metamorphosed onto the page. And to my late father Michael Coper, who never got to see the fruits of his labours to inspire my intellectual curiosity and imbue me with the skills to communicate it.

I also want to acknowledge the fact that a lot of the source material for this book came from publicly funded but privately paywalled academic literature that I was only able to access illegally through someone else's login, as I have no professional affiliation with a university. I would therefore like to acknowledge my late friend Aaron Swartz who gave his life to address this injustice. Knowledge should be free to all.

Lastly, to all the truth-tellers. To everyone who musters the courage to have an awkward conversation with someone they may not even know who has just said something misleading, mean, misogynistic, malign, or narrow-minded. Brick by tiny brick you are building a society that is based on our better parts, even though it can seem thankless and fruitless. Thank you, this book is for you.

References

This book relied on an enormous amount of scholarship on a range of topics. Below is a list of sources mentioned in the book, but if you are interested in exploring any of these threads further you will find a full list of these references (and more) with hyperlinks to the source material, study or article at: factsandotherlies.com/endnotes.

INTRO

p. 4   'Half of all the Twitter accounts . . .' Young, Virginia Alvino, 'Nearly half of the Twitter accounts discussing "Reopening America" may be bots', *CMU School of Computer Science*, 20 May 2020

p. 5   'by 2030, anti-vaxxer conspiracies . . .' Johnson, N.F., Velásquez, N., Restrepo, N.J. et al., 'The online competition between pro- and anti-vaccination views', *Nature*, 2020, vol. 582, pp. 230–233

p. 7   'It is not the voice that commands . . .' Calvino, I., *Invisible Cities*, New York: Harcourt Brace Jovanovich, 1974

PART ONE
A BRIEF HISTORY OF LIES

p. 11   'One study of primates . . .' McNally, L., & Jackson A.L., 'Cooperation creates selection for tactical deception', *Proceedings of the Royal Society B*, 2013, vol. 280

p. 11   'Researchers placed hidden cameras . . .' Talwar V., Lee K., 'Social and cognitive correlates of children's lying behavior', *Child Development*, 2008, vol. 79, pp. 866–881

p. 12   'a dinosaur because it "felt purple"' in Bhattacharjee, Y., 'Why we lie: The science behind our deceptive ways', *National Geographic*, June 2017

p. 12   'Sixty per cent of teenagers tell up to five lies a day.' Debey, E., De Schryver, M., Logan, G.D., et al., 'From junior to senior Pinocchio: A cross-sectional lifespan investigation of deception', *Acta Psychologica*, 2015, vol. 160, pp. 58–68

p. 13   'Only with the rise of Puritan morality . . .' Arendt, H. *Between Past and Future: Eight Exercises in Political Thought*, New York: Viking Press, 1968, p. 232

p. 13   '. . . all governments rest on opinion', in Arendt, p. 233

p. 14   'Crikey published a dossier of 27 . . .' Fray, P. & Beecher, E., '"Without truth, no democracy can stand": Why we are calling out the prime minister', *Crikey*, 25 May 2021

p. 15   'At an early age, he had the glory of conceiving . . .' *The Independent Chronicle and the Universal Advertiser*, 29 May 1800, quoted in Emily Sneff 'May Highlight: An Instrument which will Perpetuate the Fame of its Author', *Declaration Resources Project*, Harvard University, 4 May 2016

p. 16   'a fabrication intended to damp the festivity . . .' 'A Federal Bore', *American Citizen and General Advertiser*, New York: 5 July 1800, quoted in Sneff

p. 16   'is it the Fourth?' Martin, R., 'Jefferson's Last Words', *Thomas Jefferson Encyclopedia*, 1988, Monticello.org

p. 17   '*New York Times* described "would be divorced from religiousness" . . .' Steinhauer, Jennifer, 'Confronting ghosts of 2000 in South Carolina', *New York Times*, 19 October 2007

p. 18   'A popular Government, without popular information . . .' James Madison to W.T. Barry, 4 August 1822. Manuscript/Mixed Material. *Library of Congress*

A BRIEF HISTORY OF TRUTH

p. 21   'purple monkey dishwasher' from 'The PTA Disbands!', *The Simpsons*, Season 6, Episode 21, 1995

p. 21   'show up in London just seventeen days after . . .' Roos, D., '7 ways the printing press changed the world', *History*, 28 August 2019

p. 22   'everything *for* the people, nothing *by* the people' Attributed to Emperor Joseph II, Holy Roman Emperor

p. 22   'You can cut a man's head off . . .' 'A Pox on Hope', *The Great*, Season 1, Episode 7, 2020

p. 23   'Public opinion has now become a preponderant power . . .' Citton, Y., 'Fabrique de l'opinion et folie de la dissidence dans le "complot" selon Rousseau', *Rousseau Juge de Jean-Jacques, Études sur les Dialogues*, Presses de l'Université d'Ottawa, 1998, pp. 101–114

p. 23   'it wasn't reason that set us apart from the animals . . .' Marx, K., 'Estranged labour', *Economic and Philosophic Manuscripts of 1844*. Moscow: Progress Publishers, 1959

p. 23   'a return to The Enlightenment'. Hacker, P., 'Reason, the enlightenment, and post-truth politics', *IAI News*, Issue 54, 2 March 2017

p. 26   'They valued reason: the conviction that logic . . .' in Seppälä, E., 'A Harvard professor explains why the world is actually becoming a much better place', *Washington Post*, 13 February 2018

A BRIEF END OF HISTORY OF TRUTH

p. 28   'The End of History?' Fukuyama, F., 'The end of history?', *The National Interest*, 1989, pp. 3–18

p. 28   'What we may be witnessing is not ...' Fukuyama, p. 4

p. 29   'In Washington, a newsdealer on Connecticut Avenue ...' Atlas, James, 'What is Fukuyama saying? And to whom is he saying it?', *New York Times*, 22 October 1989, A.38

p. 30   'a moment in which a final, rational form ...' Fukyama, p. 4

p. 30   'self-congratulation raised to the status of philosophy', quoted in Atlas

p. 30   'As Thomas Piketty laid out ...' Piketty, T., *Capital in the Twenty-First Century*, Cambridge MA: The Belknap Press of Harvard University Press, 2014

p. 33   'an intellectual and cultural whirlpool ...' Clinch, J., Interview with author, 18 April 2021

p. 34   'fashionable nonsense'. Sokal, A. & Bricmont, J., *Fashionable Nonsense: Postmodern Intellectuals' Abuse of Science*, New York: Picador, 1998

p. 34   'The history that merely destroys ...' Nietzsche, F., *The Use and Abuse of History, (1873–76)*, trans. Adrian Collis, Indianapolis: Bobbs-Merrill, 1957, p. 42

p. 34   'as a nation we're over all that sort of stuff', Sheridan, G., 'Foreign regions', *Weekend Australian*, 27–28 September 2003, p. 17

p. 35   'alternative facts' Conway, K., Interview with Chuck Todd, *Meet The Press*, 22 January 2017

p. 37   'What I fear is a government of experts.' Cronin, T., *On the Presidency: Teacher, Soldier, Shaman, Pol*, London: Paradigm Publishers Boulder, 2009

p. 37   'the more learned and witty you bee ...' Cotton, J., *The Powring Out of the Seven Vials* (1642), quoted in Hofstadter, R., *Anti-intellectualism in American Life*, New York: Vintage Books, 1963, p. 46

A BRIEF HISTORY OF INFORMATION

p. 41   'The Antebellum Puzzle ...' Craig, L., 'Antebellum puzzle: The decline in heights at the onset of modern economic growth', in J. Komlos and I.R. Kelly (eds), *The Oxford Handbook of Economics and Human Biology*, New York: Oxford University Press, 2015, pp. 750–764

p. 41   'Malthusian trap ...' Malthus, T., & James, P., *An Essay on the Principle of Population*, Cambridge: Cambridge University Press, 2008

p. 42   'If you take a bale of hay ...' Wolfe, T., 'The Tinkerings of Robert Noyce: How the Sun Rose on the Silicon Valley', *Esquire Magazine*, December 1983, pp. 346–374

p. 43   'a full CD-ROM's worth of storage . . .' Hilbert, M., & López, P., 'The world's technological capacity to store, communicate, and compute information', *Science,* 2011, vol. 332, pp. 60–5

p. 43   'more than 19,000 per person', Holst, A., 'Volume of data/information created, captured, copied, and consumed worldwide from 2010 to 2025 (in zettabytes)', *Statista,* June 2021

p. 43   'grown 58 per cent per year on average . . .' Hilbert & López, 2011

p. 44   'the majority of the world's population . . .' International Telecommunication Union, 'Individuals using the Internet (% of population)', *World Telecommunication/ICT Indicators Database,* 2019

p. 45   'cost the airline $150 million . . .' Walsh, Willie, 'BA faces £80m cost for IT failure that stranded 75,000 passengers', *Financial Times,* 16 June 2017

p. 45   'technology of freedom' De Sola Pool, I., *Technologies of Freedom,* Belknap Press, 1983

p. 46   'the 'Declaration of the Independence of Cyberspace', Barlow, J.P., 'Declaration of the Independence of Cyberspace', 8 February 1996

A BRIEF HISTORY OF NEWS

p. 48   'I now write of the unfortunate Dardanelles . . .' Murdoch, K.M., & Ashmead-Bartlett, E., *Gallipoli letter from Keith Arthur Murdoch to Andrew Fisher, 1915* [manuscript], National Library of Australia, 1915

p. 50   'The last war, during the years of 1915, 1916, 1917 . . .' quoted in Knightley, P., *The First Casualty; From the Crimea to Vietnam: The War Correspondent as Hero, Propagandist and Myth Maker,* New York: Harcourt Brace Jovanovich, 1975, p. 79

p. 50   'More deliberate lies were told . . .' Knightley, p. 80

p. 51   'such knowledge as was theirs inspired silence', *The History of the Times 1785–1948, vol. 4,* London: The Times, 1935–52, p. 228

p. 51   'if the war correspondents in France . . .' Knightley, p. 103

p. 52   'Orchestra Pit Principle' Ailes, R., Interview with Judy Woodruff in David Runkel (ed.), *Campaign for President: The Managers Look at '88,* Auburn House, 1989

p. 52   'sweaty, shifty-eyed . . .' Junod, T., 'Why Does Roger Ailes Hate America?', *Esquire,* February 2011

p. 52   'If Richard Nixon was alive today, . . .' Junod, 2011

p. 53   'It's a shame a man has to use gimmicks . . .' Junod, 2011

p. 53   'In 2011, a journalist was trawling . . .' The journalist, John Cook, published his original article about this on the now-defunct *Gawker* website, 'Roger Ailes' Secret Nixon-Era Blueprint for Fox News', 30 June 2011

p. 53   'A Plan for Putting the GOP on TV News ...' 'A Plan for Putting the GOP on TV News', Richard Nixon Presidential Library, 1970

p. 54   '40 per cent lower in April 2021 ...' Johnson, T., 'Cable News Network Viewership Continued To Drop In April Vs. 2020; Fox News Tops Primetime And Total Day', *Deadline*, 27 April 2021

p. 54   'a 24/7 political campaign.' Quoted in Dickinson, T., 'How Roger Ailes Built the Fox News Fear Factory', *Rolling Stone*, 9 June 2011

p. 55   'business road trips with his living room curtains ...' in Van Ogtrop, K., *Did I Say That Out Loud?*, New York: Little, Brown Spark, 2021

p. 55   'company beach picnic ...' D'Anastasio, C., 'The secret history of a fleeting pre-internet digital media channel', *Vice*, 3 April 2017

p. 56   'fallen below where it had been in 1950 ...' Perry, M.J., 'Creative destruction: Newspaper ad revenue continued its precipitous free fall in 2014, and it's likely to continue', *American Enterprise Institute*, 30 April 2015

p. 56   'Classifieds, worth $3.7 billion ...' Australian Competition and Consumer Commission, *Digital Platforms Inquiry—Final Report*, June 2019, p. 17 (Inflation adjusted to 2018)

p. 56   '92 per cent have been from the loss of classified ads ...' AlphaBeta Australia, *Australian Media Landscape Trends*, September 2020

p. 56   'a majority of *all* US advertising ...' Hagey, K. and Vranica, S., 'How covid-19 supercharged the advertising "triopoly" of Google, Facebook and Amazon', *Wall Street Journal*, 19 March 2021

p. 57   'For every action ...' Based on an original table by Mark J. Perry on the American Enterprise Institute blog. Additional information has been sourced from Pew Research, *State of the News Media*, 2020, company SEC filings, and News Media Alliance data

p. 59   'number five on the top ten list of publisher rankings ...' NewsWhip, 'Top social publishers August 2013: Sharing way up for all publishers, and BuzzFeed on Top', 26 September 2013

p. 59   'We have a custom click testing system ...' 'What tools does Upworthy employ to test its headlines?', question on *Quora*, 2014

p. 59   '*The Atlantic* called the efforts ...' Thompson, D., 'Upworthy: I thought this website was crazy, but what happened next changed everything', *The Atlantic*, 14 November 2013

p. 60   'In May 2021 they had more than 70 million ...' NewsWhip, 'These were the top publishers on Facebook in May 2021', 10 June 2021

p. 61   'in 1983 approximately 90 per cent ...' Bagdikian, B.H., *The Media Monopoly*, Boston: Beacon Press, 1990

p. 62   'nearly 2000 newspapers have closed ...' Abernathy, P.M., *The Expanding News Desert*, Chapel Hill: University of North Carolina Press, 2018

p. 62   'behind only the state-run media giants . . .' Noam, E., & The International
         Media Concentration Collaboration, *Who Owns the World's Media?:*
         Media Concentration and Ownership around the World, New York: Oxford
         University Press, 2016

p. 62   'News Corp, controls about 70 per cent . . .' Noam, E. 2016. Subsequent to
         this report News Corp bought a further 5% of Australia's circulation

p. 62   'Australia lost more than 2000 newsroom . . .' Warren, Christopher, '2020
         was a record year for journo job losses. What comes next?', *Crikey,*
         15 December 2020

p. 63   'Prologue to a Farce or a Tragedy' James Madison to W.T. Barry, 1822

p. 63   'less likely to vote . . .' Hayes, D., & Lawless, J.L., 'As local news goes, so
         goes citizen engagement: Media, knowledge, and participation in US House
         elections', *The Journal of Politics*, April 2015, vol. 77, no. 2, pp. 447–462

p. 63   'less politically informed . . .' PEN America, *Losing the News: The*
         Decimation of Local Journalism and the Search for Solutions, 20 November
         2019

p. 63   'less likely to run for office . . .' Rubado, M.E., & Jennings, J.T., 'Political
         consequences of the endangered local watchdog: Newspaper decline and
         mayoral elections in the United States', *Urban Affairs Review*, April 2019

p. 63   'local taxes going up . . .' Gao, P., Lee, C., & Murphy, D., 'Financing dies in
         darkness? The impact of newspaper closures on public finance', *Journal of*
         Financial Economics, February 2019

p. 63   'With the decline of local news . . .' PEN America, 2019

p. 64   'It was a local paper, the Illawarra Mercury . . .' O'Shea, M., 'Rocky times:
         Local Australian newspapers are merging, closing and losing circulation
         which leaves scandals unreported', *Index on Censorship*, 2019, vol. 48(1),
         pp. 57–59

p. 64   '21 "news deserts" . . .' Australian Competition and Consumer
         Commission, 2019

p. 64   '73 per cent of them . . .' Hayes, P., et al., 'Joining the dots: using social
         media to connect to more vulnerable Victorians during emergencies',
         Australian Journal of Emergency Management, Monograph, 2019, No. 4,
         pp. 154–163

p. 64   'less likely to be vaccinated . . .' Jennings, W., et al., 'Lack of trust and social
         media echo chambers predict COVID-19 vaccine hesitancy', *medRxiv,*
         26 January 2021

A PERFECT STORM

p. 69   'We will prioritise posts . . .' 'Bringing people closer together', Facebook,
         12 January 2018

p. 70   'designers of the social platforms . . .' Wardle, C., 'Misinformation has created a new world disorder', *Scientific American*, September 2019

p. 70   '9/11 were to happen . . .' Wardle, 2019

p. 72   '300 things you had 'liked' . . .' Youyou, W., Kosinski, M., & Stillwell, D., 'Computer-based personality judgments are more accurate than those made by humans', *Proceedings of the National Academy of Sciences*, January 2015, vol. 112(4), pp. 1036–1040

p. 73   'cyber-balkanisation' Sunstein, C., *Republic.com*, Princeton: Princeton University Press, 2001

p. 73   'sites of memory', Pierre, N., 'Between memory and history: Les lieux de mémoire', *Representations*, 1989, no. 26, pp. 7–24

p. 74   'They traced his radicalisation . . .' Roose, K., 'The making of a YouTube radical', *New York Times*, 8 June 2019

p. 75   'We can really lead the users . . .' Roose, 2019

p. 76   'We've democratized propaganda . . .' Warzel, C., 'There was no midterm misinformation crisis because we've democratized propaganda', *BuzzFeed News*, 7 November 2018

p. 76   'Our political conversations are now . . .' Warzel, 2018

p. 76   'A leaked presentation in 2018 . . .' Horwitz, J., & Seetharaman, D., 'Facebook executives shut down efforts to make the site less divisive', *Wall Street Journal*, 26 May 2020

p. 76   'insiders told the *Wall Street Journal* . . .' Horwitz and Seetharaman, 2020

p. 77   'It seems significant, . . .' Arendt, p. 232

p. 77   'it was never meant to deceive literally everyone . . .' Arendt, p. 253

p. 77   'Seen from the viewpoint of politics . . .' Arendt, p. 241

PART TWO
TYPES OF DISINFORMATION

p. 82   'Thomas Rid's *Active Measures* . . .' Rid, T., *Active Measures: The Secret History of Disinformation and Political Warfare*, New York: Farrar, Straus and Giroux, 2020

p. 83   'Three Categories of Information Disorder . . .' Image: Wardle, C., 'Misinformation has created a new world disorder', *Scientific American*, September 2019

p. 84   'Wardle calls this the "atomisation" of misinformation . . .' Wardle, C., 'Fake news. It's complicated', *First Draft*, 17 February 2017

p. 84   'seven helpful categories: . . .' Wardle, C., *First Draft's Essential Guide to Understanding Information Disorder*, *First Draft*, October 2019

p. 85   'Bigger Crowd Than Auckland 9s . . .' 'White House Press Sec Insists Trump Inauguration Had Bigger Crowd Than Auckland 9s', *Betoota Advocate*, 22 January 2017 [satire]

p. 86   '*Freedom of Expression Assessment Framework . . .*' Bontcheva, K., & Posetti, J., (eds), *Balancing Act: Countering Digital Disinformation While Respecting Freedom of Expression*, ITU and UNESCO, September 2020

p. 86   'UN report lists those practices . . .' Bontcheva and Posetti, 2020, p. 23

p. 87   'set off "terror" in the heart of Washington DC' . . .' Corcoran, Mark, & Henry, Matt, 'The Tom Cruise deepfake that set off "terror" in the heart of Washington DC', *Foreign Correspondent*, ABC, 24 June 2021

THE FAKE ACCOUNT

p. 89   'We removed 3,104 accounts . . .' Twitter Safety [@twittersafety], 'Transparency is . . .' *Twitter*, 2 April 2020

p. 90   'Jobs Not Mobs' . . .' Collins, K., & Roose, K., 'Tracing a meme from the Internet's fringe to a Republican slogan', *New York Times*, 4 November 2018

p. 93   'Graham's study shows the origins . . .' Graham, T., 'The story of #DanLiedPeopleDied: how a hashtag reveals Australia's "information disorder" problem', *The Conversation*, 14 August 2020

p. 94   'Timeline of #DanLiedPeopleDied . . .' Image: Dr Timothy Graham, QUT

p. 97   'people spreading arson rumours . . .' Graham, T., & Keller, T.R., 'Bushfires, bots and arson claims: Australia flung in the global disinformation spotlight', *The Conversation*, 10 January 2020

p. 97   'bots latch onto official government feeds . . .' Ryan Ko, 'Meet "Sara", "Sharon" and "Mel": why people spreading coronavirus anxiety on Twitter might actually be bots', *The Conversation*, 1 April 2020* [*not an April Fools' joke]

p. 98   'Sara and Sharon . . .' Image: Professor Ryan Ko, University of Queensland

p. 99   'bots affect information flows . . .' Woolley, S.C. & Guilbeault, D., 'United States: Manufacturing consensus online' in S. Woolley and Howard, P.N. (eds), *Computational Propaganda: Political Parties, Politicians, and Political Manipulation on Social Media*, Oxford University Press, 2019

p. 99   'Caroline Orr . . .' Orr, C., 'Twitter bots boosted the trending #TrudeauMustGo hashtag', *National Observer*, 18 July 2019

p. 99   '#TrudeauCorruption . . .' Golberg, G., 'Justin Trudeau targeted on Twitter (Yet again)', *Medium*, 6 September 2019

p. 100 'the French #MacronLeaks disinformation . . .' Ferrara, E. et al., 'The rise of social bots', *Communications of the ACM*, 2016, vol. 59(7), pp. 96–104

p. 100 'In the time it has taken you . . .' <knightfoundation.org/features/misinfo>

THE FAKE ARTICLE

p. 101 'told Sarah Koenig . . .' Koenig, S., 'Forgive us our press passes', Episode 468: Switcheroo, *This American Life*, 29 June 2012

p. 102 'People didn't think much about the beef . . .' Tarkov, A., 'Journatic worker takes "This American Life" inside outsourced journalism', *Poynter*, 30 June 2012

p. 102 '85 per cent of Americans trusted . . .' Gallup/Knight Foundation, *State of Public Trust in Local News*, 29 October 2019

p. 102 'a Pew survey . . .' Pew Research Center, *Trust and Distrust in America*, 22 July 2019

p. 103 'The Knight Foundation conducted a . . .' Hindman, M. & Barash, V., *Disinformation, 'Fake News' and Influence Campaigns on Twitter*, The Knight Foundation, October 2018

p. 104 '450 news websites . . .' Bengani, Priyanjana, 'Hundreds of "pink slime" local news outlets are distributing algorithmic stories and conservative talking points', Tow Center Reports, *Columbia Journalism Review*, 18 December 2019

p. 104 'propaganda ordered up by dozens . . .' Alba, D. & Nicas, J., 'As local news dies, a pay-for-play network rises in Its place', *New York Times*, 18 October 2020

p. 105 'The different websites are nearly indistinguishable . . .' Sokotoff, D. & Sourine, K., 'Pseudo local news sites in Michigan reveal nationally expanding network', *Michigan Daily*, 1 November 2019

p. 105 'Jeanne Ives . . .' Federal Election Committee filings for 'Jeanne for Congress', p. 89

p. 105 'Kelli Ward . . .' Schwartz, J. & Musgrave, S., 'Kelli Ward touts endorsement from fake-news site', *Politico*, 14 February 2018

p. 106 'The GOP and the far right . . .' Memo: 'ACRONYM News Corp 2019–2020 Rapid Build Plan', 20 June 2019

p. 108 'Another guy told the actual *Washington Post* . . .' Dewey, C. 'Facebook fake-news writer: "I think Donald Trump is in the White House because of me"', *Washington Post*, 17 November 2016

p. 109 'Elvis Kafui . . .' Thompson, S., 'Fact check: As of March 7, 2020, Tanzania and Zambia had not confirmed first cases of coronavirus', *Lead Stories*, 7 March 2020

p. 110 'Frimp Eunuch . . .' Image: Lead Stories

p. 111 'A group of Yale researchers . . .' Pennycook, G. & Rand, D.G., 'Lazy, not biased: Susceptibility to partisan fake news is better explained by lack of reasoning than by motivated reasoning', *Cognition*, 2019, vol. 188, pp. 39–50

p. 111 'emergent propaganda state' Mosby, R., 'Trump, InfoWars, Breitbart and the emergent propaganda state', *Clarion Ledger*, 1 June 2018

THE FAKE AD

p. 113 'Consumer protection laws . . .' 'Social media', ACCC website, Accessed 30 August 2021

p. 114 '"intangibles" . . .' Commonwealth Parliament Joint Select Committee on Electoral Reform, *Second Report*, August 1984

p. 114 'beneath the mainstream media . . .' Karp, P., 'Labor's Medicare campaign delivered largely online, not via traditional ads', *The Guardian*, 9 July 2016

THE FAKE CITIZEN

p. 118 'We got a message from one of our folks . . .' in Riedl, M.J., et al., 'Reverse-engineering political protest: the Russian Internet Research Agency in the Heart of Texas', *Information, Communication & Society*, 2021

p. 119 'I just basically did what I always do.' in Riedl et al.

p. 119 'released samples of 3000 Facebook ads . . .' U.S. House of Representatives Permanent Select Committee on Intelligence. *Exposing Russia's effort to sow discord online: The Internet Research Agency and advertisements*. 2018 (images in this section are also taken from this report)

p. 119 'Apparently somebody there was smart enough . . .' in Riedl et al.

p. 120 'Image: Evidence of the simultaneous protests . . .' Source: US House Intelligence Committee

p. 120 'Appealing to divisive issues . . .' in Riedl et al

p. 121 'You think we are living in 2016 . . .' quoted in Ignatius, D., 'Russia's radical new strategy for information warfare', *Washington Post*, 18 January 2017

p. 122 'Image: Russian ads . . .' Source: US Senate Intelligence Committee

p. 123 'US$35 million operating budget . . .' Criminal Complaint: *United States of America v Elena Alekseevna Khusyaynova*, US District Court, 28 September 2018

p. 123 'industrial machines in a modern propaganda factory' Linvill, D.L. & Warren, P.L., 'Troll factories: Manufacturing specialized disinformation on Twitter', *Political Communication*, 2020, vol. 37(4), pp. 447–467

p. 123 'Secondary Infektion' Nimmo, B., et al., *Exposing Secondary Infektion*, Graphika, 2020

p. 124 'Frau Chancellor . . .' Post by user 'demomanz' in the 'r/germany' thread on Reddit, 10 April 2017

p. 124 'Something rather newsworthy happened . . .' From a post 'Topic: Flowers for Kim Jong-un or Operation White Chrysanthemum' on military-quotes. com, 10 November 2017

p. 125 'both correlate with spikes . . .' Sear, T. & Jensen, M., 'Russian trolls targeted Australian voters on Twitter via #auspol and #MH17', *The Conversation*, 22 August 2018

p. 125 'Troll accounts attempted to influence . . .' Ackland, R., Jensen, M., O'Neil, M., *Submission to the Senate Select Committee on Foreign Interference through Social Media*, Canberra: News & Media Research Centre, University of Canberra 2020

p. 127 'Every morning, Tamara . . .' Oxenham, S., 'I was a Macedonian fake news writer', BBC, 29 May 2019

THE FAKE REALITY

pp. 129–131 Poll numbers in this section: Pew Research Center poll conducted 4–10 June 2020; NPR/Ipsos poll conducted between 21–22 December 2020; PRRI/IFYC poll conducted between 8–30 March 2021

p. 129 'In Australia, it's 34 per cent . . .' *The Essential Report*, 26 September 2017

p. 130 'no innate correlation . . .' Moore, A., Parent, J. & Uscinski, J., 'Conspiracy theories aren't just for conservatives', *Washington Post*, 21 August 2014

p. 131 'Conspiratorial thinking can be pulled . . .' in Stanton, Z., 'You're living in the golden age of conspiracy theories', *Politico*, 17 June 2020

p. 132 'hate words from the White House' Rayman, G. & Boyer, T., 'Accused killer of Gambino mob boss was influenced by hate speak from White House and internet—lawyer', *NY Daily News*, 25 March 2019

p. 132 'QAnon is a baseless internet conspiracy . . .' Wong, J.C., 'QAnon explained: the antisemitic conspiracy theory gaining traction around the world', *The Guardian*, 26 August 2020

p. 133 'at least 315 times . . .' Kaplan, A., 'Trump has repeatedly amplified QAnon Twitter accounts', *Media Matters for America*, 11 January 2021

p. 133 'Morrison even appeared to use . . .' Hardaker, D., 'Scott Morrison's conspiracy-theorist friend claims he has the PM's ear—and can influence what he says', *Crikey*, 31 October 2019

p. 133 'No one knows where it came from,' Hardaker, D., 'PM defied his own expert panel during apology speech to child sex abuse survivors', *Crikey*, 18 November 2019

p. 133 '"I think Scott is going to do it!" ...' Event Zero TV, '#MateGate Scott Morrison was introduced to his wife Jen by Lynelle Stewart ...', *Facebook*, 27 July 2019

p. 134 'to draw otherwise sane people in ...' Warner, M., 'The geophysicist who stormed the capitol', *Politico*, 11 June 2021

p. 135 'Gesturing to his guests, he said ...' Landler, M., 'A message sent, to whom or about what is not exactly clear', *New York Times*, 7 October 2017 © 2017 The New York Times Company. All rights reserved. Used under license.

p. 136 'SUBJECT: Walnut sauce?' WikiLeaks <wikileaks.org/podesta-emails/emailid/21969>

p. 138 'Q Clearance Patriot ...' Anonymous post on the 'Calm before the Storm' thread on the /pol/ 4chan message board, 2 November 2017

p. 139 'fourth only behind ...' Gallagher, A., Davey, J. & Hart, M., 'The genesis of a conspiracy theory', *Institute for Strategic Dialogue*, 2020

p. 140 'What caught my eye ...' Hon, A. interview with Charlie Warzel, 'Is QAnon the most dangerous conspiracy theory of the 21st century?', *New York Times*, 4 August 2020

p. 141 'the number of Twitter followers ...' Levine, J., 'Twitter purge decimates GOP senators after Capitol riot, but Democrats gain', *NY Post*, 16 January 2021

p. 141 'Pauline Hanson lost 4 per cent ...' Taylor, Josh, 'One nation MPs lost more followers than other Australian politicians in Twitter purge of QAnon accounts', *The Guardian*, 20 January 2021

p. 142 'For a far greater plague is ...' Marcus Aurelius, *Meditations*, Book 9, Part II

p. 142 'One historian estimated ...' Kerr, M., '"An alteration in the human countenance": Inoculation, vaccination, and the face of smallpox in the age of Jenner' in J. Reinarz and K.P. Siena (eds), *A Medical History of Skin*, London: Pickering & Chatto, 2013, p. 131

p. 143 'Ann Davis ...' Eisen, Erica X, '"The mark of the beast" Georgian Britain's anti-vaxxer movement', *Public Domain Review*, 28 April 2021

p. 143 'An Anti-Vaccine Society pamphlet ...' Image: 'Edward Jenner vaccinating patients in the Smallpox and Inoculation Hospital at St. Pancras: the patients develop features of cows.', coloured etching by J. Gillray, 1802, Source: Wellcome Collection, (CC BY-NC 4.0)

p. 143 'The Creator stamped ...' Halket, W., *Compulsory Vaccination!! A Crime Against Nature!!*, London: G. Meyers, 1870

p. 144 'it ranked second only to fear ...' Offit, P.A., *The Cutter Incident: How America's First Polio Vaccine Led to the Growing Vaccine Crisis*, New Haven: Yale University Press, 2005

p. 144 'parents watched anxiously ...' Carroll, S.B., 'The Denialist Playbook', *Scientific American*, 8 November 2020

p. 145 'There is much that can be done ...' in Homola, S., *Bonesetting, Chiropractic, and Cultism; A Critical Study of Chiropractic*, Florida: Critique Books, 1963

p. 145 'The test tube fight against polio ...' Frame, F.D., 'Has the test tube fight against polio failed?', *Journal of the National Chiropractic Association*, March 1959

p. 145 'Your thoughtful consideration ...' in Homola, 1963

p. 145 'tracked how anti-vaccination attitudes ...' Surveys are listed in Stephen Barrett MD, 'Chiropractors and Immunization', *Quackwatch*, 10 March 2016

p. 146 'Chiropractic Board of Australia ...' Chiropractic Board of Australia, 'Statement on advertising', 7 March 2016

p. 146 '2020 Connecticut law ...' Schulson, M., 'With legislation looming, chiropractors get political on vaccines', *Undark*, 11 April 2020

p. 147 '6.2 per cent in the UK ...' Loomba, S. et al., 'Measuring the impact of COVID-19 vaccine misinformation on vaccination intent in the UK and USA', *Nature Human Behaviour*, 2021, vol. 5, pp. 337–348

p. 147 'They built a disinformation campaign ...' Nazar, S. & Pieters T., 'Plandemic revisited: A product of planned disinformation amplifying the COVID-19 "infodemic"', *Frontiers in Public Health*, 2021, vol. 9

p. 148 'just 111 accounts ...' Dwoskin, E., 'Massive Facebook study on users' doubt in vaccines finds a small group appears to play a big role in pushing the skepticism', *Washington Post*, 14 March 2021

p. 148 'advocacy group Avaaz ...' Avaaz, *Facebook's Algorithm: A Major Threat to Public Health*, 19 August 2020

p. 148 '38 times ...' Wolfe, D. & Dale, D., '"It's going to disappear": A timeline of Trump's claims that Covid-19 will vanish', CNN, 31 October 2020

p. 148 'Between March and July 2020 ...' Hamilton, L.C. & Safford, T.G., 'Elite cues and the rapid decline in trust in science agencies on COVID-19', *Sociological Perspectives*, 2021

p. 149 'greater among Trump supporters ...' NPR/PBS NewsHour/Marist poll conducted 3–8 March 2021

p. 150 'Center for Countering Digital Hate ...' The Center for Countering Digital Hate, *Pandemic Profiteers: The business of anti-vaxx*, 2021

THE MAGAPHONE

p. 152 'The sooner our politicians . . .' Moses, A., 'Obama's web strategist to advise Rudd', *Sydney Morning Herald*, 13 February 2009

p. 154 'Listen, liberals.' Roose, K., 'What if Facebook is the real "Silent majority"?', *New York Times*, 27 August 2020

p. 156 'We can't remove all of it . . .' Timberg, C., 'How conservatives learned to wield power inside Facebook', *Washington Post*, 20 February 2020

p. 156 'reality has a well-known . . .' Originally from Stephen Colbert's famous in-character roast of George W. Bush from only feet away during the 2006 White House Correspondents' Dinner, the high water mark of all political satire.

p. 156 'As Thomas Mann said . . .' Mann, T. & Ornstein, N.J., 'Let's just say it: The Republicans are the problem', *Washington Post*, 27 April 2012

p. 159 'Most engaged-with political stories . . .' Source: NewsWhip Spike from 28 May to 4 June 2021

p. 160 'a conservative Hollywood executive . . .' Nguyen, T., '"Let me make you famous": How Hollywood invented Ben Shapiro', *Vanity Fair*, 9 December 2018

p. 161 'Top Web Publishers . . .' Source: NewsWhip API from April 2021

p. 161 'a cesspool of bigotry and hatred . . .' Campbell, J., 'The Daily Wire is a cesspool of bigotry and hatred', *Media Matters for America*, 7 August 2019

p. 162 'Legum identified . . .' Legum, Judd, 'Facebook allows prominent right-wing website to break the rules', *Popular Information*, 28 October 2019

p. 162 'an ordinary American couple . . .' 'About Us', Mad World News website

p. 163 'Facebook engagement per article . . .' Source: Judd Legum, Popular Information

pp. 162–165 Sky News audience figures in this section: 'Sky News reports record 2020 audience growth', *Media Week*, 1 December 2020; 'Sky News Australia is reaching more than one third of Australians every month across its network', *Sky News Australia*, 21 July 2021; Wilson, Cam, '"In digital, the right-wing material is 24/7": How Sky News quietly became Australia's biggest news channel on social media', *Business Insider*, 6 November 2020; *Sky News Australia*, YouTube Channel

p. 164 'Facebook posts from their Page . . .' Wilson, Cam, '"In digital, the right-wing material is 24/7": How Sky News quietly became Australia's biggest news channel on social media', *Business Insider*, 6 November 2020

p. 165 'Have a look at Sky News YouTube . . .' Samios, Z., 'Alan Jones column pulled from The Daily Telegraph amid anti-lockdown, COVID-19 controversies', *Sydney Morning Herald*, 29 July 2021

p. 165 'I can be derided, . . .' Robson, F., 'By George! The controversies of an Australian government MP', *SBS*, 24 August 2017

p. 167 'messages from multiple sources . . .' Harkins, S.G. & Petty, R.E., 'Information utility and the multiple source effect', *Journal of Personality and Social Psychology*, 1987, vol. 52, pp. 260–268

p. 168 'filter bubble' See Pariser, E., 'The truth needs better marketing', *TEDxPoynterInstitute*, 2013

p. 169 'There were days when . . .' Coppins, M., 'The 2020 disinformation war', *The Atlantic*, March 2020

p. 170 'We live in two different countries . . .' Roose, 2020

p. 170 'Cambridge Analytica . . .' in Coppins, 2020

p. 170 'He took hundreds of fake news sites . . .' Albright, J., 'The #Election2016 micro-propaganda machine', *Medium*, 18 November 2016

p. 171 'They have created a web . . .' in Cadwalladr, C., 'Google, democracy and the truth about internet search', *The Guardian*, 4 December 2016

p. 171 'two-thirds of people . . .' Horwitz and Seetharaman, 2020

p. 175 'Louise Staley's bizarre press release . . .' Louise Staley MP, 'Premier owes Victorians some simple answers', Press Release issued 7 June 2021

PART THREE
2016

p. 180 '70 per cent of Trump's statements . . .' Politifact, *The Poynter Institute*

p. 181 'Extra Mile Casting agency . . .' Crouch, A. & McDermott, E., 'Donald Trump campaign offered actors $50 to cheer for him at presidential announcement', *Hollywood Reporter*, 17 June 2015

p. 182 '"Nope," Zucker was said to have replied.' Mahler, J., 'That is great television', *New York Times*, 9 April 2017, p. 40

p. 183 'US$5.8 billion . . .' Mahler, 2017

p. 184 'Was Facebook responsible . . .' Bosworth, A., 'Thoughts on 2020', post on *Facebook*, 8 January 2020

p. 185 'Stanford researchers counted 30 million shares . . .' Allcott, H. & Gentzkow, M., 'Social media and fake news in the 2016 election', *Journal of Economic Perspectives*, Spring 2017, vol. 31(2), pp. 211–236

p. 185 '171 million tweets . . .' Bovet, A. & Makse, H.A., 'Influence of fake news in Twitter during the 2016 US presidential election', *Nature Communications*, 2019, vol. 10(7)

p. 185 '20 per cent of the entire Twitter conversation . . .' Bessi, A. & Ferrara, E., 'Social bots distort the 2016 U.S. Presidential election online discussion', *First Monday*, 2016, vol. 21(11)

p. 185 'examined 25,000 messages . . .' Howard, P.N. et al., 'Junk news and bots during the U.S. election: What were Michigan voters sharing over Twitter?', *COMPROP Data Memo*, 2017.1, Oxford: Project on Computational Propaganda, 2017

p. 186 'using actual fake news headlines . . .' Pennycook, G., Cannon, T.D., & Rand, D.G., 'Prior exposure increases perceived accuracy of fake news', *Journal of Experimental Psychology: General*, 2018, vol. 147(12), pp. 1865–1880 (Emphasis added)

p. 187 'We know because we've . . .' Green, J. & Issenberg, S., 'Inside the Trump bunker, with days to go', *Bloomberg BusinessWeek*, 27 October 2016

p. 187 'Channel 4 . . .' Channel 4 News Investigations Team, 'Revealed: Trump campaign strategy to deter millions of Black Americans from voting in 2016', *4 News*, 28 September 2020

p. 187 'Ohio State University . . .' Gunther, R., Beck, P.A. & Nisbet, E.C., 'Fake news did have a significant impact on the vote in the 2016 election', *Ohio State University*, March 2018

p. 187 'Washington Post hypothetical rerun . . .' Blake, A., 'A new study suggests fake news might have won Donald Trump the 2016 election', *Washington Post*, 3 April 2018

p. 188 'I think I had come from . . .' Interview with Michael Isikoff, 'The Trump effect, one year on', *Web Summit 2017*, 8 November 2017

p. 188 'Madison Avenue gimmickry' Arendt, H., *Crises of the Republic: Lying in Politics, Civil Disobedience on Violence, Thoughts on Politics, and Revolution*, New York: Houghton Mifflin Harcourt, 1972, p. 31

p. 189 'largest data-gathering operations . . .' Speech to California Republican Party State Convention, 7 September 2019

p. 189 '3000 data points . . .' Broderick, T., 'Watch golf? Own guns? Trump data team has ads just for you', *Christian Science Monitor*, 17 December 2019

2020

p. 191 'I won the election . . .' Image: Deepa Seetharaman

p. 192 'Election Integrity Partnership . . .' Election Integrity Partnership, *The Long Fuse: Misinformation and the 2020 Election*, Stanford Digital Repository, 2021

p. 193 'Iranian disinformation campaign . . .' 'Removing more coordinated inauthentic behavior from Iran and Russia', *Facebook Newsroom*, 21 October 2019

p. 194 'were in cities with the largest . . .' Summers, J., 'Trump push to invalidate votes in heavily black cities alarms civil rights groups', *NPR*, 24 November 2020

p. 196 'shamelessly embraced disinformation . . .' Ghaffary, S., 'How fake news aimed at Latinos thrives on social media', *Recode*, 19 November 2020

p. 197 'Latinos used more . . .' Pew Research Center, *Social Media Use in 2018*, poll conducted 3–10 January 2018

p. 197 'Avaaz asked members . . .' Avaaz, *WhatsApp: Social Media's Dark Web*', 26 April 2019

p. 198 'EquisLabs . . .' EquisLabs, *2020 Post-Mortem PART ONE: Portrait of a Persuadable Latino*, April 2021

p. 199 'a 2015 analysis . . .' Sunlight Foundation, 'Capitol Words' analysis, 2015

p. 199 'We need to find and identify . . .' Viser, M., 'Inside the "malarkey factory," Biden's online war room', *Washington Post*, 19 October 2020

'THE BIG LIE' LIE

p. 203 Absentee voting figures: Survey of the Performance of American Elections, 'How We Voted in 2020'; MIT Election Data and Science Lab, February 2020

p. 203 '85 point difference . . .' Rakich, N. & Mithani, J., 'What absentee voting looked like in all 50 States', *FiveThirtyEight*, 9 February 2021

p. 203 'Champagne corks remain . . .' Coper, E., 'Why we are still waiting for the US election result', *Australian Financial Review*, 4 November 2020

p. 203 '"The AFR View" . . .' The AFR View, 'US on the brink of four more years of Trump?', *Australian Financial Review*, 4 November 2020

p. 205 '68 per cent—believing . . .' Reuters/Ipsos opinion poll conducted 13–17 November 2020

p. 205 'participatory disinformation.' Kate Starbird keynote address, 'A Changed Landscape: Conceptual and Institutional Foundations of the Conservative Dilemma', *The Conservative Dilemma conference*, GWU Institute for Data, Democracy & Politics, 4 May 2021

p. 206 'ALERT: Radical Liberals & Dems . . .' Romm, T. & Stanley-Becker, I., 'Trump-associated firm tied to unmarked texts urging vote protests in Philadelphia', *Washington Post*, 6 November 2020

p. 206 'Stop the Steal is a highly coordinated . . .' Kuznia, R., et al., 'Stop the Steal's massive disinformation campaign connected to Roger Stone', CNN, 14 November 2020

p. 207 'Image: Participatory Disinformation . . .' Source: Kate Starbird, University of Washington Human Centered Design & Engineering, and Center for an Informed Public

p. 208 'They have their own version of YouTube . . .' Helderman, Rosalind S., et al., 'Inside the "shadow reality world" promoting the lie that the presidential election was stolen', *Washington Post*, 24 June 2021

p. 209 'Zoe Lofgren published . . .' The epic 1939-page detailed takedown of her colleagues is well worth a browse on her website: Zoe Lofgren, 'Social Media Review: Members of the U.S. House of Representatives who voted to overturn the 2020 presidential election', 2021

p. 209 'Starbird called it . . .' Starbird, 2021

p. 209 'Facebook does not believe . . .' Facebook Submission to the Joint Standing Committee on Electoral Matters, *Inquiry into and report on all aspects of the conduct of the 2019 Federal Election and matters related thereto*, 8 October 2019

p. 209 'An internal report . . .' Silverman, C., Mac, R. & Lytvynenko, J., 'Facebook knows it was used to help incite the Capitol insurrection', *BuzzFeed News*, 22 April 2021

p. 210 '61 per cent of Republicans . . .' Reuters/Ipsos poll conducted 17–19 May 2021

p. 210 'County Clerk for Houghton, Michigan . . .' Helderman et al., 2021

PART FOUR
WHY DO WE FALL FOR FAKE NEWS?

p. 215 'unable to reliably distinguish . . .' Pennycook, 2019

p. 215 'six times as fast . . .' Vosoughi, S., Roy, D. & Aral, S., 'The spread of true and false news online', *Science*, 2018, vol. 359, pp. 1146–1151

p. 215 'attaching a warning . . .' Pennycook, et al., 'The implied truth effect: Attaching warnings to a subset of fake news headlines increases perceived accuracy of headlines without warnings', *Management Science*, 2020, vol. 66(11), pp. 4944–4957

p. 215 'When confronted with . . .' Cook, J., Ecker, U. & Lewandowsky, S., 'Misinformation and how to correct it', in Scott, R.A. & Kosslyn, S.M. (eds), *Emerging Trends in the Social and Behavioral Sciences: An Interdisciplinary, Searchable, and Linkable Resource*, 2015

IMPRINTS

p. 217 'food poisoning . . .' This example, and much of the psychological phenomena in this part, is drawn from: Lewandowsky, S., et al. (2020). *The Debunking Handbook 2020*. Available at <https://sks.to/db2020>.

p. 218 'myths' and 'facts' about the flu vaccine . . .' Schwarz, N., et al., 'Metacognitive experiences and the intricacies of setting people straight: Implications for debiasing and public information campaigns', *Advances in Experimental Social Psychology*, 2007, vol. 39, pp. 127–161

SHORTCUTS

p. 221 'illusory truth effect' Fazio, L.K., et al., 'Knowledge does not protect against illusory truth', *Journal of Experimental Psychology: General*, 2015, vol. 144(5), pp. 993–1002

p. 222 'easier to read fonts . . .' Reber, R., Schwarz, N., 'Effects of perceptual fluency on judgments of truth', *Consciousness and Cognition*, 1999, Vol. 8 (3), pp. 338–342

p. 222 'easily pronounced name . . .' Newman E.J., et al., 'People with easier to pronounce names promote truthiness of claims', *PLoS ONE*, 2014, vol. 9(2)

p. 222 'Disinformation featuring images . . .' Fenn, E., et al., 'The effect of nonprobative photographs on truthiness persists over time', *Acta Psychologica*, 2013, vol. 144 (1), pp. 207–211

p. 222 'that "The Atlantic Ocean . . .' Fazio, et al. 2015

p. 222 'A South Dakota nurse . . .' 'Nurse: Some patients who test positive refuse to believe they have Covid-19', CNN, 16 November 2020

SOCIAL (MEDIA) DYNAMICS

p. 224 'A bat and a ball costs $1.10 total'. Kahneman, D. & Frederick, S., 'Representativeness revisited: Attribute substitution in intuitive judgment', In T. Gilovich, D. Griffin, & D. Kahneman (eds), *Heuristics and biases: The psychology of intuitive judgment*, 2002, Cambridge: Cambridge University Press, pp. 49–82

p. 225 'by inflating its triggering stimuli . . .' Crockett, M.J., 'Moral outrage in the digital age', *Nature Human Behavior* 1, 2017, pp. 769–771

p. 226 'by 'nudging' people . . .' Pennycook, G., et al., 'Fighting COVID-19 misinformation on social media: Experimental evidence for a scalable accuracy nudge intervention,' *PsyArXiv*, 17 March, 2020

p. 226 'Social engagement metrics can strongly . . .' Avram, M., et al., 'Exposure to social engagement metrics increases vulnerability to misinformation', *Harvard Kennedy School (HKS) Misinformation Review*, 2020

p. 226 'seeing an article *one time* . . .' Effron, D.A, Raj, M., 'Misinformation and morality: Encountering fake-news headlines makes them seem less unethical to publish and share', *Psychological Science*, 2020, vol. 31(1), pp. 75–87

p. 227 'Trump supporters are more likely . . .' Swire, B., et al., 'Processing political misinformation: comprehending the Trump phenomenon', *Royal Society Open Science*, 2017

p. 227 'famous Milgram experiments . . .' Milgram, S., 'Behavioral study of obedience', *The Journal of Abnormal and Social Psychology*, 1963, vol. 67(4), pp. 371–378

p. 227 'when we read fake news . . .' Martel, C., Pennycook, G. & Rand, D.G., 'Reliance on emotion promotes belief in fake news', *Cognitive Research*, 2020, vol. 5(47)

p. 228 'likely to provoke emotion . . .' Crockett, 2017

p. 228 'robots accelerated the spread . . .' Vosoughi, et al., 2018

MOTIVATIONS

p. 229 'backfire effect . . .' Nyhan, B. & Reifler, J., 'When corrections fail: The persistence of political misperceptions', *Political Behavior*, 2010, vol. 32(2), pp. 303–330

p. 230 'death panels . . .' Nyhan, B. & Reifler, J., 'Ubel, P.A., 'The hazards of correcting myths about health care reform', *Med Care*, 2013, vol. 51(2), pp. 127–32

p. 230 'safety and efficacy of vaccines . . .' Nyhan, B., et al., 'Effective messages in vaccine promotion: a randomized trial', *Pediatrics*, 2014, vol. 133(4)

p. 231 'There is some pushback . . .' For a good summary of the debate, see: Swire-Thompson, B., DeGutis, J. & Lazer, D., 'Searching for the backfire effect: Measurement and design considerations', *Journal of Applied Research in Memory and Cognition*, 2020, Vol. 9(3)

p. 231 'recommending frequent repetition . . .' Ecker, U.K.H., Hogan, J.L., & Lewandowsky, S., 'Reminders and repetition of misinformation: Helping or hindering its retraction?', *Journal of Applied Research in Memory and Cognition*, 2017, 6(2), 185–192

p. 231 'Strengthening of the initial misinformation . . .' Cook et al., 2014

p. 232 'the "Asch experiment"' Asch, S.E., 'Effects of group pressure on the modification and distortion of judgments' in H. Guetzkow (ed), *Groups, Leadership and Men*, Pittsburgh: Carnegie Press, 1951, pp. 177–190

p. 233 'Dartmouth and Princeton . . .' Hastorf, A.H., & Cantril, H., 'They saw a game; a case study', *The Journal of Abnormal and Social Psychology*, 1954, vol. 49(1), pp. 129–134

p. 235 'militia in Beirut . . .' Vallone, R.P., Lepper, R.L., 'The hostile media phenomenon: Biased perception and perceptions of media bias in coverage of the Beirut massacre', *Journal of Personality and Social Psychology*, 1985, vol. 49(3), pp. 577–85

TRIBES

p. 236 'downloading similar songs . . .' Salganik, M., Dodds, P. & Watts, D., 'Experimental study of inequality and unpredictability in an artificial cultural market', *Science*, 2006, vol. 311, pp. 854–856

p. 236 'belief in conspiracy theories . . .' Miller, J.M., Saunders, K.L. & Farhart, C.E., 'Conspiracy endorsement as motivated reasoning: The moderating roles of political knowledge and trust', *American Journal of Political Science*, 2016, vol. 60, pp. 824–844

p. 237 '15 per cent of Trump fans . . .' Schaffner, B.F. & Luks, S., 'Misinformation or expressive responding? What an inauguration crowd can tell us about the source of political misinformation in surveys', *Public Opinion Quarterly*, 2018, vol. 82(1), pp. 135–147

p. 237 'Can you spot the difference?' Image: REUTERS/Lucas Jackson (L), Stelios Varias/Alamy Stock Photo

p. 238 'For members of the public . . .' Kahan, D., 'Why we are poles apart on climate change', *Nature*, 2012, vol. 488, p. 255

p. 239 'An Australian study . . .' Aird, M.J., et al., 'Does truth matter to voters? The effects of correcting political misinformation in an Australian sample', *Royal Society Open Science*, 2018

p. 240 'The need to belong to a tribe . . .' North, S., Piwek, L. & Joinson, A., 'Battle for Britain: Analyzing events as drivers of political tribalism in Twitter discussions of Brexit', *Policy & Internet*, 2021, vol. 13, pp. 185–208

p. 241 'we have become a set of tribes . . .' Hawkins, S., et al., 'Hidden tribes: A study of America's polarized landscape', *More in Common*, 2018

p. 241 'a "blue lie".' Fu, G., et al., 'Lying in the name of the collective good: a developmental study', *Developmental Science*, 2008, vol. 11(4), pp. 495–503

p. 241 'Dylann Roof . . .' Hersher, Rebecca, 'What happened when Dylann Roof asked Google for information about race?', NPR, 10 January 2017

p. 242 'Rachel Bernstein told *Wired* . . .' DiResta, Renee, 'Online Conspiracy Groups Are a Lot Like Cults', *Wired*, 13 November 2018

p. 243 'black swan . . .' Taleb, N., *The Black Swan: The Impact of the Highly Improbable*, New York: Random House, 2007, p. 1 (Prologue)

p. 243 'There are people who would . . .' Nichols, T., *The Death of Expertise: The Campaign Against Established Knowledge and Why it Matters*, New York: Oxford University Press, 2017

p. 244 'Italian researchers . . .' Zollo, F. et al., 'Debunking in a world of tribes', *PLoS ONE*, 2017, vol.12(7)

p. 245 'deradicalisation experts . . .' Archetti, C., 'Terrorism, communication and new media: Explaining radicalization in the digital age', *Perspectives on Terrorism*, 2015, vol. 9(1), pp. 49–59

OPINIONS

p. 247 'live in the same world . . .' Lippmann, W., *Public Opinion*, New York: Harcourt, Brace & Co., 1922, p. 5

p. 247 'For the real environment . . .' Lippmann, p. 3

p. 248 'Drew Westen started . . .' Westen, D., *The Political Brain: The Role of Emotion in Deciding the Fate of the Nation*, New York: Public Affairs, 2007

p. 249 'social intuitionism' Haidt, J., 'The emotional dog and its rational tail: A social intuitionist approach to moral judgment', *Psychological Review*, 2001, vol. 108(4), pp. 814–834

p. 250 'is more like a lawyer . . .' Haidt, 2001, p. 820

p. 250 'moral foundations theory . . .' See for example: Chapter 7 in Haidt, J., *The Righteous Mind: Why Good People Are Divided By Politics and Religion*, New York: Pantheon, 2012. You can also see a stack of resources and take the test yourself at: <moralfoundations.org>

p. 250 'analysed the speech . . .' Tasoff, H., 'An impassioned speech', *The Current*, UC Santa Barbara, 26 September 2019 based on the research: Hopp, F., et al., 'The extended moral foundations dictionary (eMFD): Development and applications of a crowd-sourced approach to extracting moral intuitions from text', *Behavior Research Methods*, 2021, vol. 53, pp. 232–246

p. 251 'How Dare You . . .' Source: Rene Weber/Frederic Hopp, Media Neuroscience Lab at UC Santa Barbara

p. 251 'We often think of communication . . .' Haidt, J. & Rose-Stockwell, T., 'The dark psychology of social networks', *The Atlantic*, December 2019

PART FIVE
WHAT NOT TO DO

p. 256 'George Lakoff . . .' Lakoff, G., *Don't Think of an Elephant! Know Your Values and Frame the Debate: The Essential Guide for Progressives*, White River Junction: Chelsea Green Pub. Co., 2004

p. 259 'cognitive psychologists have shown this can work . . .' Ecker, et al., 2017

p. 259 'it can be safe to repeat misinformation . . .' Ecker, U.K.H., Lewandowsky, S. & Chadwick, M., 'Can corrections spread misinformation to new audiences? Testing for the elusive familiarity backfire effect', *Cognitive Research*, 2020, vol. 5(41)

p. 259 'the more familiar a piece of disinformation . . .' Pennycook, 2018

p. 259 'Myth-busting familiarises people . . .' Berinsky, A., 'Rumors and health care reform: Experiments in political misinformation', *British Journal of Political Science*, 2017, vol. 47(2), pp. 241–262

p. 260 'more pronounced in older people . . .' Skurnik, I., et al., 'How warnings about false claims become recommendations', *Journal of Consumer Research*, 2005, vol. 31(4), pp. 713–724

p. 260 'biased social media feeds . . .' Luzsa, R., & Mayr, S., 'False consensus in the echo chamber', *Cyberpsychology: Journal of Psychosocial Research on Cyberspace*, 2021, vol. 15(3)

p. 260 '5G conspiracy . . .' Image: World Health Organization

p. 261 'A man has planned to meet a girl . . .' Heider, F. & Simmel, M., 'An experimental study of apparent Behavior', *The American Journal of Psychology*, 1944, vol. 57(2), pp. 243–259

p. 262 'researchers in Poland . . .' Szpitalak, M. & Polczyk, R., 'Warning against warnings: Alerted subjects may perform worse. Misinformation, involvement and warning as determinants of witness testimony', *Polish Psychological Bulletin*, 2010, vol. 41, pp. 105–112

p. 263 'We'll allow people to share . . .' Mark Zuckerberg, Facebook post, *Facebook*, 27 June 2020

p. 263 'another false post *without* a label . . .' Pennycook, et al., 'The Implied Truth Effect', 2020

p. 263 '"hoax" and "bullshit".' Christian, J., 'Is there any hope for Facebook's fact-checking efforts?', *The Atlantic*, 19 September 2017

p. 263 'the well-intentioned "trigger warning" . . .' Jones, P.J., Bellet, B.W. & McNally, R.J., 'Helping or harming? The effect of trigger warnings on individuals with trauma histories', *Clinical Psychological Science*, 2020, vol. 8(5), pp. 905–917

p. 264 'its own developers admitted . . .' Smith, J., Jackson, G. & Raj, S., 'Facebook design: "Designing against misinformation"', *Medium*, 20 December 2017

p. 264 'an average of 28 days . . .' Avaaz, *Left Behind: How Facebook is neglecting Europe's infodemic*, 20 April 2021

p. 265 'more than 21,000 times . . .' Zakrzewski, C., 'Twitter flags video retweeted by President Trump as "manipulated media"', *Washington Post*, 9 March 2020

p. 265 'to bypass the gatekeepers of free speech.' From the *Plandemic* website, now archived

p. 266 'The *MIT Technology Review* . . .' Ohlheiser, A., 'Twitter's ban almost doubled attention for Biden story', *MIT Technology Review*, 16 October 2020

p. 267 'Creepy Uncle Joe Biden . . .' Kwan, V., 'When does reporting become a megaphone for disinformation?', *First Draft*, 14 August 2019

p. 268 'Media baiting is a huge portion . . .' Wilson, C., 'Leaked neo-Nazis' manual reveals they're manipulating Australia's media to recruit new members', *Crikey*, 20 April 2021

p. 269 'mapped by researchers at Harvard . . .' Benkler, Y., et al., 'Mail-in voter fraud: Anatomy of a disinformation campaign', *Berkman Center Research Publication*, 2020

p. 269 'Just by showing up for work...' Phillips, W., *The Oxygen of Amplification: Better Practices for Reporting on Extremists, Antagonists, and Manipulators Online*, Data & Society, 2018

p. 270 'Claire Wardle's work with First Draft...' Wardle, C., '10 questions to ask before covering misinformation', *First Draft*, 29 September 2017 and '5 lessons for reporting in an age of disinformation', 27 December 2018

INFECTION CONTROL

p. 274 'Everyone should brush his...' Papageorgis, D., & McGuire, W.J., 'The generality of immunity to persuasion produced by pre-exposure to weakened counterarguments', *The Journal of Abnormal and Social Psychology*, 1961, vol. 62(3), pp. 475–481

p. 275 'an online game called *Bad News*...' <www.getbadnews.com>

p. 275 'Bad News screenshot...' Image: Bad News Company/Gusmanson

p. 276 'Across *all demographics*...' Basol, M., Roozenbeek, J., & van der Linden, S., 'Good news about bad news: Gamified inoculation boosts confidence and cognitive immunity against fake news', *Journal of Cognition*, 2020, 3(1), p. 2

p. 276 '*Go Viral!*...' <www.goviralgame.com>

p. 276 'slowly lured into an echo chamber...' Basol, M., et al., 'Towards psychological herd immunity: Cross-cultural evidence for two prebunking interventions against COVID-19 misinformation', *Big Data & Society*, January 2021

p. 277 'GoViral! screenshot...' Image: Bad News Company/Gusmanson

p. 277 'Groups wishing to cast doubt...' Cook, J., Lewandowsky, S. & Ecker, U.K.H., 'Neutralizing misinformation through inoculation: Exposing misleading argumentation techniques reduces their influence', *PLoS ONE*, 2017, vol. 12(5)

p. 278 'New Zealanders deserve a factual campaign...' Roy, E.A., 'Jacinda Ardern calls for "factual and positive" New Zealand election campaign', *The Guardian*, 23 January 2020

p. 280 'a petition of 31,000 scientists...' van der Linden, S., et al., 'Inoculating the public against misinformation about climate change', *Global Challenges*, 2017, vol. 1(2)

p. 280 'prevent Russian Facebook bots...' Zerback, T., Töpfl, F., Knöpfle, M., 'The disconcerting potential of online disinformation: Persuasive effects of astroturfing comments and three strategies for inoculation against them', *New Media & Society*, 2021, vol. 23(5), pp. 1080–1098

p. 280 'anti-conspiratorial material first...' Jolley, D., & Douglas, K.M., 'Prevention is better than cure: Addressing anti-vaccine conspiracy theories', *Journal of Applied Social Psychology*, 2017, vol. 47(8), pp. 459–469

p. 282 'obvious elite-driven triggering event . . .' Benkler, 2020

p. 282 'believe Iraq had weapons . . .' Fairleigh Dickinson University Public Mind poll conducted 8–15 December 2014

p. 284 'simple accuracy reminder' Pennycook, 'Fighting COVID-19', 2020

p. 285 *'unbelievable* 73 per cent . . .' Dwoskin, E. & Timberg, C., 'Misinformation dropped dramatically the week after Twitter banned Trump and some allies', *Washington Post*, 16 January 2021

p. 286 'original source of 20 per cent . . .' Election Integrity Partnership, *Repeat Offenders: Voting Misinformation on Twitter in the 2020 United States Election*, 29 October 2020

p. 286 'from just 111 accounts . . .' Dwoskin, 14 March 2021

p. 287 'We don't allow anyone . . .' Sowman-Lund, S., 'Advance NZ Facebook page shut down for "repeatedly" spreading Covid-19 misinformation', *The Spinoff*, 15 October 2020

p. 287 'Hindu nationalist BJP . . .' Ajmal, A., 'Facebook bans T Raja Singh of BJP, tags him as a "dangerous individual"', *Times of India*, 4 September 2020

p. 288 'GETTR . . .' McGraw, M., Nguyen, T. & Lima, C., 'Team Trump quietly launches new social media platform', *Politico*, 1 July 2021

CHANGE MINDS

p. 289 For a great summary of the psychology of changing a mind, see al-Gharbi, M., 'Three strategies for navigating moral disagreements', *Heterodox*, 16 February 2018

p. 290 *'less likely* you are to change your mind . . .' West, R.F., Meserve, R.J. & Stanovich, K.E., 'Cognitive sophistication does not attenuate the bias blind spot', *Journal of Personality and Social Psychology*, 2012, vol. 103(3), pp. 506–519

p. 290 'more difficult to sway you with facts.' Kahan, D.M., 'Ideology, motivated reasoning, and cognitive reflection: An experimental study', *Judgment and Decision Making*, 2013, vol. 8, pp. 407–424

p. 290 'more likely to discriminate . . .' Henry, P.J. & Napier, J.L., 'Education is related to greater ideological prejudice', *Public Opinion Quarterly*, 2017, Vol. 81(4), pp. 930–942

p. 291 'only polarise them further.' Kahan, D.M., 'The cognitively illiberal state', *Stanford Law Review*, 2007, Vol. 60

p. 292 'about their property values . . .' Palm, R. & Bolsen, T., *Climate Change and Sea Level Rise in South Florida: The View of Coastal Residents*, Springer: Coastal Research Library, 2020

p. 292 'Both Israeli settlers . . .' Ginges, J., et al., 'Sacred bounds on rational resolution of violent political conflict,' *Proceedings of the National Academy of Sciences of the United States of America,* 2007, vol.104(18), pp. 7357–7360

p. 292 'Sharia Law . . .' Ginges, J. & Atran, S., 'Noninstrumental reasoning over sacred values: An Indonesian case study', in B.H. Ross (ed), *Psychology of Learning and Motivation,* Cambridge MA: Academic Press, vol. 50, 2009, pp. 193–206

p. 293 'The danger of global warming . . .' Thatcher, M., Speech at 2nd World Climate Conference, 6 November 1990

p. 293 'It showed videos . . .' Goldberg, M.H., et al., 'Shifting Republican views on climate change through targeted advertising', *Nature Climate Change,* 2021, vol. 11, pp. 573–577

p. 294 'free-market conservatives . . .' Dixon, G., Hmielowski, J. & Ma, Y., "Improving climate change acceptance among U.S. conservatives through value-based message targeting', *Science Communication,* 2017, vol. 39(4), pp. 520–534

p. 295 'That's my pistol you're wearing . . .' Jones, J., *The Thin Red Line,* New York: Scribner, 1962, pp. 13–14

p. 300 'This can be as simple as listening . . .' Kalla, J.L. & Broockman, D.E., 'Reducing exclusionary attitudes through interpersonal conversation: Evidence from three field experiments', *American Political Science Review,* 2020, vol. 114(2), p. 410

p. 301 '*Dare to know!*' Kant, I., 'An answer to the question: What is enlightenment?', In M.J. Gregor (ed.), *Practical Philosophy. The Cambridge Edition of the Works of Immanuel Kant,* Cambridge: Cambridge University Press, 1999, pp. 11–12

p. 301 'small intimate "enclaves" . . .' Karpowitz, C., et al., 'Deliberative democracy and inequality: Two cheers for enclave deliberation among the disempowered', *Politics & Society,* 2009, vol. 37(4), pp. 576–615

p. 303 'Adversaries attribute . . .' Waytz, A., Young, L.L. & Ginges, J., 'Motive attribution asymmetry for love vs. hate drives intractable conflict', *Proceedings of the National Academy of Sciences,* 2014, vol. 111(44), pp. 15687–15692

p. 304 '*The Debunking Handbook.*' Lewandowsky, et al., 2020

WIN THE STORY

p. 306 '*Winning the Story Wars.*' Sachs, J., *Winning the Story Wars: Why Those Who Tell—and Live—The Best Stories Will Rule the Future,* Boston MA: Harvard Business Review Press, 2012

p. 307 'Although smaller in overall size . . .' Johnson, N.F., et al., 'The online competition between pro- and anti-vaccination views', *Nature,* 2020, vol. 582, pp. 230–233

p. 308 'Labor did not craft...' *Review of Labor's 2019 Federal Election Campaign*, 2019

p. 310 'by providing an 'alternative account'...' O'Rear, A.E., Radvansky, G.A., 'Failure to accept retractions: A contribution to the continued influence effect', *Memory & Cognition*, 2020, vol. 48, pp. 127–144

p. 311 'It's one person coming in from China', Interview with CNBC's Joe Kernen, Davos, 22 January 2020

p. 311 'We got a ton of heat...' Myers, R., 'Tara McGowan will get inside your head', *Marie Claire*, 2 November 2020

p. 312 'when UK artist Dan Baines...' 'Fairy fool sparks huge response', BBC, 1 April 2007

p. 313 'Curiosity promotes open-minded...' Kahan, D.M., et al., 'Science curiosity and political information processing', *Political Psychology*, 2017, vol. 38, pp. 179–199

p. 315 '*guess* the level of welfare...' Kuklinski, J.H., et al., 'Misinformation and the currency of democratic citizenship', *Journal of Politics*, 2000, vol. 62(3), pp. 790–816

p. 315 'messengers for their supporters...' Swire, et al., 2017

p. 316 'social media posts from peers...' Paek, H.J., et al., 'Peer or expert? The persuasive impact of YouTube public service announcement producers', *International Journal of Advertising*, 2011, vol. 30, pp. 161–188

p. 317 '83 per cent of gun owners; 85 per cent of Trump voters...' Public Policy Polling survey of gun owners conducted 11–12 November 2015; USA TODAY/ Suffolk University Poll of Trump voters conducted 20–25 August 2019

WHAT TO DO WHEN YOU SEE DISINFORMATION

p. 324 '*Mother Jones*...' Bauerlein, Monika, [@MonikaBauerlein], 'Audiences are telling us...', Twitter, 29 March 2020

p. 326 'reducing false news sharing intentions...' Mena, P., 'Cleaning up social media: The effect of warning labels on likelihood of sharing false news on Facebook', *Policy & Internet*, 2020, vol. 12, pp. 165–183

p. 328 'Social connections between fact-checkers...' Margolin, D.B., Hannak, A. & Weber, I., 'Political fact-checking on Twitter: When do corrections have an effect?', *Political Communication*, 2018, vol. 35(2), pp. 196–219

p. 328 'warning about the continued influence effect...' Ecker, U.K.H., Lewandowsky, S. & Tang, D.T.W., 'Explicit warnings reduce but do not eliminate the continued influence of misinformation', *Memory & Cognition*, 2010, vol. 38, pp. 1087–1100

p. 329 'called Eve's snake...' Flores, Rosa, 'Pope warns against "fake news" and likens it to "crafty serpent" in Genesis', CNN, 26 February 2018

PART SIX
TOWARDS A HEALTHY ECOSYSTEM

p. 333 'bullshit receptivity . . .' Pennycook, G., Rand, D.G., 'Who falls for fake news? The roles of bullshit receptivity, overclaiming, familiarity, and analytic thinking', *Journal of Personality*, 2020, vol. 88, pp. 185–200

p. 333 'function in a new environment . . .' Eshet, Y., 'Digital literacy: A conceptual framework for survival skills in the digital era', *Journal of Educational Multimedia and Hypermedia*, 2004, vol. 13(1), pp. 93–106

p. 333 'skills builds resistance . . .' Guess, A.M., et al., 'A digital media literacy intervention increases discernment between mainstream and false news in the United States and India', *Proceedings of the National Academy of Sciences*, 2020, vol. 117(27), pp. 15536–15545

p. 334 'civics-focused digital media literacy . . .' Mihailidis, P., 'Civic media literacies: Re-imagining engagement for civic intentionality', *Learning, Media and Technology*, 2018, vol. 43, pp. 1–13

p. 334 'Australian adults' media literacy . . .' Notley, T., Chambers, S., Park, S., Dezuanni, M., *Adult Media Literacy in Australia: Attitudes, Experiences and Needs*, Western Sydney University, Queensland University of Technology and University of Canberra, 2021

p. 337 'team of NYU researchers . . .' Edelson, L. & McCoy, D., 'We research misinformation on Facebook. It just disabled our accounts', *New York Times*, 10 August 2021

p. 339 'the proposed law . . .' Easton, W., 'Changes to sharing and viewing news on Facebook in Australia', *Facebook*, 17 February 2021

Further Reading

This is by no means an exhaustive list of every source used, but some of the best resources I recommend for further reading on the topic. You will find more, and hyperlinks to them, at: factsandotherlies.com/resources.

PHILOSOPHY

Arendt, H., *Between Past and Future: Eight Exercises in Political Thought*, New York: Viking Press, 1968

Plato, *Plato's The Republic*, New York: Books, Inc., 1943

AUSTRALIA

Ackland, R., Jensen, M., O'Neil, M., *Submission to the Senate Select Committee on Foreign Interference through Social Media*, Canberra: News & Media Research Centre, University of Canberra. 2020

Australian Competition and Consumer Commission, *Digital Platforms Inquiry—Final Report*, 2019

Graham, T., 'The story of #DanLiedPeopleDied: how a hashtag reveals Australia's "information disorder" problem.' *The Conversation*, 14 August 2020

O'Neil, M. & Jensen, M.J., *Australian Perspectives on Misinformation*, Canberra: News & Media Research Centre, University of Canberra. 2020

Sear, Tom & Jensen, Michael, 'Russian trolls targeted Australian voters on Twitter via #auspol and #MH17', *The Conversation*, 22 August 2018

This is a really fast-moving topic, which can stay well ahead of publishing timelines. So to keep up to date in real time with who is spreading disinformation in Australia you should follow these Twitter accounts: @cameronwilson; @timothyjgraham; @arielbogle; @ausreset; @estherswchan; @krunchymoses; @jacktheinsider; @elisethoma5

INTERNET & MEDIA

Castells, M., 'The Impact of the Internet on Society: A Global Perspective' in Benkler, Y., et al. *Ch@nge: 19 Key Essays on How the Internet is Changing Our Lives*, BBVA, 2014

Kwan, V., *Responsible Reporting in an Age of Information Disorder*, First Draft, October 2019

Mihailidis, P., 'Civic media literacies: Re-imagining engagement for civic intentionality', *Learning, Media and Technology*, 2018, vol. 43, pp. 1–13

PEN America, *LOSING THE NEWS: The Decimation of Local Journalism and the Search for Solutions*, 20 November 2019

Phillips, W., *The Oxygen of Amplification: Better Practices for Reporting on Extremists, Antagonists, and Manipulators Online*, New York: Data & Society Research Institute, 2018

Wardle, C., '10 questions to ask before covering misinformation', *First Draft*, 29 September 2017

MISINFORMATION

Coppins, M., 'The 2020 disinformation war', *The Atlantic*, March 2020

Election Integrity Partnership, *The Long Fuse: Misinformation and the 2020 Election*, Stanford Digital Repository, 2021

Hindman, M. & Barash, V., *Disinformation, 'Fake News' and Influence Campaigns on Twitter*, The Knight Foundation, October 2018

Nimmo, B., et al., *Exposing Secondary Infektion*, Graphika, 2020

Rid, T. *Active Measures: The Secret History of Disinformation and Political Warfare*, New York: Farrar, Straus and Giroux, 2020

The Center for Countering Digital Hate, *Pandemic Profiteers: The Business of Anti-vaxx*, 2021

Wardle, C., 'Misinformation Has Created a New World Disorder', *Scientific American*, September 2019

Wardle, C., *First Draft's Essential Guide to Understanding Information Disorder*, First Draft, October 2019

Woolley, S. and Howard, P.N. (eds), *Computational Propaganda: Political Parties, Politicians, and Political Manipulation on Social Media*, Oxford: Oxford University Press, 2019

DEBUNKING

Basol, M., et al. 'Towards psychological herd immunity: Cross-cultural evidence for two prebunking interventions against COVID-19 misinformation', *Big Data & Society*, January 2021

Cook, J., Ecker, U. & Lewandowsky, S., 'Misinformation and how to correct it', in R.A. Scott and S.M. Kosslyn (eds), *Emerging Trends in the Social and Behavioral Sciences: An Interdisciplinary, Searchable, and Linkable Resource*, Hoboken: John Wiley & Sons, Inc, 2015

Lewandowsky, S., et al. *The Debunking Handbook 2020*. Available at <https://sks.to/db2020>

POLITICS

Kahan, D., 'The Politically Motivated Reasoning Paradigm', in R.A. Scott and
S.M. Kosslyn (eds), *Emerging Trends in the Social and Behavioral Sciences:
An Interdisciplinary, Searchable, and Linkable Resource*, 2015

Kahan, D., 'Why we are poles apart on climate change', *Nature*, 2012, vol. 488

Lakoff, G., *Don't Think of an Elephant!: Know Your Values and Frame the Debate:
The Essential Guide for Progressives*, White River Junction: Chelsea Green
Pub. Co., 2004

Resnick, B., '9 Essential Lessons From Psychology to Understand the Trump Era',
Vox, 10 January 2019

Sachs, J., *Winning the Story Wars: Why Those Who Tell—and Live—The Best
Stories Will Rule the Future*, Boston MA: Harvard Business Review Press, 2012

Westen, D., *The Political Brain: The Role of Emotion in Deciding the Fate of the
Nation*, New York: Public Affairs, 2007

PSYCHOLOGY

Greifeneder, R., et al. (eds.). *The Psychology of Fake News: Accepting, Sharing, and
Correcting Misinformation*, London: Routledge, 2020

Haidt, J., *The Righteous Mind: Why Good People Are Divided By Politics and
Religion*, New York: Pantheon, 2012

Kahan, D., 'Ideology, motivated reasoning, and cognitive reflection: An
experimental study', *Judgment and Decision Making*, 2013, vol. 8, pp. 407–424

Lewandowsky S, et al. 'Misinformation and Its Correction: Continued Influence and
Successful Debiasing', *Psychological Science in the Public Interest*, December
2012, 13(3), pp. 106–31

al-Gharbi, M., 'Three Strategies for Navigating Moral Disagreements', *Heterodox*,
16 February 2018

Pennycook, G., Rand, D., 'The Psychology of Fake News', *Trends in Cognitive
Sciences*, vol. 25, 5, 2021, pp. 388–402

Index